HEALTH PSYCHOLOGY RESEARCH FOCUS

EMPOWERMENT

CROSS-CULTURAL PERSPECTIVES, STRATEGIES AND PSYCHOLOGICAL BENEFITS

HEALTH PSYCHOLOGY RESEARCH FOCUS

Additional books in this series can be found on Nova's website
under the Series tab.

Additional e-books in this series can be found on Nova's website
under the e-book tab.

HEALTH PSYCHOLOGY RESEARCH FOCUS

EMPOWERMENT

CROSS-CULTURAL PERSPECTIVES, STRATEGIES AND PSYCHOLOGICAL BENEFITS

RANDALL HARRIS
EDITOR

nova publishers
New York

Library of Congress Cataloging-in-Publication Data

Names: Harris, Randall B., editor.
Title: Empowerment : cross-cultural perspectives, strategies and psychological benefits / editor, Randall Harris.
Description: Hauppauge, New York : Nova Science Publishers, Inc., 2015. | Series: Health psychology research focus
Identifiers: LCCN 2015039953 | ISBN 9781634840361 (hardcover)
Subjects: LCSH: Social psychology. | Power (Social sciences)
Classification: LCC HM1033 .E5346 2015 | DDC 302--dc23 LC record available at http://lccn.loc.gov/2015039953

Published by Nova Science Publishers, Inc. † New York

CONTENTS

PREFACE

Empowerment is something that gives people hopes and dreams, brings them courage, and prompts them to be filled with the strength to live. It is a wonderful quality that should be present in everyone.

People are born with splendid abilities. And throughout their lives, they can continue to demonstrate magnificent strengths. In this book, chapter one covers the latest theories and practices of empowerment. The second chapter reviews how empowerment can be a tool in both treatment and stigma reduction for individuals with serious mental illness (SMI). Chapter three discusses empowerment as a tool to enhance social integration among mainland Chinese migrants in Hong Kong. Chapter four provides a theoretical review of experiences of sexual objectification and their consequences for women. The following chapter examines empowerment of women in the tourism and hospitality industry. Chapter six describes how, through their participation in mutual assistance groups, the wives of alcoholic men are able to re-signify conjugal relationships that are usually deeply marked by physical and psychological violence. Chapter seven provides characteristics of the empowerment of Japanese families rearing children. The final three chapters assess hope, provide lessons learned from an economic empowerment model, and examines prevention mother to child transmission programs for HIV-positive women living in West Nile Uganda.

Chapter 1 - Empowerment is something that gives people hopes and dreams, brings them courage, and prompts them to be filled with the strength to live. It is a wonderful quality that should be present in everyone.

People are born with splendid abilities. And throughout their lives, they can continue to demonstrate magnificent strengths. It is empowerment that draws out that magnificent power—in the same way that spring water flows steadily out of a natural fountain, it is empowerment that allows the vital force and potential that lie hidden deep within us to flow.

In the practice of health social services, the magnificent potential that each individual initially has is awakened, prompted to manifest, and is leveraged through activities for the good of people's lives and for the development of society. In groups of people such as in the context of a business enterprise, the potential vigor and capabilities of each employee can be drawn out skillfully and leveraged as energy to be linked to staff development and corporate growth. These are the things that empowerment—needed by organizations, groups, and people—are all about.

Empowerment is one method for realizing a society in which everyone is the hero of his or her life, where they can enjoy the differences between themselves and others and are able to embrace the joys of living alongside one another.

This chapter covers latest theories and practices of empowerment. It constructs 1) the principles of empowerment, 2) the essence of empowerment: resonance between individuals, friends and colleagues, and organizations, 3) creating an environment for empowerment, and 4) design techniques to enable empowerment for its application. The work is filled with tips that come from an array of scenes at the front lines where people stand by the brilliance of life.

Chapter 2 - This chapter reviews how empowerment can be a tool in both treatment and stigma reduction for individuals with serious mental illness (SMI). SMI is defined as a diagnosable mental health disorder that leads to, "serious functional impairment, which substantially interferes with or limits one or more major life activities." In this chapter, the authors provide a working definition of empowerment and explore how personal empowerment can be used to decrease stigma, as well as the consequences that stigma may have on help-seeking. The authors detail how empowerment fits into current treatment ideals for SMI, including Psychosocial Rehabilitation and the Substance Abuse and Mental Health Services Administration's statement on recovery. The authors discuss empowerment-oriented services and supports, including: clubhouses, supportive housing and employment, and peer support.

Finally, the authors provide tips for professionals on how to integrate empowerment throughout their services for and interactions with individuals with SMI, including: collaborative treatment, eliciting feedback from treatment participants/consumers, emphasizing strengths, and promoting community integration.

Chapter 3 - A steady influx of migrants originates from Mainland China to stay in Hong Kong, a special administrative region of China since 1997. These migrants face difficulties in integrating into Hong Kong because of discrepancy in lifestyle and sociopolitical environment between Hong Kong and Mainland China. Conceivably, the migrants need empowerment to reduce the discrepancy in order to achieve social integration. Such empowerment can come from the migrants' hometown or village fellows, superiors, and social service professionals in Hong Kong. Particularly, the professionals provide empowerment through skill training, aid for social networking, individual counseling, and family counseling to the migrants. Nevertheless, how these ways of empowerment enhance the migrants' social integration is largely uncharted. To shed light on the ways, this study employs survey data collected from 2,846 such migrants. Results revealed a significant but weak main positive effect of aid for social networking on the migrant's social integration. Moreover, very high levels of aid from superiors and from hometown or village fellows indicated significant positive effects. What is more, individual counseling, skill training, and aid for social networking displayed significant interaction effects coupled with some conditions. These results imply some strategies for empowerment to enhance the migrant's social integration efficiently.

Chapter 4 - There is an open debate regarding the notion of female sexual empowerment. Some feminist authors, headed by third-wave feminism, have supported the idea that sexuality is a way to female empowerment, whereas other authors have considered that this power is part of a sexual objectification phenomenon where women are subjugated to men. The critical point of the debate centers on whether this sense of power felt by women through their sexuality is true or false empowerment. As a consequence, this sense of power can be associated with beneficial variables for wellbeing and women´s position in society, or with mental health problems and women´s subjugation.

This debate is complex because women are surrounded by a sexualized culture in which they can assume that sexualized behaviors will be rewarded. However, the social rewards given to women when they are sexualized are the essence of benevolent sexist ideology. This ideology obliges women to keep themselves in a subordinate position to men. There is empirical evidence demonstrating how sexuality is a source of ambivalence for women, because the power they feel is rooted in the power to attract the attention and admiration of men. The power felt by women is therefore subjugated to control by men and the male sex's search for its own sexual satisfaction.

Sexual Objectification theory focuses on the consequences for women of being treated as objects and how women are reduced to their sexualized body parts to give sexual pleasure to men. This kind of gender discrimination, that usually goes unnoticed by many women and is even desired by some women, has been demonstrated to be linked to negative outcomes such as depression symptoms or high anxiety levels, amongst other mental health problems.

In this chapter, the authors will review the characteristics, etiology and consequences of the sense of power felt by women in sexual objectification encounters which combine sexual objectification and ambivalent sexism theories.

Chapter 5 – Empowerment is a practical management strategy which has been widely studied and applied by researchers and practitioners in different ways. In the past empowerment concept is related to human resources strategies which include sharing information, rewards, knowledge and power with front line employees or operational staff. Operational staff or front line employees can be described as "boundary-spanning workers". They mediate between the organization and its customers, hence are given the opportunities or empowered to make their own decisions and develop their abilities and job performance skills. Management researchers seek further to study empowerment concept of unrestricted job decision making power and job autonomy to an individual level. For instance, empowerment has been operationalized as a psychological construct reflecting an individual's feelings of self-control and self-efficacy. Hence, the definition of psychological empowerment is found in the literature.

Psychological empowerment captures an individual's orientation towards work role. It is believed to be a motivational construct manifested in namely four types of individual awareness: Meaning, Competence, Self-determination, and Impact. Meaning refers to value of one's work; Competence refers to one's ability; Self-determination refers to one's selection of actions and Impact is one's influences in the workplace. These four kinds of awareness or cognitions explain the psychological empowerment of an individual which is directly related to the perception of his or her preferred work role and context. Spreitzer advocates that psychological empowerment reflects the ongoing changes of employees' perceptions of themselves in connection with their work environment. Nevertheless, empowerment is seen to be influenced by cultural factors. When approved by the management, cultural factor or value of power-distance exerts a strong influence on employees' willingness to accept and exercise discretionary power. Discretionary empowerment depends more on the individual's preference for control of the power and can be influenced by the individual's cultural background such as power-distance. Hence, besides psychological empowerment, the definition of psychological empowerment is also found in the literature.

In the hospitality and tourism context, both discretion empowerment and psychological empowerment have been discussed by many researchers. Empowerment issues in hotels such as Ritz Carlton and Scotts' Hotels/Marriott, restaurants such as Harvester restaurants and airlines such as Scandinavian Airlines and Delta Airlines are found in the literature.

In the Asian hospitality literature context, relatively little is known about empowerment and related issues, some useful information can be identified in a few researches in China. For instance, Cheung, Baum and Wong examine the empowerment concepts in the Asian context. Using an open ended questionnaires survey and focus groups, an in-depth examination of the perceptions of hotel managers in China regarding their interpretation and practice of empowerment within their workplace is provided. Their study findings reveal the influences of empowerment practices can be individual-based as well as family based. Individual based influences are employees' virtue, skills and competency. Family or in-group based influence are family relationship between the managers and employees, trusting relationships and commitment from the managers. The significant result is family based empowerment practices are significantly dominant in China hotels. In another hotel study, Humborstad et al. empirically examines 290 hotel employees in Macau on the impact of empowerment on service willingness. Empowerment is found to have a positive relationship with delivering higher service. In a survey of hotel service employees in Beijing, the successful implementation of empowerment depended on employees' willingness to assume and exercise discretionary power approved by their managers. The three studies provide insights on how empowerment works in China hotels which has a predominately high power distance culture. Yet, whether the high power distance culture hinders the empowerment of women is not yet known.

Spreitzer, Kizilos and Nason test and find a significant relationship between gender and empowerment. Women at the middle and senior managerial positions in the hospitality industry are encountering the most important obstacle of not being thoroughly empowered. The most difficult challenge to struggle in an environment that is male dominated, informal network of "old boy network". When compare to men, women are more anxious about personal relationships and responsibilities than men. Stimpson, Neff, Jensen and Newby compare the rating of adjectives on the social desirability of men and women, women are found to rate adjectives that reflect a concern for relationships, such as likable, friendly, adaptable, etc, as more desirable than men did. Peterson and Hughey described women felt less empowered than men and proved that gender was a predictor of empowerment.

The impact of empowerment from female managers' perspective are neglected by most literature, most literature seeks insights from the perspective of managers and service employees. To fill this void in the context of a service industry such as hospitality and tourism, the present study focuses on examining the issues of empowering female hospitality and tourism managers in Asia. This study will help to provide useful and practical insights from to the senior management on the implementation of empowerment in the hospitality and tourism industry in Asia. This chapter attempts to examine the empowerment issues of tourism and hospitality women by exploring women's career in the Asia Pacific region. The objectives of this chapter are to review the women's employment situation in the hotel and tourism industry; to discuss the barriers of empowering women in the hospitality and tourism industry and to provide possible practical suggestions.

Chapter 6 – Introduction. In the wake of the feminist movement of the 20th century, women in Western societies have adopted new, more modern values that have brought changes to their lives. However, the authors observe that traditional values are still important in women's orientations and actions in Brazil, where family values are still uppermost in the female world, territorializing them in a way of life characterized by the maintenance of the bonds of affection and where the role of caregiver, the position of victim, and the idea of suffering as one's destiny and as a feminine virtue is still often present.

Objective. In this study the authors describe how, through their participation in mutual assistance groups, the wives of alcoholic men are able to re-signify conjugal relationships that are usually deeply marked by physical and psychological violence.

Methods. This is a qualitative research, with open-ended interviews with 12 female partners of male alcoholics who belonged to a support group in the city of Rio de Janeiro, Brazil. The interviews were interpreted based on the gift theory of anthropologist Marcel Mauss.

Discussion. The authors observed that when the women interviewed begin frequenting the self help group, they fell in with others whose discourse and experiences were similar to their own. Through a mutual self-identification, they began to see themselves in perspective and came to relativize situations that they never dared question before. The figure of "good mother" and "suffering wife" evoked by the majority of the women interviewed when speaking of their arrival at the mutual assistance group tended to disappear from the narratives over time. An aspect of the group's ideology is the rejection of the discourse of victimization. This can be interpreted as being a strategy to move the women towards accountability and away from their passive position as a victim of "someone else" (the partner or the situation), thus promoting a more modern, individualizing type of discourse that helps them to adopt the position of subject, leading to greater autonomy. The authors observed that as they continue to attend the meetings, the women reflected on their values and started to question their role in the family. It is as if by simultaneously belonging to the family and to the self-help group, the women were able to distance themselves from their environment of origin (the family) and gaze at themselves with a more critical eye in a process of empowerment. The authors can say that the women developed a relative individualization associated with the process of self-examination that would lead to increased reflection on their part and a broadening of their "inner horizons," which would enable them to re-position themselves in the conjugal relationship in a more satisfactory way.

Chapter 7 – The authors investigated the characteristics of the empowerment of Japanese families rearing children. The authors conducted multifaceted surveys of the attributes of children from those who are healthy to those who have moderate to serious disabilities. There has been a rapid rise in the falling birth rate and the aging population as well as more nuclear families in Japan during these past few decades, where places and human resources for sharing the struggles and stresses of the child-raising generation are essential, yet the supply or responses have not caught up with these demands, with some mothers having given up on consulting or sharing with others, and others losing confidence in raising their children. The number of incidents of child abuse has continued to escalate since these statistics have been tracked, with prior studies showing a greater sense of failure today by Japanese mothers in raising their children. In addition, Wakimizu et al. developed a Japanese version of the Family Empowerment Scale (FES) in 2010, first developed by Koren of the United States in 1992, and the results of studies on the state of empowerment in Japanese families using the Japanese version of the FES clearly zeroed in on the low values in comparison to families in the United States and Australia. The authors launched an intervention in each region around the university, based on these results, so as to improve family empowerment by combining parent training with providing local resource information. Furthermore, family empowerment in its actuality is not simply tracked cross-sectionally, but temporally and cross-sectionally. The authors will introduce in the following section 1. The history of Japanese families rearing children, 2. The state of family empowerment and 3. Intervening towards family empowerment and its results.

Chapter 8 - Depression and a sense of hopelessness have been shown to impact HIV testing, treatment adherence and health outcomes for HIV-positive women in sub-Saharan Africa. However, little has been reported on the impact of participation in Economic Empowerment (EE) programs and a sense of hope for HIV-positive individuals. The authors report the development and pilot implementation of a Hope Questionnaire with HIV-positive women living in West Nile Uganda. Focus groups with HIV-positive women in Uganda provided domains of mental health attributes which were reworded into positive affirmation statements of hope. yielding the Hope Questionnaire. This tool was piloted with HIV-positive women with 18 months of participation and women completely new to an EE sewing initiative. Each hope question score was compared to the sum of these scores using ANOVA. Results show that hope scores did not differ between women with continued participation and those new to the program. Hope may be an important by product of EE initiatives and appears to be an individually subjective outcome difficult to compare between groups.

Chapter 9 - Economic empowerment is recognized as a crucial component for alleviating poverty, social exclusion and reducing health disparities. It is necessary to build the capacity of women with technical and entrepreneurial skills in order to broaden their range of choices and give them a voice in their households and communities. In the last decade, rural non-farm (RNF) initiatives have been recognized as major actors of women's economic empowerment in developing countries. The authors report, a low-budget grassroots RNF economic empowerment model started in 2008, for HIV-positive women in West Nile Uganda. The goal of the LifeStitches model is to empower women with income-generating skills to improve their quality of life and to decrease the burdens of AIDS-related stigma. In 2012, replication in a nearby community demonstrated the model's viability. The structural aspects of this model include empowerment, sustainability and participatory evaluation and are discussed in the context of an established paradigm. The outcomes assessed by a demographic/socioeconomic outcome tool; DataThreads, supported the effectiveness of this model to address poverty and highlighted barriers to participation. Lessons learned are discussed. In conclusion, the incremental building of technical and entrepreneurial skills constitutes essential elements of empowerment.

Chapter 10 - AIDS-related stigma is a formidable barrier to uptake in Prevention Mother To Child Transmission (PMTCT) programs in sub-Saharan Africa. Poverty, lack of education, low self-efficacy, and living in rural communities also contribute. The authors report an economic empowerment initiative for HIV-positive women linked to PMTCT programs in West Nile Uganda. The classic self-efficacy model was used to develop an AIDS-related Stigma Self-Efficacy Questionnaire. Results show self-efficacy increased with participation and generalized across empowerment and stigma domains. Self-efficacy may be an effective way to measure the impact of economic empowerment initiatives on reducing AIDS-related stigma for HIV-positive women in sub-Saharan Africa.

In: Empowerment
Editor: Randall Harris

ISBN: 978-1-63484-036-1

Chapter 1

NEW EMPOWERMENT MODELS ON PRACTICAL STRATEGIES FOR WELLBEING

Tokie Anme, PhD
University of Tsukuba, Tsukuba, Ibaraki, Japan

ABSTRACT

Empowerment is something that gives people hopes and dreams, brings them courage, and prompts them to be filled with the strength to live. It is a wonderful quality that should be present in everyone.

People are born with splendid abilities. And throughout their lives, they can continue to demonstrate magnificent strengths. It is empowerment that draws out that magnificent power—in the same way that spring water flows steadily out of a natural fountain, it is empowerment that allows the vital force and potential that lie hidden deep within us to flow.

In the practice of health social services, the magnificent potential that each individual initially has is awakened, prompted to manifest, and is leveraged through activities for the good of people's lives and for the development of society. In groups of people such as in the context of a business enterprise, the potential vigor and capabilities of each employee can be drawn out skillfully and leveraged as energy to be linked to staff development and corporate growth. These are the things that empowerment—needed by organizations, groups, and people—are all about.

Empowerment is one method for realizing a society in which everyone is the hero of his or her life, where they can enjoy the differences between themselves and others and are able to embrace the joys of living alongside one another.

This chapter covers latest theories and practices of empowerment. It constructs 1) the principles of empowerment, 2) the essence of empowerment: resonance between individuals, friends and colleagues, and organizations, 3) creating an environment for empowerment, and 4) design techniques to enable empowerment for its application. The work is filled with tips that come from an array of scenes at the front lines where people stand by the brilliance of life.

1. Definition of Empowerment

The word *empowerment* consists of the word *power* with the prefix *em*, which together means drawing out and demonstrating the potential power within us.

Put simply, it means giving people hopes and dreams, offering them encouragement, and prompting them to generate within themselves the wonderful potential strength to live that everyone essentially has. It is the act of enlivening people, drawing out their power, forming bonds, and developing networks of empathy. By becoming aware of the magnificent power that lies within individuals, organizations, or communities, developing such strengths, communicating and sharing these sentiments, and having them resonate among us, it becomes possible to nurture new ways to work together. In a sense, it is an extremely creative type of power. It is a type of power that triggers the imagination, spreads, and strikes the true essence of colleagues and organizations like a pulse.

The word empowerment is used in various fields, and in fact has different definitions depending on the area in which it is used. To introduce some of them, in education it is defined as intrinsic motivation, experiences of success, a sense of competency, the development of strengths, and self-respect. In the field of social development, it is defined as respect for mankind, belief in the potential capacity of all people, and activities aimed at creating a fair and equal world where those potential abilities can be demonstrated. As to the area of business, it is creative decision-making from the delegation of authority and expanded responsibility. In social welfare, empowerment is defined as the process that a person undergoes to gain greater control over the decision-making and activities that influence a person's well-being.

2. Principles of Empowerment

There are eight principles for empowerment:

(1) A person chooses his or her own objectives.
(2) The person takes initiative and the authority to make decisions
(3) The person considers his or her issues and the ways through which to resolve them.
(4) Successes and failures are analyzed as opportunities to learn and build capacities.
(5) Inner elements within the person and their supporters are discovered and fortified to change behaviors.
(6) The person is prompted to participate in the process of resolving issues to boost their sense of responsibility.
(7) Improvements are made to networks for supporting the process of resolving issues and their resources.
(8) Motivation is boosted toward improving conditions for the person (such as the achievement of his or her objectives or their well-being).

In other words, the principles for empowerment are based on the individual. It is therefore the role of supporters—experts, superiors at work, or colleagues—to prompt an individual to generate power that oozes from within them and to improve their surroundings to enable that to happen. The individuals that we refer to here include people who are centrally involved, both people and organizations. Supporters mean people or organizations that offer them support.

These principles for empowerment apply not only to individuals but to all people and organizations (Anme, 2007). It is also essential to improve conditions when promoting empowerment in groups of people and organizations such as companies to have their individuals select their objectives and actively participate in taking initiative, the authority to make decisions, and lead the process of considering steps to resolve issues.

3. Types of Empowerment

There are three types of empowerment: self-empowerment, peer empowerment, and community empowerment. Self-empowerment means bringing out one's own capacities. Examples of this might include the use of a certain method for building motivation or to absorb oneself in a favorite pastime to relieve stress. Peer empowerment is to draw out individual capacities through peers, such as by dining together or talking with one another. Community empowerment is the leveraging of communities, organizations, the workplace, or their systems to invigorate such groups. Examples of community empowerment include activities undertaken by the entire community to organize something together such as an event or a local festival. The combined use and leveraging of these different types of empowerment are essential in order to realize something that is both sustainable and effective, and are called synergy model for empowerment (Figure 1).

Figure 1. Synergy model for empowerment (Anme, 2008).

4. Prerequisites for Empowerment

There are three prerequisite conditions for all three types of empowerment: self, peer, and community. They are:

(1) Hope: The presence of a visible goal that leads to hope.
(2) Faith: An individual's ability to believe that they have the capacity to head toward their goal. Self-efficacy and group efficacy (a sense that it is possible for an individual or a group to take approaches toward external matters).
(3) Meaning: The ability to find meaning in aiming for and working toward a goal.

What is necessary is that all three of these prerequisites are in place (Anme, 2008).

For example, let's say that a cancer has been detected in your body. You might get upset and ask, "Why me?" or deny that such a thing could happen to you. Or perhaps you would be overwhelmed with shock and fall into a state of depression or start praying to the gods to save you. But once you've settled down from the initial impact, you'll probably face reality and take some sort of action to try to resolve the issue. What is necessary in order to do that? First you need to have hope that you will recover. Next, you need to have faith that you have the strength and ability to endure treatment and recover. And by believing that such efforts have meaning, you'll be able to inspire yourself.

The same applies to peer or community empowerment. How do you cope when faced with a major crisis? You will probably establish a goal for opening up the future, have faith in your own capacities, give meaning to the efforts for moving forward a step at a time, and attempt to overcome the situation.

It is not limited to crisis situations. Whether it's daily life or work routines, people fall into a powerless state if they lose these three elements. A powerless state is a condition in which you entertain negative thoughts such as the belief that you are unable to do anything or conviction that there is no meaning to your existence. Social ignorance can be a knife that significantly cuts into the meaning of hope, a sense of efficacy, or the act of making an effort. A state of social ignorance where a person is ignored despite the presence of people around them is strongly associated with a worsening in the person's physical condition. There has also been a report that a powerless situation due to abuse or domestic violence can damage the nervous system.

5. Linking Empowerment between Individuals, Peers, and the Community

There are three criteria to link self-, peer, and community empowerment that are necessary for its promotion:

(1) A sense of pride in oneself
(2) The ability to enjoy differences
(3) Believing in the capacities of groups

First, it is necessary to believe in and have pride in yourself, as it isn't possible to have pride if you don't believe in yourself. Only by having a sense of self-pride does it become possible to recognize others.

The next requirement is to have the ability to enjoy differences with other people. Diversity is the basis for community development. In the theory of evolution, evolution is reported not as being rational but rather as the building of rationality over the irrational. It is from diversity and ambiguity that may be unclear that new values and things with meaning are given birth. Therefore, it is necessary to cherish an unorganized and ambiguous world and objects that may appear at a glance to be meaningless. It is also interrelated to a sense of playfulness and room for growth.

The next prerequisite is to believe in the capacities of peers and groups. A sense of trust, which is necessary among peers and communities, does not stop at trust between individuals. It is the ability to recognize various characteristics and to believe in the capacities of a group or community which includes such diversity.

One example is inclusive education where children with special needs spend time together with others who do not have disabilities. Each child is able to gain confidence in themselves and accept their differences as things that are simply natural while they enjoy growing together. As to adults, recognition from peers will lead to reciprocal recognition for others, which will then tie in to teamwork.

6. Three Perspectives Required of Supporters

What supporters of empowerment need to do is to clarify the needs and values of the relevant persons, assess what it is that they are able to do, and facilitate their environment.

Values of the relevant persons mean the history, culture, and sentiments that individuals and communities hold dear. Needs are the things that individuals and communities seek. It is not uncommon that such needs and values are different from what supporters expect, and communication is the first step for empowerment, which is possible by gaining an understanding of the things that people desire or consider important through language, expressions, or mannerisms. The words that are spoken by someone are not necessarily a reflection of their true needs. We hope that we can be supporters who are able to understand the deeper sentiments that lie behind speech.

As mentioned in Session 2, the principle of empowerment is that it is the people who are the main focus. They should prepare environments in which they can continuously perform within their own power. In the case of businesses, the extents that consumers want to use a company product or feel that a product is usable are indicators for company-led measurements of the levels for realizing its commercialization. Thus, there are three perspectives that are required among supporters:

(1) The values or sense of worthiness among the subjects of empowerment
(2) Their needs
(3) What they are able to do (or sense or mutual sense of feasibility)

In business, the establishment of systems where companies and consumers support one another—or empower one another—is what brings on development. A company will grasp the needs and values of consumers and their sense of what products are usable and offer high quality products and services to offer them empowerment. Likewise, consumers will empathize in their own way with the values, needs, and wonders of such products and services, offer high ratings for the value of the brand, and communicate information to society to empower the company. In these ways, the promotion of such interactive empowerment is essential for the development of the community.

As another example, we'll consider a case where a new employee is unable to adapt to his workplace. In such a situation the people around him need to understand his situation and accept him. They need to get involved with the employee to draw out his potential by giving thought to what types of dreams he had embraced when he joined the company, what he believes to be his strengths, and what activities bring him joy.

Let us now consider a case from the health and welfare scene. We have an elderly person who would like to continue to live at home but has a problem with walking. We can respect their wish to live at home and remove the different levels of the floor to make it flat. A durable walker that is strong enough to support the person's weight can be used for their shopping needs or when they want to take a stroll. A meal delivery service can be used for dinner, and a professional caregiver can come to check on them once a day. The ability to manage independent daily living in these ways will lead to pride and dignity.

7. Three Elements for Developing Empowerment

Three elements for developing empowerment are plasticity, diversity, and integrality (see Figure 2, Anme, 2015).

Plasticity: Plasticity of and adaptability to objectives, procedures, and methods.
Diversity: Inclusion of various possibilities
Integrality: Coherence from a long-term perspective

Plasticity refers to the act of making improvements in a person's plasticity of and adaptability to objectives, procedures, and methods. It's a strength that enables them to cope with change. With plasticity, they are able to endure difficulties and always face tasks with a positive attitude. It is a crucial element for empowerment.

The original meaning of plasticity is to deal with things in a smooth manner and the nature of changing while adapting to conditions. It is a term that is used at various levels, from molecules to internal organs, solid matter, the environment, to the universe.

Among these, three types of plasticity are particularly closely related to the deployment of empowerment: neuroplasticity, cognitive plasticity, and environment plasticity (Figure 3).

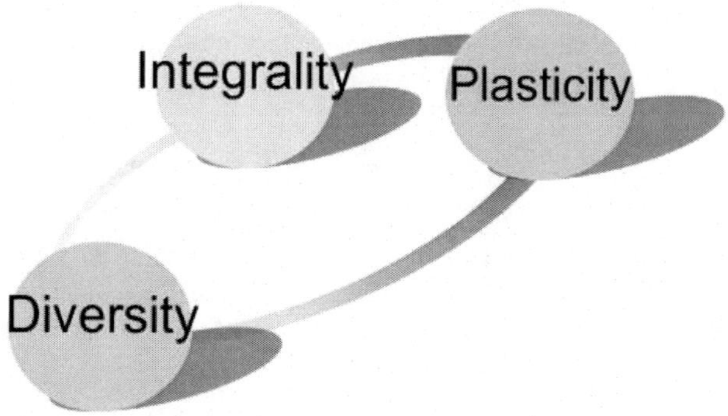

Figure 2. The three elements of empowerment.

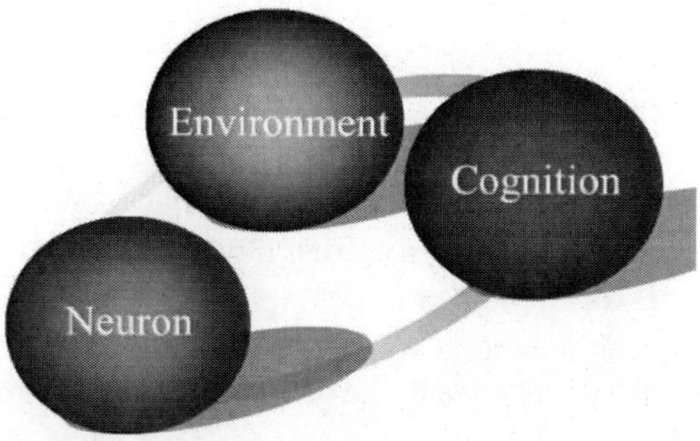

Figure 3. Plasticity.

Neuroplasticity is a characteristic of the cerebral nerve, and it builds associations within the nerves depending on conditions. It is the modification of the way that things are viewed and adapting. Environment plasticity, an ecological nature of the environment, refers to its modification for stability and balance amid changes in various conditions such as climate change and social backgrounds.

These three types of plasticity are actually deeply interrelated. If a person modifies the way that they view things and exercise their cognitive plasticity, adjustment is also made to connections within the nervous system. Taking action and stimulating the environment will bring change to its conditions.

In other words, it is possible to change any one of the types of plasticity by intentionally modifying any one of the others, regardless of the order, and we often do this unconsciously. But conscious modification now and then can enable further enhancements in the results of our plasticity.

Cognitive plasticity, or changing the way that we see things, is probably the easiest way for us to exercise our plasticity in our daily lives. We can vigorously leverage our cognitive plasticity and adjust the circuitry in our brain for dealing more effectively as we aim to fulfill our objectives or improve our environment to enable easier action.

Diversity is the breadth of our capacity to contain various possibilities. It is a treasure for the next step in development, a principle that exists in a large number of fields such as evolution, genetics, and neuroscience.

Integrality is a state in which overall coherence is exercised over a long-term period. While people and communities may appear to be moving about separately from one another, there is a need for a framework to integrate them as a whole. There may be ups and downs at times, but growth continues as balance is maintained from a long-term perspective.

Plasticity, diversity, and integrality may be described as the pillars for empowerment.

8. Dynamic Model for Empowerment

Section 3 mentioned that there are three types of empowerment: self-empowerment, peer empowerment, and community empowerment, and also touched on combinations between them for synergistic models of empowerment (see Figure 1).

Of the three, community empowerment can further be broken down into three levels. They are community empowerment in a strict sense of the term, social empowerment within markets or communities, and system empowerment for systems and frameworks. There are five elements when self- and peer empowerment are included, and the dynamic association of these types of empowerment is called a dynamic model for empowerment (Figure 4). Such a dynamic model is a model that demonstrates complicated associations between the five levels of empowerment, with strengthening or weakening between them. They are similar to the five practices written in the Book of Changes which indicate characteristics such as *sosho*, or relationships, or *sokoku*, or conflict. *Sosho* refers to relationships in which elements positioned next to each other help and strengthen each other while *sokoku* stands for relationships of conflict and rivalry between elements that are positioned two items apart.

The different levels of empowerment—self, peer, community, society, and system—affect each other and are linked in a circle. Thus, they fall under a *sosho* relationship, while a *sokoku* association is also in presence.

Here are some examples of these types of relationships:

(1) An individual who is too strong may weaken an organization.

In an organization where individual independence is given weight, it may be difficult at times to make decisions as a group.

(2) The presence of some groups which are too strong may weaken systems as standards.

Strong groups or divisions that assert their claims may sometimes distort the logic of the system as a whole.

(3) A system that is too strong can bind and weaken the strengths of peers with regulations. Totalitarian control can sometimes eliminate outside groups.

(4) Peers who are too strong may create factions and weaken their society. Groups of peers who pursue their self-interests may at times pretend to be ignorant toward the well-being of society as a whole.

(5) A society that is too strong may weaken individuals.

Figure 4. Dynamic model for empowerment.

It may enforce social norms and restrict individual freedom. The application of these models will allow the true essence of something to be seen in an overall manner and enable the observer to understand changing conditions in a flexible way.

For example, in the practice of healthcare and welfare it can go beyond simply paying attention to the well-being of individuals and enable systematic understanding of the changes in integral relationships while paying attention to the families, peers, organizations, communities, systems and frameworks, culture, or history behind individuals or other relevant factors which correspond to individual growth or aging. As to corporate environments, in addition to market development, interest has recently been focusing on how to link new technology to empowerment that involves individual consumers, their peers and communities, as, for example, how to make consumers fans of a brand as its partners. Particularly through the development of social networking services using the Internet, attention has been focusing on methods to reach out to individuals through peers and social communities. The use of a dynamic model for empowerment offers possibilities to create more effective.

9. Eight Elements for Creating an Empowering Environment

In order to create an environment that enables empowerment, there is a need to have eight values for empowerment (Anme, 2008). These elements are necessary for exercising empowerment and can also be used as indicators for evaluation for measuring results.

(1) Empathy

Empathy is indispensable for an empowering environment. Empathy means individuals have their own will and also recognize that likewise, others also have their own clear will. Individuals can accept the intentions of others, apply these to themselves, and understand them. That is what empathy is about.

Empathy does not stop at associations between people. Empathy with the purposes and details of their business, projects, or programs and their results and contributions can have a significant influence on the realization of empowerment. Programs that have high levels of empathy and ties between its members will have strong momentum for empowerment.

(2) Self-Actualization

Self-actualization is a sense among each and every member that through their individual activities, they are able to realize their values. Regardless of whether they are children or senior citizens, people take action when they feel enjoyment and have a sense of meaning. Activities that offer high rates of self-actualization will arouse people's desires to take part and remain involved in such activities.

(3) Inter-Sectoral Characteristics

Inter-sectoral characteristics are measured to indicate the ways in which each member is involved in the affairs of others, as if they were matters that pertained directly to them. Personal involvement indicates a state in which they are convinced in the presence of their roles for achieving objectives.

When a person is unable to clearly see where they stand it becomes difficult to grasp the issue at hand as their own affair. Particularly in the case of projects or corporate environments where a large number of people are involved, people are often a part of such groups for vague reasons and unable to gain an inter-sectoral sense that they are directly involved.

To promote empowerment it is necessary to have some sort of role and contribute to the whole, regardless of how small that part may be.

(4) Participation

Participation is an indicator for the extent to which each member actually feels that they are impacting their activities. Not limited to physical participation, this is an indicator for how people feel that they are clearly involved in some way.

The difference between inter-sectoral characteristics and participation is that participation includes specific actions for involvement which are visible and recognizable by both individuals and by others. People are able to give meaning to themselves when they are recognized by others. It is possible to establish the presence of their participation or involvement, which become opportunities to gain such recognition.

It is important that measures are considered so that by having people work together to create something, such efforts become positioned as invaluable experiences in their daily lives. Establishing frameworks that will lead to internal motivation—one idea for that is to promote regular participation as events in themselves.

(5) Equality

Equality, or fairness, is essential for promoting solidarity between members. They will not be able to perform unless they feel that a project or program is being conducted fairly, as well as the feedback that is given and the treatment of each member. Without a sense of equality, they will end up losing their motivation.

One way for presenting fairness when dealing with situations where equal treatment to all members may not be possible is to explain rational reasons that will convince them and to facilitate an environment that everyone is willing to accept.

(6) Diversity of Strategies

The presence of diversity in strategies is a significant strength for individuals, groups, and also for the environment, which ties in to the procurement of a multitude of resources that are aimed at the development of a project or program. In addition to the diversity among members, consideration should also be made for the diversity of resources to be used.

(7) Plasticity

Plasticity is an indicator for assessing whether it is possible to deal flexibly with various changes in conditions and presents significant impact on the development of an individual or an organization. Performance assessments are made on the extent to which members, the project or program, or the process for achieving objectives may be carried forward while implementing modifications, regardless of changing conditions or changes among members.

(8) Innovation

Innovation for future development and possibilities for sustainability will bring members a sense of security. This is because by envisioning the future, it becomes possible to establish standards for behavior and determine roles in a strategic manner. Performance assessments are made for projects and programs by examining whether there are prospects for innovation for growth and stable sustainability.

10. Seven Tips for Creating an Empowering Environment

Tips for the effective promotion of empowerment (Table 1) are as explained below.

Table 1. Seven tips for promoting empowerment (Anme, 2008)

1.Have clear objectives
2.Enjoy relationships
3.Create networks of empathy
4.Produce a sense of comfort
5.Offer flexible forms of participation
6.Always aim for development
7.Have a perspective of evaluation

(1) Have Clear Objectives

First it is necessary to involve the relevant subjects. By subjects we do not only mean the people who are directly involved in the matter at hand; they include everyone with whom the subjects come into contact: those who are in need of support, employers, friends and families of consumers, and residents of the community who are associated with the particular project. Clear objectives, which reflect the values of the subjects, are established based on their needs. These values include standards and policies that must be maintained within the process for realizing the targeted conditions. The values of each and every member are brought together and the basic ways of thinking of the group, its principles, guidelines, and guidelines for action shared.

The presentation to subjects of results that match their values will often lead to a sense of unity and a will to participate, while it is difficult to achieve a sense of satisfaction by simply sharing values to suit the occasion for a particular project or exercise. The reason for that is because we are able to affirm the meaning of our existence or our work when we achieve a sense of connection and empathy with our peers or with the people in our society. The effective steps to take are to give importance to individual values while always recognizing the values that the group or organization aims to achieve and affirming such matters verbally.

A need will arise for values that are based on empathy, which will enable members to understand and feel that they can make an impact on knowledge that is worth sharing with others, issues, new ideas, and future activities. Such values are determined by participating members.

Another recommendation is to have someone other than the members of the group, such as a person in a supporting role or an external expert, set such values. It is preferable to obtain multifaceted opinions from experts on the social values of a particular initiative or how it might be possible to draw out more capacities.

(2) Enjoy Relationships

This means finding enjoyment in associations between people and communities or the process of working on a theme in itself.

Sharing enjoyment with others is the most important principle of empowerment, as it relies largely on self-actualization based on empathy. The important things that enable people to share enjoyment are an open atmosphere that invites voluntary involvement and prompts people to enjoy associating with others; a sense of reciprocity that gives them a sense that they are gaining something, although there is no need to be able to clearly identify what that something is; and above all, a sense of trust. Confucius said, "One who knows is no match for one who likes. One who likes is no match for one who enjoys." The most effective way to achieve something is to enjoy it.

Empowerment may be described as empowerment through connections. There is a need to boost ties between people and communities and to create environments that enable people to enjoy those ties.

(3) Create Networks of Empathy

Networks of empathy are for enabling subjects to have a sense of closeness and stimulation while experiencing a feeling of connection. Closeness means a relaxed sense of security while stimulation refers to a sharp sense of tension. The combination of both aspects is known to invigorate empowerment.

When personal relationships between people are strong and a high level of closeness exists, activities within the community as a whole will be enriched, as the trust that is nurtured through daily personal exchange will be tied in to new activities. Conversely, close associations can be developed through overall activities as well. On the other hand, a sense of stimulation will increase if there are opportunities to belong to multiple groups depending on the situation. Stimulus is obtained through a new position in a new group outside the constraints of daily associations.

To promote the development of networks of empathy, regular activities and stimulating new activities can be combined intentionally, taking steps to boost personal relationships with new people and expanding the scope of stimulating topics.

(4) Produce a Sense of Comfort

Neuroscience has revealed that the brain is an organ that experiences comfort from rhythms. Everything that exists in the natural world has been demonstrated to have a rhythm. From the rhythm of plants and animals during growth to the rhythm of the expanding universe, periods of growth or suspension, repetition and change, a rhythm is something that is found in all processes of growth and development. The same may be said for the growth of individuals, communities, and society: the growth of relationships between people, people and communities, or people and society.

So to promote growth and development, it is crucial to intentionally create rhythm. Whether the subject is an individual or a community or organization, a rhythm promotes growth. For example, even if a person is facing challenges and is biding his or her time, when viewed from a long-term perspective it is often an opportunity for the person to take the next major step for growth. The science of lifelong development indicates that the presence of vulnerability makes it possible for people to develop the strength to overcome difficulties and the empathy to be considerate of others. The area of aquaculture occasionally introduces large fish to intentionally create a tense environment for the smaller fish, which is said to actually invigorate the smaller specimens and extend their longevity or improve their state of reproduction.

A rhythm is a wave motion. It serves as a wave motion in the human body, such as a heartbeat or a brain wave, to ensure that energy is spread throughout the body. It can also invigorate a particular subject, people, or communities.

The following types of initiatives are effective for generating a sense of comfort:

1) Maintaining a balance between stimulation from coming into contact with a large number of people and opportunities to create close relationships.
2) Maintaining a balance.... between debates for coming up with new ideas and training sessions aimed at disseminating existing knowledge.
3) Creating a rhythm of the comings and goings of various people and conducting an array of activities.
4) Developing an awareness of the pulsation felt toward actions such as personal interaction or development.
5) Intentionally generating a rhythm that matches occasions.

In order to promote empowerment, a rhythm should be created for periods for making efforts for dealing with change, as well as for maintaining order. Change stands for a person's acute sensitivity to changes in his or her surroundings, and order is the effort to organize the methods which have been developed for adapting and expanding them more effectively and efficiently.

Efforts for coping with change should start by reviewing the standards of value that people and communities have, without realizing it, as the basis for decision-making. An assessment should be made on whether they are desirable or require modification and then flexibly adjusted according to need. What is necessary is the clarification and review of such bases.

In dealing with change, it is necessary to eliminate past concepts and methods. In reality, however, many people and communities are not skilled at discarding such conventional beliefs and tend to adhere to what they are familiar with, particularly if things have been going well in the past. Rather than changing the course of their direction to what is necessary, they try to continue to use the same concepts and methods in a more efficient way.

It is essential to identify the things that should be modified and those for which order should be maintained. Change is the opposite of order, and it means the destruction of preconceptions, or is itself the object of destruction.

Initiatives for coping with change: a review of the preconditions and frameworks behind the concepts, actions, and decision-making of people or communities, an assessment of desirability, and modification if so required. Initiatives for order: the dissemination of shared values. It is an opportunity for individuals and communities to show their skills in just how beautiful a rhythm they can weave these together to give life to empowerment.

(5) Offer Flexible Forms of Participation

A fundamental rule for the roles and state of people's participation is that flexible leeway is given so that periodical changes can be recognized. Examples of the forms of participation include the following (Figure 5):

1) Coordinator: A person who takes on a role for making adjustments to plans as well as for the organization.
2) Core member: A person who is proactively involved in planning and operations.
3) Active member: A person who is involved in activities on a daily basis.
4) Cooperating member: A person who takes part when they are interested.
5) Consulting member: A person who offers expert information and technical skills according to need.

Consideration should be made for planning activities so that members at each level will feel that they can fulfill their roles at any time.

Rather than enforcing participation, an effective way to exercise successful empowerment is to create a mood that attracts people like a magnet and enables people to take part in a casual and natural way. It is also important that the forms of participation are made flexible and interchangeable so that any member can be active as a core or active member based on need.

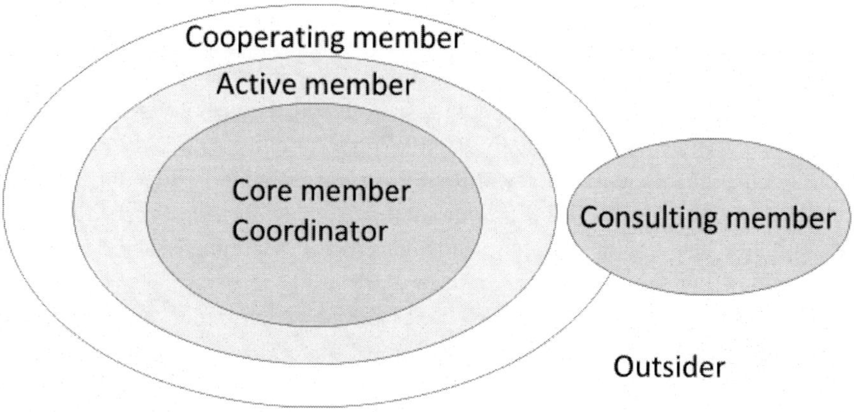

Figure 5. Types of participation.

(6) Always Aim for Development

People and communities are both entities that cannot remain unchanged in a single state. They are invigorated by moving toward the future, always aiming for growth. Instead of becoming fixed, various members are accepted in a flexible manner. Dynamic activities get underway while they adapt to their environment.

What empowerment aims to achieve are people and communities that are invigorated. By prompting them to generate their potential power, it becomes possible to bring them change.

Charles Dederich, who founded a self-help community for drug abusers in the United States, introduced the expression, "Today is the first day of the rest of your life."

What is important is to be prepared with a plan for always aiming for development in order to maintain a lively perspective for the future.

(7) Have a Perspective of Evaluation

To appreciate the significance of conducting activities, it is necessary to have a perspective for understanding their meaning, to be able to evaluate them. By being aware of the meaning of things that are associated with the community and their activities and understanding their objectives, results from activities, impact, and costs, it will be possible to achieve a sense of satisfaction and develop outlooks for the future.

In order to promote empowerment, it is necessary to always reveal the value of activities that take place. They are assessed over the course of activities as required for the purpose of conducting objective evaluations. The level of strength, both apparent and potential—the amount of strength that is present and the level of potential strength that potentially exists—are made clear. And furthermore, new methods are proposed and predictions are made on issues that may arise in the future.

By presenting values based on assessment, it will become possible to identify the motivation for people and communities to proactively participate. Effective assessments are those made by both internal and external parties who can see through the essence of the community.

The purpose of an evaluation is to leverage the findings in the next stage. Like Edison, who said that he had never failed and only found ten thousand ways that won't work, an attitude is needed to use assessments as a step for further growth.

CONCLUSION

Living alongside each other— which we express in Japanese with the word kyosei—does not simply mean living together. The Buddhist term for this is gusho, which has the meaning of living with one another while mutually stimulating each other. However, when used in the context of Buddhist terminology, the meaning of the word is slightly different. Whereas jisho stands for "self-existence" and tasho refers to "a person who exists on account of others," kyosei (gusho) indicates a state in which jisho and tasho are combined, where one exists as an individual while at the same time, he or she is also made to exist because of others. The meaning of a person's existence becomes clear due to the presence of others, enabling a person to acknowledge his or her self. That type of state is what we envisioned with our subtitle: "New ways to live together where everyone is a hero."

The science of empowerment is the product of plasticity, diversity, and holistic attributes. The reason for this is that plasticity is the power to change oneself and the environment, which is accelerated within diversity, and then integrated as a holistic action.

REFERENCES

Anme T, McCall M. Culture, Care and Community Empowerment: International Applications of Theory and Methods, Kawashima Press, 2008.

Anme T. Intergenerational Activities and Aging Well: Plasticity as a Fundamental Strength of Lifespan Development, Systems Sciences for Health-Social Services, 21(2), 2015.

In: Empowerment
Editor: Randall Harris
ISBN: 978-1-63484-036-1

Chapter 2

Empowerment as a Tool for Individuals with Serious Mental Illness

***Lindsay A. Phillips*[1], *Jennifer McIntyre*[1], *Zach Greth*[2], *Chris Kichline*[1] *and Esther Bird*[1]**
[1]Albright College, Reading, PA, US
[2]The University of North Carolina at Charlotte, Charlotte, North Carolina, US

Abstract

This chapter reviews how empowerment can be a tool in both treatment and stigma reduction for individuals with serious mental illness (SMI). SMI is defined as a diagnosable mental health disorder that leads to, "serious functional impairment, which substantially interferes with or limits one or more major life activities" (National Institute of Mental Health 2012, para. 2). In this chapter, we provide a working definition of empowerment and explore how personal empowerment can be used to decrease stigma, as well as the consequences that stigma may have on help-seeking. We detail how empowerment fits into current treatment ideals for SMI, including Psychosocial Rehabilitation and the Substance Abuse and Mental Health Services Administration's (2006) statement on recovery. We discuss empowerment-oriented services and supports, including: clubhouses, supportive housing and employment, and peer support.

Finally, we provide tips for professionals on how to integrate empowerment throughout their services for and interactions with individuals with SMI, including: collaborative treatment, eliciting feedback from treatment participants/consumers, emphasizing strengths, and promoting community integration.

Introduction

Serious mental illness (SMI) is characterized by a marked decline in mental, behavioral, or emotional functioning sufficient for daily living. The National Institute of Mental Health defines SMI as a diagnosable mental health disorder that leads to, "serious functional impairment, which substantially interferes with or limits one or more major life activities" (National Institute of Mental Health, n.d., para. 2). Some of the following disorders may be classified as SMI, depending on an individual's symptoms: schizophrenia and other psychotic disorders, mood disorders (in some cases, bipolar disorder and major depression), and others.

In 2012, there were 9.6 million individuals 18 years or older diagnosed with SMI (National Institute of Mental Health, n.d.). However, this figure may not fully represent the true number, as many people with mental health concerns are reluctant to seek professional help. Some reluctance to seek treatment may be attributed to the presence of stigma and discrimination in society today. This chapter reviews empowerment; the following sections outline how empowerment can be used as a tool in both treatment and stigma reduction for individuals with SMI.

Defining Empowerment

Empowerment is a means by which individuals take control of their own lives. It occurs on a micro (individual) and macro (social) level (Page and Czuba 1999). The process of taking control of the environment – whether individually or within a group – helps people overcome life's challenges and increase overall well-being. We will begin by providing two definitions of empowerment: an applied, consumer/participant focused definition, and a newer, theoretical definition. To begin, the Substance Abuse and Mental Health Services Administration's (2006) statement on recovery identified empowerment as one of the ten "fundamental components of recovery" (p. 1). They defined empowerment in an applied fashion to treatment in this manner:

> Consumers have the authority to choose from a range of options and to participate in all decisions—including the allocation of resources—that will affect their lives, and are educated and supported in so doing. They have the ability to join with other consumers to collectively and effectively speak for themselves about their needs, wants, desires, and aspirations. Through empowerment, an individual gains control of his or her own destiny and influences the organizational and societal structures in his or her life (Substance Abuse and Mental Health Services Administration 2006, p. 1).

More recently, Cattaneo and Chapman (2010) defined empowerment as, "an iterative process in which a person who lacks power sets a personally meaningful goal oriented toward increasing power, takes action toward that goal, and observes and reflects on the impact of this action" (p. 647).

Background: How Empowerment Has Reached the Forefront

According to Phillips (2013), "a shift has occurred in the past six decades due to political acts, social movements, funding changes, and improvements in treatments for mental health disorders" (p. 21).

Specifically, due to the Community Mental Health Act of 1963 and improved pharmacological treatments, fewer individuals with SMI live in institutions and more reside and receive treatment in communities. Improved treatments and community living has led to individuals with all types of mental health concerns taking a larger role in directing their own treatment and making their own life choices (Substance Abuse and Mental Health Services Administration 2006).

A key to individuals taking a larger role in their treatment is empowerment. As previously discussed by Phillips (2013), there are three overlapping movements in mental health treatment that inform the current views of systems and providers of mental health services. These movements include mental health recovery, psychiatric rehabilitation, and community integration.

All three movements seek to place a greater emphasis on use of community-based resources, reduced stigma, and of most significance to this chapter, all seek emphasis on empowerment of mental health service participants/consumers. These movements all seek to move away from models in which individuals with SMI are viewed as passive patients, and instead promote that individuals with SMI actively engage in all elements of treatment planning and the treatment process as service participants or consumers. These movements should not be viewed as discrete and separate, as they all promote similar concepts in treatment and community involvement of individuals with mental illness.

Regarding the recovery movement, in 2002, the President's New Freedom Commission on Mental Health established a proposal to improve the mental health system to promote integration of people with mental illness into the community and to practice mental health treatment from a recovery-based standpoint. The Substance Abuse and Mental Health Service Administration defines mental health recovery as, "a journey of healing and transformation enabling a person with a mental health problem to live a meaningful life in a community of his or her choice while striving to achieve his or her full potential" (Substance Abuse and Mental Health Services Administration, n.d., p. 1).

Another movement within current mental health treatment is psychiatric or psychosocial rehabilitation (US Psychiatric Rehabilitation Association, n.d.), which implements recovery principles, and is explained as follows:

> Psychiatric rehabilitation promotes recovery, full community integration and improved quality of life for persons who have been diagnosed with any mental health condition that seriously impairs their ability to lead meaningful lives. Psychiatric rehabilitation services are collaborative, person-directed and individualized. These services are an essential element of the health care and human services spectrum, and should be evidence-based. They focus on helping individuals develop skills and access resources needed to increase their capacity to be successful and satisfied in the living, working, learning, and social environments of their choice (US Psychiatric Rehabilitation Association, n.d., para. 2).

An overarching goal of both mental health recovery and psychiatric rehabilitation is involvement of individuals with SMI in their communities. This movement in mental health treatment and advocacy is often called "community integration." Yasui and Berven (2009) describe community integration in the following manner:

> The basic principle of the community integration movement is that all people, including those who have disability labels, have a right to full community participation and membership. Within this movement, community integration is considered to be a product of self-help, peer support and professional services; in addition, housing, jobs, and relationships with community members (p. 761).

Community integration means that treatment providers are encouraged to help individuals with all levels of seriousness of mental illness to actively participate within their communities, including in community employment settings, community housing, and community activities. King, Lloyd, and Meehan (2007) stress the fundamental role support serves in community integration, "This goes beyond provision of supported housing and supported employment. Inclusion involves a feeling of belonging, of having a niche or meaningful role to play in the life of the community" (p. 131-132).

STIGMA AND OVERCOMING WITH EMPOWERMENT

As previously noted, individuals with SMI are members of our communities, and recovery, psychiatric rehabilitation, and community integration are all movements that aim to increase involvement of individuals with mental illness in their communities. Despite these movements, research indicates that stigma toward individuals with SMI continues.

Corrigan and Kosyluk (2014) discussed four different types of stigma: public, self, label avoidance, and structural. They defined these as follows:

- Public stigma occurs when people accept stereotypes of mental illness and use them to discriminate against an individual.
- Self-stigma is when individuals with mental illness accept and internalize the discrimination and prejudice they experience.
- Label avoidance deters individuals from seeking appropriate treatment.
- Structural stigma occurs when there is an absence of necessary mental health services.

When seeking appropriate treatment, some people fear that they will be judged by friends and family, and others may believe that they would be perceived as weak if they sought psychological help (Pedersen and Paves 2014). Topkaya (2014) discussed gender differences in stigma. Specifically, men may be less likely to seek help because they tend to experience higher levels of both self and social stigma. Chen, Fang, Liu, Hu, Lan and Deng (2014) found that young adults with more mental health issues also experienced significantly more stigma than those with only one issue. Young adults are also less likely to disclose that they have a mental health issue, and they are more likely to share with friends and family rather than seek professional help (Quinn, Wilson, MacIntyre and Tinklin 2009). As far as ethnicity and stigma, the research is limited, but mostly finds that attitude contributes to how individuals of different races deal with stigma. Older African American women, for example, may be less likely to seek help because of the stereotype that they are supposed to be strong and take care of the family (Ward, Clark and Heidrich 2009).

Additionally, Krajewski, Burazeri, and Brand (2013) found that there may be differences in self-stigma between people from various countries in their research comparison of individuals from six European countries.

One can see how stigma could greatly compromise an individual's ability to achieve empowerment. Therefore, specialists from multiple disciplines (psychology, sociology, education, economics, politics, etc.) have sought to overcome this concern (Page and Czuba 1999). A key recommended method for reduction of self-stigma is personal empowerment (Corrigan and Calabrese 2005, Substance Abuse and Mental Health Services Administration 2006, Substance Abuse and Mental Health Services Administration, n.d.). In fact, Corrigan and Calabrese (2005), describe, "self-stigma as the opposite of personal empowerment" (p. 246) and note that:

> Persons who have a strong sense of personal empowerment can be expected to have high self-efficacy and self-esteem. They are not overwhelmed by their symptoms and psychiatric labels but have a positive outlook and take an active role in their recovery. Empowerment approaches may be considered among the best ways to deal with self-stigma. Though the active involvement of the consumer is essential to this goal, communities and health service providers can foster personal empowerment among mental health consumers in a variety of ways that involve giving consumers greater control over their own treatment and reintegration into the community (Corrigan and Calabrese 2005, p. 249).

The benefits of empowerment include improved self-image, self-efficacy, confidence, and hopefulness, as well as increased ability to cope with daily life, greater satisfaction with treatment, and higher likelihood of reaching treatment goals (Linhorst, Hamilton, Young and Eckert 2002). Empowerment oriented services are discussed next, and this chapter concludes with tips for integrating empowerment into treatment.

Empowering Services and Supports

We now shift to a discussion of several empowerment-oriented services and supports for use in collaborative treatment with individuals with SMI. Empowerment can play an important role in coping with and/or recovering from SMI. Two of the goals of empowerment are to help an individual gain social skills and to learn how to advocate for themselves (Hollander and Offerman 1990, Ralph 2000, Salzer 1997, as cited by Schutt and Rogers 2009). The services we discuss are those identified as empowering services by Corrigan (2004), including clubhouses, supportive housing, supportive employment, and peer support. We also include a brief discussion about the possibility of utilizing empowerment psychoeducation (Phillips and Schade 2012), as well as a discussion of how wellness planners can increase empowerment (Marchinko and Clarke 2011). This is not an all-inclusive list of empowering services and supports, as King et al. (2007) also suggested activities to promote recovery and empowerment, including community gardening, community arts, holistic health, supported education, supported socialization, leisure participation, religious and spiritual participation, and volunteer work.

Clubhouses. The clubhouse model is one strategy implemented in order to combat stigma and influence empowerment. A clubhouse program provides an open community for individuals with SMI (Herman, Onaga, Pernice-Duca, Oh and Ferguson 2005). Members interact with one another as a support group, as they work to reintegrate themselves back into an adaptive pattern of living. There are four underlying components that reflect each clubhouse program: (1) the clubhouse belongs to its members, (2) everyday attendance is preferred and shown to influence other members, (3) members feel like contributors, and (4) members feel needed. In a clubhouse design, members and staff share a similar level of responsibility for work-related activities and decision-making (Herman et al. 2005).

These elements stress the importance for commitment, active participation, and belongingness needed to motivate the individual towards empowerment.

Supportive housing. More than 610,000 individuals are homeless on any given night in the United States (US Department of Housing and Development 2013). Of those individuals, an estimated 26% have some type of mental illness and 6% have SMI (US Conference of Mayors 2008). For this reason, individuals with SMI can benefit from supportive housing, which Glauber (1996) defined for the National Housing Institute as:

> Supportive housing, in its broadest definition, is housing linked with social services tailored to the needs of the population being housed. Supportive services can be either on-site or off-site. Nonprofit housing developers and social service providers have long recognized the importance of comprehensively addressing the needs of their residents and clients. Housing and supportive services are interdependent; both are less effective in the absence of the other (para. 3).

The utilization of supportive housing keeps individuals with SMI connected to supportive relationships, such as family, friends and mental health professionals (National Coalition for the Homeless 2009).

Supportive employment. An important and challenging piece of recovery from SMI is the ability to obtain and retain employment. Difficulties, such as not having access to sustainable, supportive, and non-discriminatory employment (Paluch, Fossey and Harvey 2012, Williams, Fossey and Harvey 2010), add to an already difficult proposition. Conversely, employment brings desirable results such as financial independence, greater self-esteem, and better functioning (Lehman et al. 2002) to the individual.

The philosophy of supportive employment is that individuals with SMI have the ability to work if the appropriate job and job environment can be found for them (US Department of Health and Human Services 2009). Bond (2004) defined supportive employment as, "competitive work in integrated work settings… for individuals with the most significant disabilities for whom competitive employment has not traditionally occurred" (p. 346). National Alliance on Mental Illness (NAMI) added the important aspect to the definition that included supporting the individual both in the job search and while being employed (NAMI 2003). Peer support. Another method of empowering individuals that is growing in popularity is peer support. One definition of peer support is, "social emotional support, frequently coupled with instrumental support that is mutually offered or provided by persons having a mental health condition to others sharing a similar mental health condition to bring about a desired social or personal change" (Solomon 2004, p. 393, as cited by Schutt and Rogers 2009).

Schutt and Rogers (2009) found that adults in an Empowerment Center were able to not only learn how to care for others, but also how to express their own needs to others.

Individuals felt a sense of belonging, improved their social interactions, and experienced less alienation and stigma than they had at regular mental health institutions (Schutt and Rogers 2009). While the results are promising, further research still needs to be conducted to measure the effectiveness of similar peer support programs.

Empowerment psychoeducation. Although this concept has not been the subject of research, Phillips and Schade (2012) advocated for empowerment psychoeducation. They discussed using participant feedback to create a regularly scheduled psychoeducational group that implements empowerment topics, including applications of empowerment, motivation, overcoming stigma, and personal recovery process. They note that this is not an all-inclusive list, and that other service providers may benefit from using participant feedback to incorporate empowerment in a psychoeducational format.

Wellness Planners. Marchinko and Clarke (2011) investigated participants/consumers using a wellness planner in their treatment. This particular wellness planner sought to help individuals with daily plans and goals. The planner included a crisis plan, names and numbers of supports, goal planning information, a calendar, inspirational quotes, and self-help suggestions. Quantitative and qualitative findings suggested that the wellness planner was empowering and was not viewed as stigmatizing.

INTEGRATING EMPOWERMENT IN TREATMENT

Finally, we now provide tips for professionals on how to integrate empowerment throughout their services for and interactions with individuals with SMI. King et al. (2007) caution:

> Reorienting services based on recovery and empowerment necessitates a shift from the old entrenched cultures, which many practitioners may find difficulty in letting go. The challenge is for practitioners to think about people with mental illness as individuals and to explore alternate means of delivering services that are more directly in tune with what clients want and need to assist them in their recovery. This involves practitioners thinking about recovery, the importance of hope and collaborative relationships, and providing interventions or strategies that emphasize social inclusion (p. 131).

As previously discussed by Phillips and Schade (2012), Linhorst and Eckert (2003) discussed seven factors that promote empowerment. To begin, some degree of symptom control is needed so that individuals are able to engage in decision-making. This statement is supported by research that indicates that psychiatric symptoms likely need to be managed or decreased before empowerment can be attained (Strack, Deal and Schulenberg 2007). Second, per Linhorst and Eckert (2003), the individual must possess decision-making skills required to make meaningful, thoughtful, and deliberate decisions. Third, the individual needs access to resources (e.g., emotional support, social support, advocates, logistical resources, etc.). Social support, for example, might serve as a "protective factor" to decrease or prevent self-stigma (Krajewski et al. 2013, p. 1140).

Marchinko and Clarke (2011) echoed the focus on resources, "Persons must have opportunities to make meaningful choices and must also have the resources to make these choices a reality" (p. 280).

Fourth, per Linhorst and Eckert (2003), concrete incentives for participation in decision-making will promote empowerment. Fifth, the setting/environment of services must have structures and processes through which individuals can participate in decisions. Sixth, individuals should have meaningful and abundant information about their options when making choices. Finally, a supportive culture that welcomes and nurtures involvement in decision-making promotes an individual's empowerment.

Beyond these initial factors being present, treatment providers should aspire to engage in collaborative treatment, elicit feedback from treatment participants/consumers, emphasize strengths and desires of treatment participants/consumers, and promote community integration. Corrigan and Calabrese (2005) also state that treatment participants/consumers can create and provide their own services (for example, our previous section on peer support provides just one illustration of this). These factors are all examples of participant/consumer involvement in treatment. Research by Tambuyzer and Van Audenhove (2013) indicated that participant/consumer involvement is associated with increases in both satisfaction and empowerment.

Conclusion

In closing, there were 9.6 million adults diagnosed with SMI in 2012 (National Institute of Mental Health, n.d.). Despite the prevalence of SMI and progress in empowering and community-oriented treatments and supports, stigma continues. "Through empowerment, an individual gains control of his or her own destiny and influences the organizational and societal structures in his or her life" (Substance Abuse and Mental Health Services Administration 2006, p. 1). Empowering treatments and services help individuals with SMI to combat stigma and engage in activities that support their wellness and their own desires in life.

References

Bond, G. R. (2004). Supported employment: Evidence for an evidence-based practice. *Psychiatric Rehabilitation Journal*, 27, (4), 345-359.

Cattaneo, L. B. and Chapman, A. R. (2010). The process of empowerment: A model for use in research and practice. *American Psychologist*, 65, 646-659. doi: 10.1037/a0018854.

Chen, H., Fang, X., Liu, C., Hu, W., Lan, J. and Deng, L. (2014). Associations among the number of mental health problems, stigma, and seeking help from psychological services: A path analysis model among Chinese adolescents. *Children and Youth Services Review*, 44356-362. doi:10.1016/j.childyouth.2014.07.003.

Corrigan, P. W. (2004). Enhancing personal empowerment of people with psychiatric disabilities. *American Rehabilitation*, 10-21.

Corrigan, P. W. and Calabrese, J. D. (2005). Strategies for assessing and diminishing self-stigma. In: P. W. Corrigan (Ed.), *On the stigma of mental illness: Practical strategies for research and social change* (pp. 239-256). Washington, DC: American Psychological Association.

Corrigan, P. W. and Kosyluk, K. A. (2014). Mental illness stigma: Types, constructs, and vehicles for change. In: P. W. Corrigan, P. W. Corrigan (Eds.), The stigma of disease and disability: Understanding causes and overcoming injustices (pp. 35-56). Washington, DC, US: American Psychological Association. doi: 10.1037/14297-003.

Glauber, D. (1996). *The evolution of supportive housing.* National Housing Institute (NHI). Retrieved from http://www.nhi.org/online/issues/88/suphousing.html.

Herman, S., Onaga, E., Pernice-Duca, F., Oh, S. and Ferguson, C. (2005). Sense of community in clubhouse programs: Member and staff concepts. *American Journal of Community Psychology*, 34(3-4), 343-356.

King, R., Lloyd, C. and Meehan, T. (2007). *Handbook of psychosocial rehabilitation.* Oxford, UK: Blackwell Publishing.

Krajewski, C., Burazeri, G. and Brand, H. (2013). Self-stigma, perceived discrimination and empowerment among people with a mental illness in six countries: Pan European stigma study. *Psychiatry Research*, 210(3), 1136-1146. doi: 10.1016/j.psychres.2013.08.013.

Lehman, A. F., Goldberg, R., Dixon, L. B., McNary, S., Postrado, L., Hackman, A. and McDonnell, K. (2002). Improving employment outcomes for persons with severe mental illness. *Archives of General Psychiatry*, 59, 165-172.

Linhorst, D. M. and Eckert, A. (2003). Conditions for empowering people with severe mental illness. *Social Services Review*, 77(2). 279-305. doi: 10.1086/373909.

Linhorst, D. M., Hamilton, G., Young, E. and Eckert, A. (2002). Opportunities and barriers to empowering people with severe mental illness through participation in treatment planning. *Social Work*, 47(4), 425-434.

Marchinko, S. and Clarke, D. (2011). The wellness planner: Empowerment, quality of life, and continuity of care in mental illness. *Archives of Psychiatric Nursing*, 25(4), 284-293. doi: 10.1016/j.apnu.2010.10.003.

National Alliance for Mental Illness. (2003). *Treatments and services: Supported employment.* Retrieved from http://www2.nami.org/Content/NavigationMenu/Inform_Yourself/About_Mental_Illness/About_Treatments_and_Supports/Supported_Employment1.htm.

National Coalition for the Homeless. (2009). *Mental illness and homelessness*. Retrieved from http://www.nationalhomeless.org/factsheets/Mental_Illness.pdf.

The National Institute of Mental Health. (n.d.). *Serious mental illness (smi) among US adults.* Retrieved from http://www.nimh.nih.gov/health/statistics/prevalence/serious-mental-illness-smi-among-us-adults.shtml.

Page, N. and Czuba, C. (1999). Empowerment: What is it? *Journal of Extension*, 37(5). Retrieved from http://www.joe.org/joe/1999october/comm1.php.

Paluch, T., Fossey, E. and Harvey, C. (2012). Social firms: Building cross-sectoral partnerships to create employment opportunity and supportive workplaces for people with mental illness. *IOS Press*, 43, 63-75. doi: 10.3233/WOR-2012-1448.

Pedersen, E. R. and Paves, A. P. (2014). Comparing perceived public stigma and personal stigma of mental health treatment seeking in a young adult sample. *Psychiatry Research*, 219(1), 143-150. doi: 10.1016/j.psychres.2014.05.017.

Phillips, L. A. (2013). Modern perceptions of mental illness and movements to decrease stigma. In: T. G. Plante (Ed.), *Abnormal Psychology across the Ages, Vol. III: Future Directions and Current Trends*, pp. 107-117. Santa Barbara, CA: Praeger/ABC-CLIO.

Phillips, L. A. and Schade, D. N. (2012). Implementing empowerment psychoeducation in a psychosocial rehabilitation setting. *The International Journal of Psychosocial Rehabilitation*, 16(1), 112-119.

Quinn, N., Wilson, A., MacIntyre, G. and Tinklin, T. (2009). 'People look at you differently': Students' experience of mental health support within higher education. *British Journal of Guidance and Counselling*, 37(4), 405-418. doi: 10.1080/03069880903161385.

Schutt, R. K. and Rogers, E. S. (2009). Empowerment and peer support: Structure and a process of self-help in a consumer-run center for individuals with mental illness. *Journal of Community Psychology*, 37(6), 697-710. doi: 10.1002/jcop.20325.

Strack, K. M., Deal, W. P. and Schulenberg, S. E. (2007). Coercion and empowerment in the treatment of individuals with serious mental illness: A preliminary investigation. *Psychological Services*, 4(2), 96-106. doi: 10.1037/1541-1559.4.2.96.

Substance Abuse and Mental Health Services Administration (2006). *SAMHSA issues consensus statement on mental health recovery.* Retrieved from http://www.samhsa.gov/news/newsreleases/060215_consumer.htm.

Substance Abuse and Mental Health Services Administration (n.d.). *National Consensus statement on mental health recovery*. Retrieved from http://store.samhsa.gov/shin/content//SMA05-4129/SMA05-4129.pdf.

Tambuyzer, E. and Audenhove, C. (2013). Is perceived patient involvement in mental health care associated with satisfaction and empowerment?. *Health Expectations: An International Journal of Public Participation In Health Care and Health Policy*, doi: 10.1111/hex.12052.

Topkaya, N. (2014). Gender, self-stigma, and public stigma in predicting attitudes toward psychological help-seeking. *Kuram Ve Uygulamada Eğitim Bilimleri*, 14(2), 480-487.

US Conference of Mayors. (2008). *Hunger and homeless survey.* Retrieved from http://usmayors.org/pressreleases/documents/hungerhomelessness report_121208.pdf.

US Department of Health and Human Services. (2009). *Supported employment: Building your program.* (DHHS Pub. No. SMA-08-04364). Retrieved from https://store.samhsa.gov/shin/content/SMA08-4365/BuildingYourProgram-SE.pdf.

US Department of Housing and Urban Development. Office of Community Planning and Development (HUD-OCPD). (2013). *The annual homeless assessment report to Congress* (2013). Retrieved from https://www.hudexchange.info/resources ahar-2013-part1.pdf.

US Psychiatric Rehabilitation Association. (n.d.). Retrieved from: http://www.uspra.org.

Ward, E. C., Clark, L. O. and Heidrich, S. (2009). African American women's beliefs, coping behaviors, and barriers to seeking mental health services. *Qualitative Health Research*, 19(11), 1589-1601. doi: 10.1177/1049732309350686.

Williams, A., Fossey, E. and Harvey, C. (2010). Social firms: Sustainable employment for people with mental illness. *IOS Press*, 43, 53-62. doi: 10.3233/WOR-2012-1447.

Yasui, N. Y. and Berven, N. L. (2009). Community integration: Conceptualization and measurement. *Disability and Rehabilitation*, 31(9), 761-771. doi: 10.1080/09638280802306638.

In: Empowerment
Editor: Randall Harris

ISBN: 978-1-63484-036-1

Chapter 3

EMPOWERMENT TO ENHANCE SOCIAL INTEGRATION AMONG MAINLAND CHINESE MIGRANTS IN HONG KONG

Chau-kiu Cheung
City University of Hong Kong, Hong Kong, China

ABSTRACT

A steady influx of migrants originates from Mainland China to stay in Hong Kong, a special administrative region of China since 1997. These migrants face difficulties in integrating into Hong Kong because of discrepancy in lifestyle and sociopolitical environment between Hong Kong and Mainland China. Conceivably, the migrants need empowerment to reduce the discrepancy in order to achieve social integration. Such empowerment can come from the migrants' hometown or village fellows, superiors, and social service professionals in Hong Kong. Particularly, the professionals provide empowerment through skill training, aid for social networking, individual counseling, and family counseling to the migrants. Nevertheless, how these ways of empowerment enhance the migrants' social integration is largely uncharted. To shed light on the ways, this study employs survey data collected from 2,846 such migrants. Results revealed a significant but weak main positive effect of aid for social networking on the migrant's social integration. Moreover, very high levels of aid from superiors and from hometown or village fellows indicated significant positive effects. What is more, individual counseling, skill training, and aid for social networking displayed significant interaction effects coupled with some conditions. These results imply some strategies for empowerment to enhance the migrant's social integration efficiently.

Social integration into host society, empowerment, and their relationship in the immigrant are crucial for research to inform policies and practices. For the immigrant, social integration means living harmoniously with people in host society, and empowerment means receiving aid to enhance capability (Bourhis et al. 2009; Gullan et al. 2013). The aid can stem from formal as well as informal sources (Cox 2002; Hung 2012). Whereas empowerment from the formal source includes skill training, aid for social networking, individual counseling, family counseling, and aid from superiors, empowerment from the informal source includes aid from hometown or village fellows of the origin. While empowerment is generally supposed to contribute to the immigrant, existing research findings have not offered a clear and detailed picture about the various kinds and ways of the contribution. Notably, such a detail is germane to policy and practice for enhancing immigrants' social integration into host society (Dierckx and Van Dam 2014; Hung 2012). A possible reason for the unclear picture is the diversity of empowerment and related conditions for the contribution. That is, a different form of empowerment can have a differential effect on the immigrant's social integration under a different condition. For grasping the differentials in the real-life picture, the present study examines the main and conditional effects of the various forms of empowerment on the immigrant's social integration into host society in Hong Kong, China.

Hong Kong has been a paradise for immigrants, mainly from the bordering place in Mainland China (Law and Lee 2006; Wong 2006). Those immigrants from Mainland China, properly called migrants in Hong Kong, come to Hong Kong mainly for family, work, and political reasons. Obviously, many residents in Hong Kong maintain familial relations with inhabitants in Mainland China (So 2011). Migrants thus are primarily the spouses, offspring, and other relatives of residents in Hong Kong (Zhang and Wu 2011). Despite the familial linkage, nevertheless, migrants and Hong Kong people have differences in sociocultural and political contexts that would retard migrants' social integration into Hong Kong (Sautman and Kneehans 2002). Such retardation can stem from discrimination, marginalizing, and thus disempowerment by people in Hong Kong against migrants (Law and Lee 2006). To expedite migrants' social integration, empowerment is thereby of concern in policy and practice in Hong Kong (Hung 2012). Anyhow, development in migrants is a crucial goal of public policy there (Wong 2006).

The migrant's social integration in host society is important in Hong Kong as well as in other societies. Intrinsically, social integration is a valued property in the individual and society as well and represents a social expectation or norm (Horenczyk and Tatar 1998). Social integration is also intrinsically meaningful as a representation of social identity, which is integral to everyone's psychosocial development (Kosic 2002). Furthermore, social integration is extrinsically vital as a precursor to achievement (Freeman 2000). Essentially, social integration counts as an achievement as well. Social integration has also appeared to be a precondition for well-being or happiness and academic achievement among immigrants (Bankston and Zhou 1995; Rose et al. 2014). Conversely, the lack of social integration is problematic, such as a generator of inequality, discrimination, and conflict (Freeman 2000). What is more, the lack of social integration has appeared to be a determinant of risk taking and substance abuse (Bankston and Zhou 1995; Ramirez-Valles et al. 2010). The significance of social integration further hinges on its inadequacy among immigrants (Rosenthal et al. 2007).

Empowerment is also essential intrinsically and extrinsically. In the first place, empowerment counters powerlessness, which is the source of many social problems in the immigrant (Dierckx and Van Dam 2014). By contrast, having power is meaningful and instrumental as a basis for the immigrant's competence, autonomy, and social integration, in according with the self-determination view about empowerment (Gullan et al. 2013). In general, empowerment is significant from the following perspectives. First, the perspective of oppression hints that empowerment is useful for tackling oppression to remove alienation, discrimination, and marginalization, which can lead to poverty (Bartle et al. 2002; Langley

2001; McWhirter 1994). Second, the ecological perspective states that empowerment means or contributes to the person's adaptation, exchange, and fit to the environment (Wise 2005). Third, the feminist perspective maintains that empowerment is necessary to dispel gender inequality and oppression (Lee 2001). Fourth, the systems perspective indicates that empowerment is necessary to sustain the person's flexibility, interconnection, participation, and distinctiveness in order to uphold the functioning of the total system (Wise 2005). Fifth, the liberation perspective posits that empowerment is crucial for human liberation in order to fulfill human nature (Lee 2001). Sixth, the strengths perspective reasons that empowerment is required to build and consolidate the person's strengths (Pease 2002). Nevertheless, empowerment remains a concern for clarification and research because it appears to be rhetoric (Pease 2002). That is, research evidence has not been blatant to demonstrate the power of empowerment as proposed. A worse case is that empowerment degenerates into the complicity of oppression in sustaining and legitimizing oppression (Yip 2004). This argument rests on the premise that the context of power imbalance cannot give empowerment effectively or genuinely. As the ubiquity of such a context is undeniable, clarification of the power of empowerment is necessary to address the issue.

EXPECTED CONTRIBUTIONS OF VARIOUS FORMS OF EMPOWERMENT TO SOCIAL INTEGRATION

The contribution of empowerment is not straightforward because of the presence of the various forms of empowerment, including aid from hometown or village fellows, aid from superiors, skill training, aid for social networking, individual counseling, and family counselling provided by informal or formal sources. That is, the diverse forms of empowerment are likely to engender diverse effects on the immigrant's social integration in host society. Nevertheless, the contributions represent a key proposition of empowerment theory. Empowerment theory obviously posits that empowerment is beneficial through the enhancement of information, knowledge, skill, control, resources, connectedness, social integration, and generally power in the person (Fuchsel 2014; Gullan et al. 2013). In other words, power encompasses strengths, autonomy, rationality, cohesion, collaboration and others that represent usable energy for practice (Hung 2012; Stacki and Monkman 2003). The key of the theory is a person's acquisition of power to enable practices beneficial to the person. More critically, empowerment theory asserts that the benefit is contingent on the person's initial state of powerlessness (Lee 2001). Powerlessness in turn is a reflection of oppression and injustice (Chapin and Cox 2001). Thus, empowerment would be more beneficial in the case of greater powerlessness, oppression, and injustice. Furthermore, empowerment theory envisions the synergistic effect of combination of various forms of power. Notably, combination of personal and collective power would generate an extraordinarily greater benefit than either power (Bohem and Staples 2002; Lee 2001).

Aid from other people generally benefits the immigrant. With respect to empowerment theory, the aid injects power to the person to activate the person's action for the person's benefit. The benefit has appeared in the person's enhancement of health, self-esteem, adjustment, social adjustment, well-being, academic engagement, college attendance, career commitment, and reduction in anxiety, distress, depression, and discrimination felt (De

Garms et al. 2006; Diwan and Jonnalagadda 2001; Finch et al. 2000; Garcia-Reid 2007; Kovacev and Shute 2004; Leal-Muniz 2005; Lee et al. 2012; Oppedal et al. 2004; Ryabov 2009; Sumer et al. 2008; Tsang 2001; Yeh et al. 2014; Zimmerman et al. 2000). Notably, the aid has indicated shown a positive effect on the receiver's social integration (Kovacev and Shute 2004). Moreover, a mentor's support has shown a positive effect on the protégé's social integration (Sanchez et al. 2008). Support from host people has also shown a positive effect on social integration (Murphy 2013). Aid from colleagues has displayed a positive effect on the immigrant's adjustment (Liu and Shaffer 2005). Nevertheless, aid from hometown fellows has also appeared to be unhelpful to the immigrant, such as the raising of stress and discrimination experienced (Landale and Oropesa 1999; Portes 1995a). Hence, the contributions of aid from various sources can have different effects on the immigrant.

Skill training is likely to confer a positive effect on the migrant's social integration into host society. In light of empowerment theory, skill training upgrades the migrant's power to integrate into host society. Existing supportive research findings are as follows. First, direct evidence for the contribution of training on social integration is available (Lu et al. 2013). Second, indirect evidence stems from the contribution of training to income or wages and civic responsibility (Gullan et al. 2013; Knight and Song 2005; Lu et al. 2013).

Individual counseling (i.e., involving the immigrant), family (i.e., involving the immigrant and his or her family as well) counseling, and other formal aid represent the formal intervention or program to enhance the immigrant's power. Such formal intervention has exhibited contributions to the immigrant's conduct, social networking, distress reduction, school achievement, parenting efficacy or skill, employment, and abstinence from substances (Bjorknes et al. 2015; Delander et al. 2005; Leung et al. 2011; Springer et al. 2004; Taylor and Lopez 2005; Williamson et al. 2014). Nevertheless, the intervention or programs have not always been helpful in empowering the immigrant. Such programs include those involving children, big brothers, family strengthening (Leung et al. 2011; Royse 1998; Spoth et al. 2003).

RESEARCH QUESTIONS

Given the uncertainty concerning the effects of various forms of empowerment on the migrant's social integration, the research questions of the study are about main and conditional effects. Conditions for examination include background characteristics. Each of the characteristics can also affect social integration as well as empowerment experienced. Some existing findings regarding the characteristics are as follows.

The female immigrant has appeared to have higher social integration into host society has the male immigrant (Liang 1994). She may have greater ability for social interaction and thus social integration (Feingold 1994).

The older immigrant has appeared to have greater social integration into host society (Baker et al. 2000; Rubin et al. 2012). With respect to empowerment theory, the older person has more resources to facilitate the immigrant's social integration (Freeman 2000; Hallerod 2006). Such resources include knowledge and social class as well (Parrado 2005; Price et al. 2006). The proximity of the origin, indicated by the neighboring provinces of Guangdong and Fujian in Mainland China, may facilitate social integration. From the perspective of empowerment theory, the proximity may expedite access to resources from the origin and that would raise the migrant's power. In this regard, proximity has been an indicator of the immigrant's social capital (Dominguez and Watkins 2003). Education, notably before arrival at host society, has appeared to facilitate social integration into host society (Mastinovic et al. 2009). In line with empowerment theory, eduation is a basis for power, competence, or efficacy (Cerin and Leslie 2008). Such power, notably in terms of language proficiency, has appeared to underlie social integration into host society (Braun and Glockner-Rist 2011).

Disability before arrival at host society is likely to impede social integration into host society. This is because physical functioning due to disability has appeared to impede social functioning (Henry et al. 2009). For instance, physical and cognitive disabilities have appeared to reduce social integration in general (Cornwall 2009; Granzin and Haggard 2000).

Membership in the Chinese Community Party is likely a source of power or resources to facilitate social integration in host society. This membership has appeared to characterize Chinese with higher education (Zhang and Treiman 2012). Thus, the membership is an indicator of power or resources, which would be conducive to social integration.

The presence of the immigrant's parents and/or siblings in Hong Kong is likely to facilitate social integration there by offering needed resources. This presence would be another indicator of power or resources. Notably, family resources are conducive to the immigrant's social integration (Liang 1994).

Having friends in Hong Kong is likely to facilitate the immigrant's social integration into Hong Kong. This is in line with existing research findings (Kovacev and Shute 2004; Ying 2002). Friends would represent a source of resources or power (Carbery and Buhrmester 1998).

The year of arrival at Hong Kong indicates how recent the migration is. Conceivably, recent migration leaves little time for the migrant to gather power to sustain social integration into Hong Kong. Conversely, residency in host society is likely to accumulate resources for the social integration. This has appeared to be the case (Braun and Glockner-Risk 2011; Yue et al. 2013).

Study in Hong Kong is likely to enhance resources or power for social integration in Hong Kong. This is simply the case of acculturation. Acculturation has appeared to facilitate the immigrant's social integration (Birman et al. 2005; Wenzel 2006; Yoon et al. 2008). Moreover, studying in host society has indicated a contribution to social integration into the society (Mastinovic et al. 2009). According to empowerment theory, studying in host society consolidates resources, known as cultural capital, conducive to social integration.

The number of years taken to learn the host dialect of Cantonese would indicate a lower level of language capability and this low level would impede the migrant's social integration into Hong Kong. This aligns with the finding that host language proficiency facilitates social integration into host society (Braun and Glockner-Risk 2011; Mastinovic et al. 2009).

Welfare reception may facilitate social integration into the host society through obtaining financial and social resources from connection with social welfare agencies and personnel. Notably, the connection may provide opportunities for acculturation. Such cultural and social resources have appeared to contribute to the immigrant's social integration into host society (Shih 1998; Yue et al. 2013).

The asset, monthly family income, and flat size of the immigrant's residence indicate wealth or economic power, According to empowerment theory, such power is conducive to social integration. This contribution of economic power has been evident (Baker et al. 2000; Freeman 2000).

METHOD

Participants

Data came from a survey of 2,846 migrants from Mainland China in the special administrative region of Hong Kong. Recruitment of these migrants relied on the support of 50 social service agencies in Hong Kong. These agencies maintained some contact with or rendered services to migrants. With the help of the agencies, research personnel managed to contact the recruited migrants to conduct the survey with them individually.

The migrants who participated in the survey had an average of 31.9 years in age, 23.4 years in age at arrival at Hong Kong, 8.1 years in education, and 7.0 years in education in Mainland China (see Table 1). Among them, 62.3% were female, 80.6% coming from the neighboring province Guangdong, 9.1% coming from the next neighboring province of Fujian, 41.5% having both parents in Hong Kong at arrival, and 17.5% receiving welfare. On average, the immigrant took 3.7 years to learn Cantonese.

Measurement

Social integration at the time of the survey was a composite (i.e., average) of six seven-point rating items: liking Hong Kong, liking the Hong Kong lifestyle, being a Hongkonger, joining activities in Hong Kong, interacting with the people of Hong Kong, and having no wish to return to Mainland China (Keyes and Shapiro 2004). These items were randomly interspersed in the questionnaire to reduce unnecessary influences among them due to adjacency. Each item gave a score on a 0-100 scale, with a score of 0 for the first point, 16.7 for the second point, 33.3 for the third point, 50 for the fourth point, and 63.3 for the fifth point, 86.7 for the sixth point, and 100 for the seventh point. The internal-consistency reliability of the composite was .725.

Social integration at the time of arrival at Hong Kong was a composite (i.e., average) of four seven-point rating items: liking Hong Kong, liking the Hong Kong lifestyle, being accustomed to the Hong Kong lifestyle, and having no wish to return to Mainland China (Keyes and Shapiro 2004). These items were randomly interspersed in the questionnaire to reduce unnecessary influences among them due to adjacency. Each item gave a score on a 0-100 scale, with a score of 0 for the first point, 16.7 for the second point, 33.3 for the third point, 50 for the fourth point, and 63.3 for the fifth point, 86.7 for the sixth point, and 100 for the seventh point. The internal-consistency reliability of the composite was .572.

Empowerment since arriving at Hong Kong comprised six seven-point rating items: aid from hometown/village fellows, aid from superiors, skill training, aid for social networking, individual counseling, and family counseling. Each item gave a score on a 0-100 scale, with a score of 0 for the first point, 16.7 for the second point, 33.3 for the third point, 50 for the fourth point, and 63.3 for the fifth point, 86.7 for the sixth point, and 100 for the seventh point. These items were randomly interspersed in the questionnaire to reduce unnecessary influences among them due to adjacency. Notably, the indicators reflected real-life empowerment rather than any laboratory form of empowerment created provisionally for research.

Table 1. Means and standard deviations (*N* = 2,846)

Variable	Scoring	*M*	*SD*
Aid from hometown/village fellows	0-100	43.9	33.5
Aid from superiors	0-100	41.4	33.1
Skill training	0-100	42.5	36.8
Aid for social networking	0-100	46.1	35.3
Individual counseling	0-100	39.9	35.6
Family counseling	0-100	32.1	33.7
Acquiescence	0-100	49.7	15.2
Female	0, 100	62.3	48.5
Age	0, 100	31.9	17.8
Guangdong origin	0, 100	80.6	39.5
Fujian origin	0, 100	9.1	28.8
Age at arrival	0, 100	23.4	14.8
Education before arrival	years	7.0	2.9
Disability before arrival	0, 100	4.0	19.5
Communist Party member	0, 100	2.4	15.5
Father in Hong Kong at arrival	0, 100	15.7	36.4
Mother in Hong Kong at arrival	0, 100	9.7	29.6
Both parents in Hong Kong at arrival	0, 100	41.5	49.3
Siblings in Hong Kong at arrival	persons	1.0	1.2
Siblings in Mainland China at arrival	persons	1.3	1.8
Friends in Hong Kong at arrival	persons	3.6	10.1
Application years	years	4.8	4.1
Year of arrival	year	1998.6	10.3
Social integration at arrival	0-100	56.7	22.1
Studying in Hong Kong	months	26.0	35.2
Years to learn Cantonese	years	3.7	17.8
Education	years	8.1	3.0
Welfare reception	0, 100	17.5	38.0
Welfare reception months	0, 100	3.4	12.8
Asset	0, 100	3.8	19.2
Monthly family income	US$	1418.9	1499.3
Flat size	sq. ft.	463.2	255.8
Social integration	0-100	65.1	19.1

Acquiescence was the composite of all rating items. This served as a control variable to minimize the method artifact of the acquiescence response set.

Analytic Procedure

Linear regression analysis proceeded with four steps to analyze the effects of predictors on the outcome of current social integration into the host society of Hong Kong. The first entered basic background characteristics. In the second step, details about welfare reception, assets, family income, and residential flat size were additional predictors to check their more detailed effects. The third step entered empowerment indicators. Lastly, the four step added significant interactions between empowerment indicators and background characteristics. In this connection, the stepwise selection procedure ensured that the interactions were significant (i.e., showing significant effects on social integration). To minimize the problem of multicollinearity in regression analysis, each interaction referred to the product of an empowerment indicator and background characteristics using their standard scores. Similarly, the square of each indicator of empowerment was also an additional entered in the fourth step. This was to reveal any quadratic effect of empowerment.

RESULTS

Social integration in the average migrant displayed some rise since arriving at Hong Kong (M = 56.7 to 65.1, see Table 1). Eventually, the average social integration level was moderately high. Meanwhile, empowerment since the arrival in terms of six indicators was at a modest level (M= 32.1-46.1).

In analyzing the effects of predictors on social integration, the first step of regression analysis revealed that age and welfare reception manifested significant positive effects, whereas the Fujian origin, disability before arrival, and the year of arrival displayed significant negative effects (see Table 2). In other words, the older migrant or the welfare recipient maintained greater social integration into Hong Kong, whereas the migrant who had come from Fujian rather than another place, had a disability before arrival, or a recent arrival had lower social integration. Nevertheless, these effects on social integration were very weak. Other main background characteristics in this step did not show significant effects. Evidently, social integration at the time of arrival was the major predictor of current social integration. The analysis controlled for acquiescence, which represented some bias and thus required controlling in the analysis.

Table 2. Standard effects on social integration

Predictor	(1)	(2)	(3)	(4)
Acquiescence	.221***	.223***	.225***	.242***
Female	.001	.001	-.001	-.001
Age	.095***	.089***	.079**	.058*
Guangdong origin	-.006	-.006	-.006	.006
Fujian origin	-.044*	-.044*	-.044*	-.041*
Education before arrival	-.016	-.013	-.010	.001
Disability before arrival	-.038*	-.042*	-.040*	-.040*
Communist Party member	.005	.004	.002	.008

Predictor	(1)	(2)	(3)	(4)
Father in Hong Kong at arrival	.036	.035	.035	.029
Mother in Hong Kong at arrival	.030	.030	.029	.027
Both parents in Hong Kong at arrival	.013	.011	.010	.009
Siblings in Hong Kong at arrival	-.012	-.012	-.011	-.012
Siblings in Mainland China at arrival	-.011	-.009	-.005	-.002
Friends in Hong Kong at arrival	.028	.028	.025	.009
Application years	-.001	-.003	-.006	-.014
Year of arrival	-.102***	-.103***	-.106***	-.113***
Social integration at arrival	.491***	.490***	.489***	.487***
Studying in Hong Kong	-.002	-.002	-.002	.006
Years to learn Cantonese	-.028	-.031	-.032*	-.032*
Education	-.011	-.011	-.012	-.004
Welfare reception	.038*	.020	.020	.008
Welfare reception months		.038*	.034	.035
Asset		-.010	-.010	-.017
Monthly family income		-.006	-.006	-.014
Flat size		.005	.006	.003
Aid from hometown/village fellows			.006	-.005
Aid from superiors			.008	-.009
Skill training			-.011	.001
Aid for social networking			.041*	.018
Individual counseling			-.034	-.037
Family counseling			-.010	.012
Aid from superiors squared				.077***
Aid from hometown/village fellows squared				.072***
Individual counseling × Welfare reception				.097***
Individual counseling × Age at arrival				-.093***
Individual counseling × Communist Party member				-.057***
Individual counseling × Guangdong origin				-.057***
Individual counseling × Acquiescence				-.055**
Aid for social networking × Age				.075***
Skill training × Aid for social networking				.053**
R^2	.316	.317	.318	.353

The second step of regression analysis manifested that duration in welfare reception in Hong Kong was the additional significant predictor of social integration. This duration displaced the state of welfare reception as a significant predictor. Nevertheless, the effect of welfare duration remained trivial, despite its statistical significance. Meanwhile, family assets did not introduced significant effects.

The third step of regression analysis introduced empowerment indicators as the predictors of current social integration into Hong Kong. Among the six indicators, only aid for social networking manifested a significant positive but very weak effect. The empowerment indicators thus made a very little difference in explanation for social integration (R^2 = .318 vs. .317).

The fourth step of regression analysis revealed a squared empowerment indicator and eight interactions involving empowerment and background characteristics to indicate significant effects on current social integration. First, the square of aid from superiors revealed a significant positive effect. This effect meant that social integration was higher in either the high end or low end of the aid. Second, the square of aid from hometown or village fellows evolved a positive effect. This meant that social integration was higher in both the high and low ends than in the middle. Third, the interaction between individual counseling and welfare reception indicated a positive effect. That is, the effect of individual counseling was more positive on the welfare recipient. Fourth, the interaction between individual counseling and age at arrival manifested a negative effect. That is, the effect of individual counseling was weaker on the migrant with higher age at arrival. Fifth, the interaction between individual counseling and Chinese Communist Party membership rendered a negative effect. This effect meant that individual counseling was less helpful to the party member. Sixth, the interaction between individual counseling and Guangdong origin registered a negative effect. That is, the effect of individual counseling was less positive on the migrant coming from Guangdong. Seventh, the effect of the interaction between individual counseling and acquiescence was negative. That is, individual counseling had a less positive effect on one with great a acquiescent response style. Eighth, the interaction between aid for social networking and age displayed a positive effect. That is, the effect of the aid was more positive on the older migrant. Ninth, the interaction between skill training and aid for social networking generated a positive effect. This meant that the presence of both forms of empowerment introduced a particularly greater positive effect. In other word, the two forms reinforced the effect of each other.

DISCUSSION

Results principally reveal that empowerment exerted conditional effects rather than main effects on the migrant's social integration into the host society of Hong Kong. The conditional effects appear to fit empowerment theory in two ways, such that empowerment is effective in the case of powerlessness and empowerment is effective by combining its various forms. This fit happens in the significant interaction effects involving empowerment indicators and background characteristics. First, individual counseling had a more positive effect on social integration when the migrant was a welfare recipient, younger at the time of arrival, not being a Chinese Communist Party member, and not coming from Guangdong. Welfare reception, younger age at arrival, not being the party member, and not coming from Guangdong tend to reflect less power than not receiving welfare, older age at arrival, party membership, and coming from Guangdong do (Herrnstein and Murray 1994; Hess et al.

2005). Notably, the Guangdong origin represents the closest place to Hong Kong, and thus the greatest access to resources. Similarly, membership in the Chinese Communist Party is an indication of power (Johnson and Ali 2004; Karstedt 2003). Welfare reception, nevertheless, can be a form of empowerment to acquire financial and social resources (Delander et al. 2005; Morris 2007). The reception may reinforce the help of individual counseling and vice versa. Second, aid for social networking appeared to be more helpful to the older migrant. The results also notably show that the older migrant maintained greater social integration. Thus, the older migrant is likely to receive empowerment or resources to raise social integration (Baker et al. 2000; Rubin et al. 2012). The aid might thereby reinforce other forms of empowerment to boost the social integration of the older migrant. This is the synergistic effect of combining multiple forms of empowerment. Third, combination of aid for social networking and skill training tended to manifest an extra contribution to social integration. This combination, incorporating human capital and social capital, appears to be extraordinarily helpful.

Results also reveal that aid for social networking was the only empowerment indicator delivering a significant main effect on the migrant's social integration. This positive effect, nevertheless, was very weak. In addition, aid for social networking combined with age and skill training to yield positive interaction effects on social integration. Hence, the aid appears to be more important than the other empowerment indicators. The importance tends to rest on collective empowerment by the aid, which can be much powerful than personal empowerment. This inevitably indicates the unique contribution of collective power (Cox 2002; Fuchsel 2014; Gullan et al. 2013). Apparently, help from collective power can be unlimited, unlike that from personal power. The help evidently reflects the powerful influence of collective power on the immigrant social integration (Kovacev and Shute 2004; Ying 2002). Thus, the aid is a means to empower the migrant to acquire collective power to install social integration. Besides, the aid for social networking is clearly the most relevant form of empowerment for social integration.

The squares of aid from supervisors and hometown fellows revealed significant positive effects on the migrant's social integration. Notably, the quadratic rather than linear effects of the two sources of aid were influential. The quadratic effects reflect the profound function of empowerment. A simple interpretation of the profound function is that the aid is helpful only when it is large in volume. One reason for this is that a small volume of the aid is too commonplace to make any difference. Thus, aid from supervisors and hometown fellows still appeared to be effective empowerment, when they were in large volumes. This reflects the critical mass perspective of empowerment (Campbell and Russo 2003; Gregg 2012; Oliver and Marwell 2001; Swaroop and Morenoff 2006).

Background characteristics reflective of empowerment are age, the origin of Fujian, disability before arrival at Hong Kong, the year of arrival, years to learn Cantonese, and welfare reception. Age and welfare reception displayed significant positive effects on social integration. The effects reflected power related to age and welfare reception for social integration (Baker et al. 2000; Rubin et al. 2012). Specifically, welfare reception can facilitate the acquisition of financial and social resources (Delander et al. 2005; Morris 2007). Conversely, disability, recent arrival, time to learn Cantonese, and the origin of Fujian represent a lower level of power than do the others. For instance, Fujian is farther away from Hong Kong than is Guangdong. The migrant from Fujian might receive fewer resources from the origin than might the migrant from Guangdong.

Limitations and Future Research

The study has limitations in the single city and single time design. That is, it involved only migrants from Mainland China to the Chinese metropolis of Hong Kong. The migrants only reported their experiences retrospectively at the time of the survey. These migrants were also limited to those accessible through social service agencies. The limitations mean that results are somehow most relevant to Hong Kong and their generalizability to other places and the world is in need of future research. In this regard, future research needs to sample from various places with diverse sociocultural characteristics to gauge any variation among the places regarding the results of the present study. Future research can also go further to explain and predict the variation using the sociocultural characteristics of the places. To enhance the validity of the explanation and prediction, the desirable sampling used in future research is to secure representative samples in various places. That is, future research would need to approach immigrants not accessible by social service agencies. Another desirable feature for future research is the use of a panel design to track social integration and other factors prospectively. This is to minimize problems due to retrospective report, especially when the retrospective time is long. Analysis of panel data in future research also gives credence to causal inference concerning social integration. A further means to enhance validity is the incorporation of measures from multiple informants in future research. Remarkably, social integration involves multiple parties and thus multiple informants. The integration of the migrant thus naturally engages host society members who integrate with the migrant.

Elaboration of empowerment theory, regarding the main and conditional effects of empowerment, is also a vital task for future research. The two conditions for empowerment effectiveness, pertaining to powerlessness and the complementarity of the forms of empowerment, are in need of detailed investigation. That is, explicit measures of powerlessness and complementarity need to be present in future research to enable the investigation. Future research will then examine if the two conditions sustain the effectiveness of empowerment. Future research also needs to elaborate the linear and quadratic effects of various forms of empowerment. For the quadratic effect, future research essentially needs to scrutinize the threshold of the critical mass to make empowerment effective. An initial step of the scrutiny is the differentiation of aid and its helpfulness. That is, receiving much aid does not mean experiencing high helpfulness. Another factor for scrutiny is the cost for acquiring aid, which would neutralize the helpfulness of the aid (Oliver and Marwell 2001). According to the critical mass perspective, only when the cost plateaus does the aid become helpful.

Implications

The study reveals the effectiveness of real-life empowerment in the migrant's social integration into host society. Specifically, the study indicates that aid for social networking is effective generally and conditionally, whereas aid from superiors and hometown fellows, individual counseling, and skill training are effective conditionally. Notably, aid from superiors and hometown fellows would be effective when they are in large volumes, individual counseling would be effective for the powerless migrant, and skill training would be effective for the older migrant or in the presence of aid for social networking. These findings would provide a clear guideline for leveraging empowerment to enhance the migrant's social integration. Such a guideline would propound the following to foster the migrant's social integration. First, providing aid for social networking is generally helpful. Second, a condition for raising the effectiveness of empowerment is providing empowerment to powerless migrants. Third, another condition for raising the effectiveness is rendering multiple forms of empowerment, for instance, skill training and aid for social networking. Fourth, raising a high level of aid from superiors or hometown fellows is necessary to make it effective. In addition, social welfare arrangement can be a means to empower migrants by helping their engagement with formal and informal welfare services. The engagement is undeniably integral to migrants' social integration into host society.

REFERENCES

Baker, Susan Gonzalez. & Marilyn, Espitia (2000). "From Latin American Immigrant to Hispanic Citizen: The Role of Social Capital in Seeking U.S. Citizenship." *Social Science Quarterly*, *81*(4), 1053-1064.

Bankston, Carl L., III. & Min, Zhou (1995). "Religious Participation, Ethnic Identification, and Adaptation of Vietnamese Adolescents in an Immigrant Community." *Sociological Quarterly*, *36*(3), 523-534.

Bartle, Elizabeth E., Couchonnal, Graciela, Canda, Edward R. & Staker, Martha D. (2002). "Empowerment as a Dynamically Developing Concept for Practice: Lessons Learned from Organizational Ethnography." *Social Work*, *47*(1), 32-43.

Birman, Dina., Trickett, Edison. & Buchanan, Rebecca M. (2005). "A Tale of Two Cities: Replication of a Study on the Acculturation and Adaptation of Immigrant Adolescents from the Former Soviet Union in a Different Community Context." *American Journal of Community Psychology*, *35*(1/2), 83-101.

Bjorknes, Ragnhild, Marit, Larsen, Fungisai, Gwanzura-Ottemoller & John, Kjobli (2015). "Exploring Mental Distress among Immigrant Mothers Participating in Parent Training." *Children and Youth Services Review*, 51, 10-17.

Bohem, Amnon & Staples, Lee H. (2002). "The Functions of the Social Worker in Empowering: The Voices of Consumers and Professionals." *Social Work*, *47*(4), 449-460.

Bourhis, Richard Y., Genevieve Barrette, Shaha El-Geledi. & Ronald Schmidt, Sr. (2009). "Acculturation Orientations and Social Relations between Immigrant and Host Community Members in California." *Journal of Cross-Cultural Psychology*, *40*(3), 443-467.

Braun, Michael. & Angelika, Glockner-Rist (2012). "Patterns of Social Integration of Western European Migrants." *Journal of International Migration and Integration*, *13*(4), 403-422.

Campbell, Scott W. & Russo, Tracy C. (2003). "The Social Construction of Mobile Telephony: An Application of the Social Influence Model to Perceptions and Uses of Mobile Phones within Personal Communication Networks." *Communication Monographs*, *70*(4), 317-334.

Carbery, Julie & Duane, Buhrmester (1998). "Friendship and Need Fulfillment during Three Phases of Young Adulthood." *Journal of Social & Personal Relationships*, *15*(3), 393-409.

Cerin, Ester & Eva, Leslie (2008). "How Socio-economic Status Contributes to Participation in Leisure-time Physical Activity." *Social Science & Medicine*, *66*, 2596-2609.

Chapin, Rosemary & Enid Opal, Cox (2001). "Changing the Paradigm: Strengths-based and Empowerment-oriented Social Work with Frail Elders." *Journal of Gerontological Social Work*, *36*(3/4), 165-179.

Cornwall, Benjamin (2009). "Good Health and the Bridging of Structural Holes." *Social Networks*, *31*, 92-103.

Cox, Carole B. (2002). "Empowering African American Custodial Grandparents." *Social Work*, *47*(1), 45-53.

De Garms, David S. & Martinez, Jr. Charlos R. (2006). "A Culturally Informed Model of Academic Well-being for Latino Youth: The Importance of Discriminating Experiences and Social Support." *Family Relations*, *55*, 267-278.

Delander, Lennart, Mats, Hammarstedt, Jonas, Monsson & Erik, Nyberg (2005). "Integration of Immigrants: The Role of Language Proficiency and Experience." *Evaluation Review*, *29*(1), 24-41.

Dierckx, Danielle & Sylvie, Van Dam (2014). "Redefining Empowerment Interventions of Migrants Experiencing Poverty: The Case of Antwerp, Belgium." *British Journal of Social Work*, *44*(suppl 1), i105-i122.

Diwan, Badhna & Jonnalagadda, Satya S. (2001). "Social Integration and Health among Asian Indian Immigrants in the United States." *Journal of Gerontological Social Work*, *36*(1/3), 45-62.

Dominguez, Silvia & Celeste, Watkins (2003). "Creating Networks for Survival and Mobility: Social Capital among African-American and Latin-American Low Income Mothers." *Social Problems*, *50*(1), 111-135.

Feingold, Alan (1994). "Gender Differences in Personality: A Meta-analysis." *Psychological Bulletin*, *116*(3), 429-456.

Finch, Brian Karl, Bohdan, Kolody & Vega, William A. (2000). "Perceived Discrimination and Depression among Mexican-origin Adults in California." *Journal of Health & Social Behavior*, 41, 295-313.

Freeman, Lance (2000). "Minority Housing Segregation: A Test of Three Perspectives." *Journal of Urban Affairs*, *22*(1), 15-35.

Fuchsel, Catherine L. Marrs (2014). "Exploratory Evaluation of Si, Yo Puedo: A Culturally Competent Empowerment Program for Immigrant Latina Women in Group Settings." *Social Work with Groups*, *37*(4), 279-296.

Garcia-Reid, Pauline (2007). "Examining Social Capital as a Mechanism for Improving School Engagement among Low Income Hispanic Girls." *Youth & Society*, *39*(2), 164-181.

Granzin, Kent L. & Haggard, Lois M. (2000). "An Integrative Explanation for Quality of Life: Development and Test of a Structural Model." Pp.31-64 in *Advances in Quality of Life Theory and Research*, edited by Ed Diener and Don R. Rahtz. Dordrecht, Netherlands: Kluwer Academic.

Gregg, Benjamin (2012). *Human Rights as Social Construction*. Cambridge, UK: Cambridge University Press.

Gullan, Rebecca L., Power, Thomas J. & Leff, Stephen S. (2013). "The Role of Empowerment in a School-based Community Service Program with Inner-city Minority Youth." *Journal of Adolescent Research*, *28*(6), 664-689.

Hallerod, Bjorn (2006). "Sour Grapes: Relative Deprivation Adaptive Preferences and the Measurement of Poverty." *Journal of Social Policy*, *35*(3), 371-390.

Henry, Julie D., William, von Hippel & Kate, Baynes (2009). "Social Inappropriateness, Executive Control, and Aging." *Psychology & Aging*, *24*(1), 239-244.

Herrnstein, Richard J. & Charles, Murray (1994). *The Bell Curve: Intelligence and Class Structure in American Life*. New York: Free Press.

Hess, Thomas M., Osowski, Nicole L. & Leclerc, Christina M. (2005). "Age and Experience Influences on the Complexity of Social Inferences." *Psychology & Aging*, *20*(3), 447-459.

Horenczyk, Gobriel & Moshe, Tatar (1998). "Friendship Expectations among Immigrant Adolescents and Their Host Peers." *Journal of Adolescence*, *21*, 69-82.

Hung, Suet Lin (2012). "Empowerment Groups for Women Migrating from China to Hong Kong." *Social Work with Groups*, *35*(1), 4-17.

Johnson, Daniel K. N. & Ayfer, Ali (2004). "ATale of two Seasons: Participation and Medal Counts at the Summer and Winter Olympic Games." *Social Science Quarterly*, *85*(4), 974-993.

Karstedt, Susanne (2003). "Legacies of a Culture of Inequality: The Janus Face of Crime in Post-communist Countries." *Crime, Law & Social Change*, *40*, 293-320.

Keyes, Corey L. M. & Shapiro, Adam D. (2004). "Social Well-being in the United States: A Descriptive Epidemiology." pp.350-372 in *How Healthy Are We: A National Study of Well-being at Midlife*, edited by Orville Gilbert Brim, Carol D. Ryff and Ronald C. Kessler. Chicago, IL: University of Chicago Press.

Knight, John & Lina, Song (2005). *Towards a Labour Market in China*. Oxford, UK: Oxford University Press.

Kosic, Ankica. (2002). "Acculturation Attitudes Need for Cognitive Closure and Adaptation of Immigrants." *Journal of Social Psychology*, *142*(2), 179-201.

Kovacev, Lydia. & Rosalyn, Shute. (2004). "Acculturation and Social Support in Relation to Psychosocial Adjustment of Adolescent Refugees Resulted in Australia." *International Journal of Behavioral Development*, *28*(3), 259-267.

Landale, Nancy S. & Oropesa, R. S. (1999). "Does Americanization Have Adverse Effects on Health? Stress Health Habits and Infant Outcomes among Puerto Ricans." *Social Forces*, *78*(2), 613-641.

Langley, Jackie. (2001). "Developing Anti-oppressive empowering Social Work Practice with Older Lesbian Women and Gay Men." *British Journal of Social Work*, *31*, 917-932.

Law, Kam-yee. & Lee, Kim-ming (2006). "Citizenship, Economy and Social Exclusion of Mainland Chinese Immigrants in Hong Kong." *Journal of Contemporary Asia*, *36*(2), 217-242.

Leal-Muniz, Veronica. (2005). "Predictors of the Career Commitment Process in Mexican-American College Students." *Journal of Career Assessment*, *13*(2), 204-215.

Lee, Judith A. B. (2001). *The Empowerment Approach to Social Work Practice: Building the Beloved Community* (2nd ed.). New York: Columbia University Press.

Lee, Mohd Najib Redzuan, Andanastuti, Muchtar, Shahrum, Abdullah & Khairul & Anwar Mastor (2012). "Malaysian Students' Manifestation of Cultural Adaptation and Resilience during Theory Sojourn in Germany." *Asian Social Science*, *8*(16), 96-103.

Leung, Cynthia, Sandra, Tsang & Suzanne, Dean (2011). "Outcome Evaluation of the Hands on Parent Empowerment (HOPE) Program." *Research in Social Work Practice*, *21*(5), 549-561.

Liang, Zai (1994). "Social Contact, Social Capital, and the Naturalization Process: Evidence from Six Immigrant Groups." *Social Science Research*, *23*, 407-437.

Liu, Xiangyang & Shaffer, Margaret A. (2005). "An Investigation of Expatriate Adjustment and Performance: A Social Capital Perspective." *International Journal of Cross Cultural Management*, *5*(3), 235-354.

Lu, Yao, Danching, Ruanb & Gina, Laib (2013). "Social Capital and Economic Integration of Migrants In Urban China." *Social Networks*, *35*(3), 357-369.

Mastinovic, Borja, Frank, van Tauergen & Ineke, Maas (2009). "Dynamics of Interethnic Contact: A Panel Study of Immigrants in the Netherlands." *European Sociological Review*, *25*(3), 303-318.

McWhirter, Ellen Hawley (1994). *Counseling for Empowerment*. Alexandra, VA: American Counseling Association.

Morris, Lydia (2007). "New Labour's Community of Rights: Welfare Immigration and Asylum." *Journal of Social Policy*, *36*(1), 39-57.

Murphy, Esther (2013). "It's Funny I feel Much More Stigmatized by My Own Home Community: Investigating Visually Impaired Migrants' Experiences of Unsupportive Ethnic Community." *International Journal of Migration, Health & Social Care*, *9*(1), 4-16.

Oliver, Pamela E. & Gerald, Marwell (2001). "Whatever Happened to Critical Mass Theory? A Retrospective and Assessment." *Sociological Theory*, *19*(3), 292-311.

Oppedal, Brit, Espen, Roysamb & David, Lackland Sam (2004). "The Effect of Acculturation and Social Support Change in Mental Health among Young Immigrants." *International Journal of Behavioral Development*, *28*(6), 481-494.

Parrado, Emilio A. (2005). "Globalization and the Transition to Adulthood in Mexico." pp.327-348 in *Globalization, Uncertainty and Youth in Society*, edited by Hans-Peter Blossfeld, Erik Klijzing, Melinda Mills and Karin Kurz. London: Routledge.

Pease, Bob (2002). "Rethinking Empowerment: A Postmodern Reappraisal for Emancipatory Practice." *British Journal of Social Work*, *32*, 135-147.

Portes, Alejandro (1995a). "Children of Immigrants: Segmented Assimilation and Its Determinants." Pp.248-280 in *The Economic Sociology of Immigration: Essays on Networks, Ethnicity, and Entrepreneurship*, edited by Alejandro Portes. New York: Russell Sage Foundation.

Price, Vincent, Clarissa, David, Brian, Goldthorpe, Marci, Mccoy Roth & Cappella, Joseph N. (2006). "Locating the Issue Public: The Multi-dimensional Nature of Engagement with Health Care Reform." *Public Behavior*, *28*(1), 33-63.

Jesus, Ramirez-Valles, Kuhns, Lisa M., Campbell, Richard T. & Rafael, Diaz (2010). "Social Integration and Health: Community Involvement, Stigmatized Identities, and Sexual Risk in Latino Sexual Minorities." *Journal of Health & Social Behavior*, *51*(1), 30-47.

Rose, Theda, Sean, Joe., Joseph, Shields & Caldwell, Cleopatra H. (2014). "Social Integration and the Mental Health of Black Adolescents." *Child Development*, *85*(3), 1003-1018.

Rosenthal, Doreen Anne., Jean, Russell & Garry, Thomson (2007). "Social Connectedness among International Students at an Australian University." *Social Indicators Research*, *84*, 71-82.

Royse, David (1998). "Mentoring High-risk Minority Youth: Evaluation of the Brothers Project." *Adolescence*, *33*(129), 145-158.

Rubin, Mark, Watt, Sue E. & Marcella, Ramelli (2012). "Immigrants' Social Integration as a Function of Approach-Avoidance Orientation and Problem-Solving Style." *International Journal of Intercultural Relations*, *36*(4), 498-505.

Ryabov, Igor (2009). "The Role of Peer Social Capital in Educational Assimilation of Immigrant Youths." *Sociological Inquiry*, *79*(4), 453-480.

Sanchez, Bermadette, Patricia, Esparza & Yari, Colon (2008). "Natural Mentoring under the Microscope: An Investigation of Mentoring Relationships and Latino Adolescents' Academic Performance." *Journal of Community Psychology*, *36*(4), 468-482.

Sautman, Barry & Ellen, Kneehans (2002). *The Politics of Racial Discrimination in Hong Kong*. Baltimore, MY: University of Maryland School of Law.

Shih, Tzymei Alexasia (1998). "Finding the Niche: Friendship Formation of Immigrant Adolescents." *Youth & Society*, *30*(2), 209-240.

So, Alvin Y. (2011). "One Country, Two Systems and Hong Kong-China National Integration: A Crisis-transformation Perspective." *Journal of Contemporary Asia*, *41*(1), 99-116.

Spoth, Richard, Max, Guyll, Wei, Chao & Virginia, Molgaard (2003). "Exploratory Study of a Preventive Intervention with General Population: African American Families." *Journal of Early Adolescence*, *23*(4), 435-468.

Springer, J. Fred, Elizabeth, Sale, Rafa, Kasim, William, Winter, Soledad, Sambrano & Sandra, Chipungu (2004). "Effectiveness of Culturally Specific Approaches to Substance Abuse Prevention: Findings from CSAP's National Cross-site Evaluation of High Risk Youth Programs." *Journal of Ethnic & Cultural Diversity in Social Work*, *13*(3), 1-23.

Stacki, Sandra L. & Karen, Monkman (2003). "Change through Empowerment Processes: Women's Stories from South Asia and Latin America." *Compare*, *33*(2), 173-189.

Sumer, Seda, Senel, Poyrazli & Kamini, Grahame (2008). "Predictors of Depression and Anxiety among International Students." *Journal of Counseling & Development*, *86*, 429-437.

Swaroop, Sapna & Morenoff, Jeffrey D. (2006). "Building Community: The Neighborhood Context of Social Organization." *Social Forces*, *84*(3), 1665-1695.

Taylor, Ronald D. & Lopez, Elizabeth I. (2005). "Family Management Practice, School Achievement, and Problem Behavior in African American Adolescents: Mediating Processes." *Applied Developmental Psychology*, *26*, 39-49.

Tsang, Eric W. K. (2001). "Adjustment of Mainland Chinese Academics and Students to Singapore." *International Journal of International Relations*, *25*, 347-372.

Wenzel, James P. (2006). "Acculturation Effects on Trust in National and Local Government among Mexican Americans." *Social Science Quarterly*, *87*(5), 1073-1087.

Williamson, Ariel A., Lyndee, Knox., Nancy, Guerra. & Williams, Kirk R. A. (2014). "Pilot Randomized Trial of Community-Based Parent Training for Immigrant Latina Mothers." *American Journal of Community Psychology*, *53*(1-2), 47-59.

Wong, Siu-lun (2006). *Enhancing Population Potential for a Sustainable Future*. Hong Kong, China: Council for Sustainable Development.

Yeh, Christine J., Liao, Hsin-Ya, Winnie, Pei-Wen Ma, Munyi, Shea, Yuki, Okubo, Kim, Angela B. & Atkins, Marc S. (2014). "Ecological Risk and Protective Factors of Depressive and Anxiety Symptoms among Low-Income, Chinese Immigrant Youth." *Asian American Journal of Psychology*, *5*(3), 190-199.

Ying, Yu-Wen (2002). "Formation of Cross-cultural Relationships of Taiwanese International Students in the United States." *Journal of Community Psychology*, *30*(1), 45-55.

Yip, Kam-shing (2004). "Controversies in Psychiatric Services in Hong Kong: Social Workers' Superiority and Inferiority Complexities." *International Social Work*, *47*(2), 240-258.

Yoon, Eunju, Lee, Richard M. & Michael, Joh (2008). "Acculturation, Social Connectedness, and Subjective Well-being." *Cultural Diversity & Ethnic Minority Psychology*, *14*(3), 246-255.

Yue, Zhongshan, Shuzhuo, Li, Xiaoyi, Jin & Feldman, Marcus, W. (2013). "The Role of Social Networks in the Integration of Chinese Rural Urban Migrants: A Migrant Resident Tie Perspective." *Urban Studies*, *50*(9), 1704-1723.

Zhang, Zhuoni & Treiman, Donald J. (2012). "Social Origins, Hukou Conversion, and the Wellbeing of Urban Residents in Contemporary China." *Social Science Research*, *42*, 71-89.

Zhang, Zhuoni & Wu, Xiaogang (2011). "Social Change, Cohort Quality and Economic Adaptation of Chinese Immigrants in Hong Kong, 1991-2006." *Asian & Pacific Migration Journal*, *20*(1), 1-29.

Zimmerman, Marc, Jesus, Ramirez-Vallez, Zapert, Kinga M. & Maton, Kenneth I. (2000). "A Longitudinal Study of Stress-buffering Effects for Urban African-American Male Adolescent Problem Behavior and Mental Health." *Journal of Community Psychology*, *28*(1), 17-33.

In: Empowerment
Editor: Randall Harris

ISBN: 978-1-63484-036-1

Chapter 4

Sexual Objectification: A Double-Edged Sword for Female Empowerment

Gemma Sáez, Inmaculada Valor-Segura and Francisca Expósito
University of Granada, Granada, Spain

Abstract

There is an open debate regarding the notion of female sexual empowerment. Some feminist authors, headed by third-wave feminism, have supported the idea that sexuality is a way to female empowerment, whereas other authors have considered that this power is part of a sexual objectification phenomenon where women are subjugated to men. The critical point of the debate centers on whether this sense of power felt by women through their sexuality is true or false empowerment. As a consequence, this sense of power can be associated with beneficial variables for wellbeing and women´s position in society, or with mental health problems and women´s subjugation.

This debate is complex because women are surrounded by a sexualized culture in which they can assume that sexualized behaviors will be rewarded. However, the social rewards given to women when they are sexualized are the essence of benevolent sexist ideology. This ideology obliges women to keep themselves in a subordinate position to men. There is empirical evidence demonstrating how sexuality is a source of ambivalence for women, because the power they feel is rooted in the power to attract the attention and admiration of men. The power felt by women is therefore subjugated to control by men and the male sex's search for its own sexual satisfaction.

Sexual Objectification theory focuses on the consequences for women of being treated as objects and how women are reduced to their sexualized body parts to give sexual pleasure to men. This kind of gender discrimination, that usually goes unnoticed by many women and is even desired by some women, has been demonstrated to be linked to negative outcomes such as depression symptoms or high anxiety levels, amongst other mental health problems.

In this chapter, we will review the characteristics, etiology and consequences of the sense of power felt by women in sexual objectification encounters which combine sexual objectification and ambivalent sexism theories.

This chapter was made possible thanks to the financing provided by the Spanish Ministerio de Educación y Ciencia for the R&D project 'Sexist ideology and power inequality in the development and maintenance of Sexual Harassment' (Ref. PSI2011–29720) and by a Grant from the FPU (AP12–01619) Program of the Spanish Ministerio de Educación, Cultura y Deporte given to the first author.

When I got out of the car and went to pay at the parking meter, I sensed how two men about 15 meters away were looking at me and saying something to each other. I could feel their eyes glued to my body. I got coins out of my purse to put into the meter, but I was so nervous that I dropped some of them and when I bent down to pick them up, the men kept staring at me. I felt embarrassed, but at the same time admired and desired. I managed to get the coins into the meter and I left with my head held high, knowing their gaze would follow me until I was out of sight.

The description of events you have just read is an example of something commonly and routinely experienced by women. It is a form of sexist discrimination but is not identified as such by many women, who actually even enjoy it and get a sense of power from it.

This chapter provides a theoretical review of experiences of sexual objectification and their consequences for women (section I); the ambiguous nature of the phenomenon of sexual objectification: feelings of sexual power obtained through experiences of sexual objectification and enjoyment of sexualization (section II); sexist ideology as an ideology accommodating women's enjoyment of experiences which are discriminatory and relegate them to a subordinate position (section III), and conclusions and practical implications (section IV).

Women as Sexual Objects: Psychosocial Consequences

Sexual objectification is one of the components of sexualization. According to the American Psychological Association (APA), sexualization is defined as the assessment of women exclusively on the basis of their physical features, treating them as sexual objects (APA, 2007). There are four components to sexualization: (a) equating a person's value with their sexuality; (b) defining a person's attractiveness as sexuality; (c) sexual objectification, and (d) imposing sexuality on a person; only one of these four components need be present for the event to be qualified as sexualized (APA, 2007).

Specifically, *sexual objectification* is a component of sexualization which reduces a woman to her body or body parts and presents the erroneous perception that she can be represented entirely and exclusively by her body or body parts (Bartky, 1990).

Feminist theories have underlined the importance of social construction in women's development and construction of self-image. This idea was taken up and developed in the Objectification Theory formulated by Fredrickson and Roberts in 1997, which provides an ideal theoretical framework for understanding how the socialization of women and experiences of sexual objectification affect their physical, psychological and social wellbeing (Fredrickson and Roberts, 1997). According to this theory, there are numerous forms of sexual objectification which can be classified along a continuum ranging from the most subtle (body evaluation) to the more extreme (unwanted explicit sexual advances) (Fredrickson and Roberts, 1997). *Female body evaluation* is the action of observing and analyzing a woman's body or body parts, whilst *unwanted explicit sexual advances* are sexual approaches made against a woman's wishes (Kozee, Tylka, Augustus-Horvath and Denchik, 2007).

The main thrust of this theory highlights the strong presence of female sexual objectification in current society and how it affects women's physical, psychological and social wellbeing (Fredrickson and Roberts, 1997). Sexual objectification events can take place in multiple contexts, for example in the media, in interpersonal interactions, in the workplace, in the educational environment and on the street, to name just a few (Fredrickson and Roberts, 1997).

Continuous exposure to situations in which women are sexually objectified leads them to perceive themselves as objects and to internalize the gaze of the external observer. This is termed *self-objectification* and it manifests itself as excessive self-monitoring, understood as the "persistent monitoring of body appearance" (Fredrickson and Roberts, 1997, p. 180).

Both self-objectification and body self-monitoring can lead women to experience negative emotions such as shame, anxiety and reduced awareness of internal bodily states (Fredrickson and Roberts, 1997).

Sexual objectification is a form of sexist discrimination (Klonoff and Landrine, 1995) and as such is more prevalent among women than among men (Swim, Hyers, Cohen and Ferguson, 2001). Although it is more prevalent among women, sexual objectification has also been the subject of empirical study among men given that today, demands for the ideal body also extend to the male sex (Leit, Pope and Gray, 2001) and makes them less satisfied with their body image than they were in the past (Garner, 1997).

Empirical research has shown that men who score higher in self-objectification score lower in body esteem (McKinley, 2006). However, experiences of sexual objectification do not appear to affect men and women in the same way. Empirical evidence shows that there is a link between more reported instances of sexual objectification in interpersonal relationships and higher levels of self-esteem among men, whilst this link has not been observed among women (Sáez, Valor-Segura and Expósito, 2012). This can be explained by different gender socialization, where women work on their bodies in order to be looked at whilst for men, being evaluated on the basis of their physical appearance is an added value, generating positive feelings in them and improving their self-concept (Spitzack, 1990). Women, however, whose socialization inextricably links their value as a person with their value in terms of physical appearance, have fewer positive feelings about themselves (Cash, Winste and Janda, 1986), this body evaluation being perceived as a threat and causing feelings of fear that they might "fail" this evaluation.

Numerous studies have demonstrated the negative consequences of sexual objectification for women's wellbeing. These consequences can be classified into those which affect psychological wellbeing, those which affect cognitive performance and those which act on the social level.

a) Regarding the consequences on psychological wellbeing, Russo (1995) explains the gender differences in specific mental problems as the result of different exposure to acts of sexist discrimination, considering them as gender-specific stressors which affect women more strongly.

Eating disorders are one of the consequences of sexual self-objectification on which there is substantial empirical evidence. We live in a society where women attach a great deal of importance to their weight and body image.

Calogero, Tantleff-Dunn and Thompson (2011) claim that there is sufficient empirical evidence to support applying objectification theory to eating disorders in both clinical and sub-clinical samples. Peat and Muehlenkamp (2011) have found empirical evidence of the relationship between self-objectification and eating disorders, this relationship being mediated by social anxiety and poor interoceptive awareness.

Another consequence of sexual objectification is poor overall and body self-esteem, due fundamentally to sexual objectification experiences leading women to internalize a particular body ideal as an essential element of their self-concept (Crocker and Wolfe, 2001). When this takes place and the beauty ideal is perceived as unattainable, this has a negative effect on women's self-esteem (Irving, 1990). The effect of objectification on self-esteem can be two-pronged: on the one hand, the physical and sexual attractiveness that many women have can increase their self-esteem at a given moment, although in the long term these levels of self-esteem will not be maintained (Breines, Crocker and García, 2008). On the other, women who do not achieve established ideals of beauty experience feelings of personal failure (Wolf, 1991) which in turn cause feelings of shame harmful to their self-esteem (Crocker, Luhtanen, Cooper and Bouvrette, 2003; Crocker and Wolfe, 2001).

Sexist discrimination is one of the main causes of gender differences in symptoms of depression (Klonoff, Landrine and Campbell, 2000). Such symptoms have been linked both to being the victim of sexist discrimination (Landrine et al., 1995; Swim et al., 2001) and to exposure to experiences of sexual objectification (Tiggemann and Kuring, 2004).

The literature has linked exposure to sexual objectification events with higher levels of anxiety (Fiske, Cuddy, Glick and Xu, 2002). Specifically, Fredrickson and Roberts (1997) describe in their theory how the persistent body evaluation that women are subjected to causes increased body monitoring on their part with the resulting higher anxiety (Noll and Fredrickson, 1998).

a) Sexual objectification has also been linked to sexual dysfunction and problems. Steer and Tiggemann (2008) have shown how self-objectification and body monitoring are associated with body shame, appearance anxiety and self-awareness of body image during sexual intercourse, causing poor sexual function.

b) Regarding the cognitive consequences of sexual objectification, both objectification and self-objectification can have a negative impact on women's performance and lead them to perform below their potential. Calogero et al. (2011) argue that there may be three possible mechanisms through which self-objectification affects women's performance: one, that an individual who self-objectifies adopts the perspective of the external observer; two, that when an individual self-objectifies they are monitoring their body and comparing its appearance with a culturally prescribed standard, and three, self-objectification is accompanied by negative emotions which may interfere with correct performance.

Fredrickson and Roberts (1997) argue that increased self-objectification is related to poorer awareness of flow states. Numerous studies have supported evidence of the link between diminished cognitive performance and self-objectification (Calogero et al., 2011). Considering that flow state is an important indicator of cognitive performance, Tiggemann and Kuring (2004) observe that self-objectification is related indirectly to poorer flow state and that this is explained by body monitoring. Szymanski and Henning (2007) observe a direct and negative relationship between self-objectification and flow state, in addition to an indirect and negative relationship through self-monitoring.

c) Social consequences of sexual objectification. These refer to the time, money and effort invested by women in attempting to improve their appearance, at the expense of investing in activities which could help improve their real skills and enable them to access areas traditionally dominated by men. Acting in this way is instrumental in keeping women relegated to more lowly qualified employment posts and in a subordinate position.

An experimental study by Saguy, Quinn, Dovidio and Pratto (2010) revealed the social consequences of sexual objectification, showing that women who self-objectified participated less in a conversation with men than women who did not self-objectify. According to the authors, women speak less or are less socially participative when they are objectified, because they are attempting to adjust their behavior and appearance to socially expected norms and therefore the cognitive resources required for organizing and expressing their views are directed at regulating elements relating to their appearance, not their discourse (Saguy et al., 2010).

Self-objectification results in women being more concerned with how they are being seen by men than with their performance and real achievements, therefore they are not able to stake their claim to an equal position in society and can even end up legitimizing their position of inferiority.

Sexual objectification is thus a tool for female subjugation. However, for this tool to be effective and sustainable, society must create the mechanisms which make women find enjoyment in interactions where they occupy the role of sexual object, rather than challenging such situations. This comes about as a result of the ambivalent nature of the sexual objectification phenomenon; this ambivalence is due on the one hand to the negative consequences of being victims of persistent sexual objectification, and on the other but at the same time, to the feelings of enjoyment and power that envelope these experiences.

The Ambiguous Nature of The Sexual Objectification Phenomenon: Feelings of Power by Women during Objectification Experiences and Enjoyment of Sexualization

In spite of the negative consequences of sexual objectification for women, some women enjoy sexualization and seek to attract the gaze of men by engaging in self-sexualizing behavior (Nowartzki and Morry, 2009). Such behavior reflects a desire for male attention and indicates that such women feel power and enjoyment during the sexual objectification experience (Liss, Erchull and Ramsey, 2011). *Enjoyment of sexualization* occurs when women find sexual attention based on their appearance pleasing (Liss et al., 2011).

Female sexual empowerment is an area which has received particular interest in the public and academic spheres (Erchull and Liss, 2014). Female empowerment is generally a term used by feminists to refer to the mechanisms through which women accentuate their own power by achieving social changes (Yuval-Davis, 1994).

Differences are inferred between the sexual empowerment felt by women when their bodies are being observed by men and the sexual empowerment felt by women as a social group when they achieve milestones in the gender equality struggle. In order to understand these different types of empowerment, we must look at how the concept has changed in recent decades; a change in which "third-wave feminism" has played a fundamental role.

This feminist movement champions empowerment in individual terms, training the spotlight on the kind of empowerment which leads to taking decisions at the individual level, rather than empowerment at the group level (Shugart, Whaggoner and Hallstein, 2001). Specifically as regards sexual empowerment, this new feminist current claims that women can feel empowered through freely choosing to sexualize themselves and that these feelings of empowerment are positive, since they indicate that women are taking control of their sexuality (Baumgardner and Richards, 2004).

The expression of sexual empowerment at the individual level can be seen in the numerous media representations of women using their sexuality freely to increase their popularity and climb the social ladder. By means of monitoring and self-objectification, women obtain the attention of men and this makes them feel powerful (Cato, Dillman and Carpentier, 2010).

The link between power and sexualization is based on the relationship between sexualization and attractiveness (APA, 2007; Liss et al., 2011). In the society we live in today, being attractive is considered good and desirable, and people who conform to the established beauty canons reap social rewards (Fiske, Bersoff, Borgida, Deaux and Heilman, 1991). Physical attractiveness thus becomes a mechanism through which women attempt to win these social rewards. And since there are rewards associated with being attractive, women enjoy being sexualized as they consider it a sign of their attractiveness and an indicator that the social rewards are within their grasp (Liss et al., 2011).

Although some women experience feelings of power and are rewarded for sexualizing themselves, these positive feelings are in stark contrast to the negative consequences of sexualization for girls and women, according to the American Psychological Association (2007) (Cato el al., 2010). This contradiction is the fundamental core of the debate surrounding the real sexual power of women (Lamb and Peterson, 2012). On the one hand, female power felt through sexuality is not considered real because it is not controlled by women, but rather operates in the framework of male sexuality (see for example: Lamb, 2012). On the other, such power may be considered real because women can experience genuine feelings of intrapersonal power whilst simultaneously being disempowered at the interpersonal level (Peterson, 2010).

The point of discord between both positions arises when we consider whether the subjective feeling of empowerment experienced through sexualization is authentic or illusory, and to clarify this we need to examine whether the presence of desire and pleasure can be considered necessary and sufficient signals of sexual empowerment (Peterson, 2010).

Sexualization can be used by women themselves as a strategy for increasing their power and gaining a higher position in the patriarchal hierarchy (Erchull and Liss, 2013). Through this prism, sexualization is considered an empowerment tool and not a harmful and dangerous process which has a negative impact on women (Leum and Dworkin, 2005). Vanwesembeek (2009) considers the importance of sexualization, since deprived of the right to be sexual and sexualize themselves, women cannot attain a healthy sex life.

During their socialization, women learn that they can become stronger through using their "feminine wiles" (Smolak and Murnem, 2011). Girls internalize the message that they can gain power if they manage to enjoy their sexuality and if they behave in a sexualized manner (Griffin et al., 2013). These feelings of power through sexualization itself are considered by some authors as legitimate empowerment (Peterson, 2012).

The significance of exposure to sexualization during women's socialization has been demonstrated by a number of studies, which link greater exposure to sexualized images of females in the media with more sexualized behavior among women and the acceptance of sexualized behavior in other women (Nowatzki and Morry, 2009).

The feelings of power experienced by women during sexual objectification events have been analyzed in diverse empirical studies. These studies show how women experience feelings of empowerment when being looked at by men (Liss et al., 2011).

The positive feelings which come from self-sexualization are linked to the belief that it is a matter of free choice to use the body as a way of gaining individual power, rather than as a way of collectively obtaining social change for women as a group (McRobbie, 2004). That is to say, women who enjoy experiences of sexual objectification are seeking individual empowerment, rather than social change aimed at achieving the empowerment of women as a collective (Liss and Erchull, 2013).

Women who choose to gain power at the individual level by using their bodies do so in the belief that they are distancing themselves from the collective of oppressed women, but they are still following the guidelines and path marked out by the traditional female role (Liss and Erchull, 2013).

By contrast, some authors state that sexualization cannot be an empowerment strategy given its negative consequences on women's autonomy, wellbeing and psychological health, and on their academic and professional performance (APA, 2007). This argument holds that female empowerment and the enjoyment of female sexualization sit firmly within the framework of a heterosexual schema of sexuality that perpetuates power inequalities, since men are in control of the sexual act and women must carefully control their own sexuality, on occasion even being blamed for "provoking" acts of sexual aggression (Smolak and Murden, 2011).

Fredrickson and Roberts (1997) argue that representations which sexualize women are an essential element of objectification, rather than a process of female empowerment. Supporting this claim, Aubrey (2006) highlights the relationship between women's exposure to television programmes which sexualize the female body and higher rates of self-objectification. Saguy et al. (2010) link female objectification to lower participation in social interaction, which can be considered a clear example of loss of power.

If forms of sexual objectification cause loss of power among women, then the feelings of enjoyment and empowerment associated with these experiences should likewise be linked to indicators of disempowerment. Supporting this hypothesis, enjoyment of sexualization is related to traditional beliefs about gender and patriarchal standards which exacerbate the negative effects of self-objectification (Liss et al., 2011). The subjective feeling of empowerment felt by women who enjoy sexualization thus has no relationship with behavior aimed at social change, understood as the wish to improve women's situation in society (Tolman 2012), but rather is only the desire to obtain personal power through sexualization.

Specific instruments have been developed to measure the enjoyment and empowerment felt by women through sexualization. One of these instruments, the "Sex Is Power Scale," shows that there is a relationship between the aforementioned construct, sexist ideology and increased self-objectification (Erchull and Liss, 2013).

Liss, Erchull and Ramsey (2011) developed the Enjoyment of Sexualization Scale (ESS) and found that enjoyment of sexualization is linked to the idea that women need to be cared for and protected by men, and to certain traditional ideas about femininity including the power an attractive woman has in controlling men (Liss et al., 2011).

Objectification is therefore perceived as an instrument of subjugation through which the needs, interests and experiences of persons with less power are subordinate to those with more power (Gruenfeld, Inesi, Magee and Galinsky, 2008). Objectification is defined as the process which leads to viewing people as tools to be used for personal benefit (Bartky, 1990). Narrowing this down to sexual objectification, this is described as evaluation of a person, usually a woman, as regards the usefulness of her sexual parts or sexual functions (Gruenfeld et al., 2008). As stated by Calogero (2013), in a classic heterosexual sexual objectification interaction, the woman's body becomes the possession of the observer.

Thus, and in line with the thoughts of Gavay (2012), the social changes which have taken place for the advancement of gender equality over the course of history have been changes at the societal level which have required impetus by collective action. However, the sexual empowerment felt by women during sexual objectification experiences is associated with a feeling of power arising from individual benefits; this feeling of power cannot be equated with the real power that women can attain when acting as a group.

Undoubtedly, one of the characteristics which sets sexual objectification apart from other types of sexual discrimination is that in the former, women may experience feelings of enjoyment and this leads to their behaving in a way that presents them as sexual objects, even though female self-sexualization entrenches male dominance more than it promotes female empowerment (Infanger, Rudman and Sczesny, 2013) and prevents women from engaging in collective action for gender equality (Calogero, 2013).

The Ideology Underlying the Power Felt by Women Through Their Sexuality: Benevolent Sexism

Women's bodies are tools that men and women alike can make use of to gain or maintain power in the social hierarchy. The ideology which justifies using the female body as a tool for gaining power is sexist ideology (Glick and Fiske, 2001; Vescio, Schelenker and Lenes, 2010).

In the most traditional notion of sexism, understood as prejudice against women based on their supposed inferiority as a group (Glick and Fiske, 1996), explicit reference is made to the real power that women have through using their sexuality. In this respect, traditional sexism presupposes that women are weaker than men, that they are different and inferior to them and dangerous because of their sexual power, thus causing hostile feelings towards women (Glick and Fiske, 1996; Expósito, Moya and Glick, 1998).

Over the course of time, sexist ideology has transformed itself in order to adjust to current social norms so that it can continue to be used as an ideology for perpetuating inequality between men and women today. Glick and Fiske (1996), looking at the duality of this new sexism, developed the theory of ambivalent sexism where positive feelings towards women coexist with the traditional hostility towards them. One of the main characteristics of ambivalent sexism is the notion that men and women are complementary and interdependent beings (Fiske, Cuddy, Glick and Xu, 2002). This interdependence is based principally on the sexual power that women have and men desire (Glick and Fiske, 1996).

The function of sexist ideology lies in its role in maintaining and assimilating power inequalities between men and women. Specifically, benevolent sexist ideology, with its more subtle forms of discrimination, is more significant for keeping gender inequalities in place than more overtly hostile forms (Glick and Fiske, 2001). The power inequalities promoted by benevolent sexist ideology would not be possible using more explicit forms of sexist ideology (Glick and Fiske, 2001), since women would reject this (Vescio, Schelenker and Lenes, 2010). Empirical studies endorse this idea, showing how complementary gender stereotypes, a feature of benevolent sexism, serve as a mechanism for justifying the status quo (Jost and Kay, 2005).

Persons in disadvantaged groups who subscribe to such beliefs tend to stay in their inferior position in exchange for minimizing uncertainty and sharing a social reality with others (Jost et al., 2008). The role of women in keeping inequality in place by assimilating sexist ideology is fundamental and can make them accomplices to their own subordination (see for example: Jackman, 1994).

These beliefs that justify inequality are associated with positive emotions, increased life satisfaction and subjective wellbeing (Jost and Hunyady, 2002). Benevolent sexism thus increases women's satisfaction with the social system (Jost and Kay, 2005), although it restricts their participation in collective action to combat sexist discrimination (Becker and Wright, 2011) and diminishes the perception of certain types of behavior as sexist since they are not explicitly hostile (Barreto and Ellemers, 2005).

In the same way as experiences of sexual objectification have negative consequences for women's emotional wellbeing whilst simultaneously producing feelings of enjoyment and empowerment, benevolent sexism leads to greater satisfaction with the system even though it is associated with negative consequences. The consequences of benevolent sexism are evidenced both in the sphere of employment ambitions (Moya, Glick, Expósito, de Lemus and Hart, 2007) and in interpersonal relationships, leading women to accept sexist discrimination to a greater extent, reinforcing power differences between the sexes (Glick and Fiske, 1996) and even increasing the tolerance of domestic abuse (Expósito, Herrera, Moya and Glick, 2010) or other kind of gender violence (Herrera, Herrera and Expósito, 2014).

That women assimilate benevolent sexism has to do with the benefits this ideology provides them (Glick and Fiske, 1996). Benevolent sexism provides women with the admiration and protection of men, so gaining sexual attention from men becomes a strategy for women and being successful in this respect gives them feelings of enjoyment.

In this way, by subscribing to benevolent sexism, women justify using their sexuality to gain male attention and thus experience feelings of enjoyment and power (Liss et al., 2011).

Women are exposed to all kinds of sexist events on a daily basis. The literature shows that women are exposed to sexism more than men and experience one to two sexist events each week (Swim et al., 2001).

However, we may expect that for women who have assimilated an ideology which leads them to invest large amounts of time and money in adjusting their appearance to what men desire, the experience of being evaluated solely on the basis of their body will not cause them to suffer the same consequences as women who identify such experiences as a form of sexist discrimination. Empirical evidence endorses the relationship between enjoyment of sexualizing oneself and subscribing more closely to sexist ideology (Sáez et al., 2012), and being exposed to greater sexual objectification and developing sexist attitudes (Kalof, 1999; Ward and Friedman, 2006).

Women who have assimilated benevolent sexism more fully make efforts to adjust their appearance to what is desirable by men in an attempt to improve their position in the power hierarchy. This hypothesis is in line with studies showing that women who subscribe more strongly to benevolent sexism use more cosmetic products (Forbes, Doroszewicz, Card, and Adams-Curtis, 2004; Franzoi, 2001), have internalized the slimness canon to a greater extent (Forbes, Collinsworth, Jobe, Braun, and Wise, 2007) and undertake activities designed to manage their physical appearance (Calogero and Jost, 2011).

Numerous studies have demonstrated the relationship between social rewards and physical beauty for women (Davis, 1990; Fiske, Bersoff, Borgida, Deaux and Heilman, 1991). Physical attractiveness thus becomes a way to obtain certain social advantages more easily (Fredrickson and Roberts, 1997; Unger, 1979), but can also relegate the status of women to a lower level than that of men in the social hierarchy (Jost and Kay, 2005), as women invest more time and effort in making their appearance conform to a culturally prescribed ideal (Calogero, Boroughs and Thompson 2007).

By contrast and from the perspective of men as the dominant group, sexualized women can be perceived as a threat to the status quo because of the power they can obtain through their sexuality, which can cause increased hostility and male dominance as a reaction to this threat (Infanger, Rudman and Sabine, 2013). Prejudice against sexualized women feeds ideologically off hostile sexism (Sibley and Willson, 2004), in a similar way to the prejudice aroused by women with successful careers, or feminists (Glick, Diebold, Bailey-Werner and Zhu, 1997).

Hostile sexism reflects resistance to female power and aims to punish women who have sexual power and pose a threat to the established gender hierarchy (Glick and Fiske, 2001). Empirical evidence demonstrates the relationship between exposure of men to sexualized women and higher acceptance of rape myths, sexual harassment myths, gender role stereotypes and interpersonal violence (Ward, 2002; Aubrey, Hopper and Mbure, 2011).

Conclusion and Practical Implications

Forms of sexual objectification are types of behavior linked to female submission and the assimilation of women's inferiority to men. The literature quoted in this chapter alerts us to the negative impact of sexual objectification on women's psychosocial wellbeing and to the fact that sexist ideology legitimizes objectifying behavior and plays a part in women viewing themselves as sexual objects (Calogero and Jost, 2011).

Women are at a loss as to how to address experiences of sexual objectification and focus exclusively on accepting and internalizing such experiences, increasing their self-objectification. If a sexual objectification experience results in positive evaluation of their appearance, women therefore feel enjoyment and power. But if they receive a negative evaluation of their appearance, women will embark on activities to change their appearance as the only way to obtain the power and control promised by society (Petterson, Gripo and Tantleff-Dunn, 2008).

Faced with the expectations of an objectification experience where women expect their body to be evaluated, they can experience self-directed feelings of guilt and attempt to make body changes so that they receive positive evaluation. In order to change these feelings, it is necessary to change the mental schemata which blame women for sexual objectification (Tylka and Augustus-Horvath, 2011). For this, it is important for mental health professionals to focus on reducing the impact of objectification and self-objectification on women's wellbeing and to try to reduce the actual incidence of female sexual objectification at the social level. Research on sexual objectification must be taken into account for the development of preventive and action programmes which aim to palliate the negative effects of the more subtle forms of gender discrimination.

In order to augment true women's empowerment and lessen self-objectification, women should be taught to respond assertively to comments on their appearance instead of responding passively as they usually do (Tylka and Augustus-Horvath, 2011). Programmes must be included which aim to encourage men not to treat women as sexual objects so frequently, and action to change attitudes is the most effective way of changing these types of behavior.

As we have argued in this chapter, sexism is the ideological foundation of female sexual objectification and the patriarchal system works to keep women in a subordinate position by rewarding them for self-objectifying. Working in society to lessen sexist beliefs among both men and women is therefore the effective way to challenge sexual objectification.

References

American Psychological Association, Task Force on the Sexualization of Girls. (2007). *Report of the APA Task Force on the Sexualization of Girls.* Washington, DC: American Psychological Association.

Aubrey, J. S., Hopper, K. M. & Mbure W.G. (2011). Check that body! The effects of sexually objectifying music videos on college men's sexual beliefs. *Journal of Broadcasting & Electronic Media 55 (3)*, 360-379.

Aubrey, J. S. (2006). Effects of sexually objectifying media o self-objectification and body surveillance in undergraduates: Results old a 2-Year panel Study. *Journal of communication, 56*, 366-386.

Barreto, M., & Ellemers, N. (2005). The burden of benevolent sexism: How it contributes to the maintenance of gender inequalities. *European Journal of Social Psychology, 35*, 633–642.

Bartky, S. L. (1990). Femininity and domination: Studies in the phenomenology of oppression. New York, NY: Routledge.

Baumgardner, J., & Richards, A. (2004). Feminism and femininity: Or how we learned to stop worrying and love the thong. In A. Harris and M. Fine (Eds.), *All About the Girl.* (pp. 59-69). London: Routledge.

Becker, J. C., & Wright, S. C. (2011). Yet another dark side of chivalry: Benevolent sexism undermines and hostile sexism motivates collective action for social change. *Journal of Personality and Social Psychology, 101*, 62-77.

Breines, J. G., Crocker, J., & Garcia, J. A. (2008). Self-objectification and well-being in women's daily lives. *Personality and Social Psychology Bulletin, 34,* 583-598.

Calogero, R. M. (2013). Objects don't object: Evidence that self-objectification disrupts women's social activism. *Psychological Science, 24*(3), 312-318.

Calogero, R. M., & Jost, J. T. (2011). Self-subjugation among women: Exposure to sexist ideology, self-objectification, and the protective function of the need to avoid closure. *Journal of Personality and Social Psychology, 100(2*), 211-228.

Calogero, R.M., Tantleff-Dunn, S., & Thompson, J.K. (2011). Future directions for research and practice. *Self-objectification in Women; Causes, Consequences and Counteractions*, (pp. 217–231). Washington, DC: American Psychological Association.

Calogero, R.M., Boroughs, M., & Thompson, J.K. (2007). The impact of Western beauty ideals on the lives of women and men: A sociocultural perspective. In V.Swami & A.Furnham (Eds.), *Body beautiful: Evolutionary and sociocultural perspectives* (pp. 259-298). New York: Palgrave Macmillan.

Cash, T.F., Winstead, B.W., & Janda, L.H. (1986). The great American shape-up: Body image survey report. *Psychology Today, 19* (4), 30-37.

Cato, M., & Dillman Carpentier, F. R. (2010). Conceptualizations of female empowerment and enjoyment of sexualized characters in reality television. *Mass Communication and Society, 13(3)*, 1-19.

Crocker, J., & Wolfe, C.T. (2001). Contingencies of self-worth. *Psychological Review, 108*, 593–623.

Crocker J., Luhtanen R., Cooper M.L., & Bouvrette S.A. (2003). Contingencies of self-worth in college students: Measurement and theory. *Journal of Personality and Social Psychology, 85,* 894–908.

Davis, S. (1990). Men as success objects and women as sex objects: A study of personal advertisements. *Sex Roles, 23*, 43–50.

Dion, K. L., Dion, K. K., & Keelan, P. (1990). Appearance anxiety as a dimension of social-evaluative anxiety: Exploring the ugly duckling syndrome. *Contemporary Social Psychology, 14*, 220–224.

Erchull, M. J., & Liss, M. (2013). Exploring the concept of perceived female sexual empowerment: Development and validation of the Sex is Power Scale. *Gender Issues, 30*, 39–53.Erchull, M. J., & Liss, M. (2014). The object of one's desire: How perceived sexual empowerment through objectification is related to sexual outcomes. *Sexuality & Culture*, 1-16.

Expósito, F., Herrera, M.C., Moya, M., & Glick, P. (2010). Don't Rock the Boat: Women's Benevolent Sexism Predicts Fears of Marital Violence. *Psychology of Women Quarterly, 34*, 36-42.

Expósito, F., Moya, M., & Glick, P. (1998) Sexismo ambivalente: medición y correlatos. *Revista de Psicología Social, 13*, 159-170.

Fiske, S. T., Bersoff, D. N., Borgida, E., Deaux, K., & Heilman, M. E. (1991). Social science research on trial: Use of sex stereotyping research in Price Waterhouse *v.* Hopkins. *American Psychologist, 46,* 1049-1060.

Fiske, S. T., Cuddy, A. J. C., Glick, P., & Xu, J. (2002). A model of (often mixed) stereotype content: Competence and warmth respectively follow from perceived status and competition. *Journal of Personality and Social Psychology, 82*, 878-902.

Forbes, G. B., Doroszewicz K., Card, K., & Adams-Curtis, L. (2004). Association of the thin body ideal, ambivalent sexism, and self-esteem with body acceptance and the preferred body size of college women in Poland and the United States. *Sex Roles, 50(5)*, 331-345.

Forbes, G. B., Collinsworth, L. L., Jobe, R. L., Braun, K. D., & Wise, L. M. (2007). Sexism, hostility toward women, and endorsement of beauty ideals and practices: Are beauty ideals associated with oppressive beliefs? *Sex Roles, 56*, 265-273.

Franzoi, S. L. (2001). Is female body esteem shaped by benevolent sexism? *Sex Roles, 44*, 177-188.

Fredrickson, B. L., Roberts, T., Noll, S. M., Quinn, D. M., & Twenge, J. M. (1998). That swimsuit becomes you: Sex differences in self-objectification, restrained eating, and math performance. *Journal of Personality and Social Psychology, 75*, 269–284.

Garner, D.M. (1997). The 1997 body image survey results. *Psychology Today, 30*, 30 41.

Glick, P., & Fiske, S. T. (1996). The Ambivalent Sexism Inventory: Differentiating hostile and benevolent sexism. *Journal of Personality and Social Psychology, 70*, 491-512.

Glick, P., & Fiske, S. T. (2001).Ambivalent sexism. In M. P. Zanna (Ed.), *Advances in experimental social psychology (Vol. 33, pp. 115-188).* San Diego, CA: Academic Press.

Glick, P., Diebold, J., Bailey-Werner, B., & Zhu, L. (1997). The two faces of Adam: Ambivalent sexism and polarized attitudes toward women. *Personality and Social Psychology Bulletin, 23*, 1323–1343.

Griffin, C., Szmigin, I., Bengry-Howell, A., Hackley, C., & Mistral, W. (2013). Inhabiting the contradictions: Hypersexual feminity and the culture of intoxication among young women in the UK. *Feminism & Psychology, 23*, 184-206.

Gruenfeld, D. H., Inesi, M. E., Magee, J. C., & Galinsky, A. D. (2008). Power and the objectification of social targets. *Journal of Personality and Social Psychology, 95*, 111-127.

Herrera, M. C., Herrera, A., y Expósito, F. (2014). Stop harassment! Men's reactions to victims' confrontation. The European Journal of Psychology Applied to Legal Context, 6, 1-8.

Infanger, M., Rudman, L. A., & Sczesny, S. (2014). Sex as a source of power? Backlash against self-sexualizing women. *Group Processes and Intergroup Relations 22*,1-15.

Irving, L. M. (1990). Mirror images: Effects of the standard of beauty on the self- and body-esteem of women exhibiting varying levels of bulimic symptoms. *Journal of Social and Clinical Psychology, 9(2)*, 230-242.

Jackman, M. R. (1994). *The velvet glove: Paternalism and conflict in gender, class, and race relations*. Berkeley: University of California Press.

Jost, J.T., Ledgerwood, A., & Hardin, C.D. (2008). Shared reality, system justification, and the relational basis of ideological beliefs. *Social and Personality Psychology Compass, 2*, 171-186.

Jost, J.T., & Hunyady, O. (2002). The psychology of system justification and the palliative function of ideology. *European Review of Social Psychology, 13*, 111-153.

Jost, J.T., & Kay, A.C. (2005). Exposure to benevolent sexism and complementary gender stereotypes: Consequences for specific and diffuse forms of system justification. *Journal of Personality and Social Psychology*, 88, 498-509.

Kalof. L. (1999). The Effects of Gender and Music Video Imagery on Sexual Attitudes. *The Journal of Social Psychology, 139(3)*, 378-385.

Klonoff, E.A., & Landrine, H. (1995). The Schedule of Sexist Events: A measure of lifetime and recent sexist discrimination in women's lives. *Psychology of Women Quarterly, 19*, 439 – 472.

Klonoff, E. A., Landrine, H., & Campbell, R. (2000). Sexist discrimination may account for well-known gender differences in psychiatric symptoms. *Psychology of Women Quarterly, 24*, 93–99.

Kozee, H. B., Tylka, T. L., Augustus-Horvath, C. L., & Denchik, A. (2007). Development and psychometric evaluation of the Interpersonal Sexual Objectification Scale. *Psychology of Women Quarterly, 31*, 176-189.

Lamb S., & Peterson Z. (2012). Adolescent girls' sexual empowerment: Two feminists explore the concept. *Sex Roles, 66, 703–712.* Landrine, H., Klonoff, E.A., Gibbs, J., Manning, V., & Lund, M. (1995). Physical and psychiatric correlates of gender discrimination: An application of the Schedule of Sexist Events. *Psychology of Women Quarterly, 19,* 473-492.

Leit, R. A., Pope, H. G., & Gray, J. J. (2001). Cultural expectations of muscularity in men: The evolution of playgirl centerfolds. *International Journal of Eating Disorders, 29,* 90–93.

Lerum, K., & Dworkin, S. L. (2009). "Bad girls rule": An interdisciplinary feminist commentary on the report of the APA Task Force on the Sexualization of Girls. *Journal of Sex Research*, *46*, 250-263.

Liss, M., Erchull, M.J., & Ramsey, L. R. (2011). "Empowering or Oppressing? Development and exploration of the Enjoyment of Sexualization Scale." *Personality and Social Psychology Bulletin, 37(1)*, 55-68.

McKinley, N. M. (2006). Longitudinal gender differences in objectified body consciousness and weight-related attitudes and behaviors: Cultural and developmental contexts in the transition from college. *Sex Roles*, *54*, 159–173.

McRobbie, A. (2004). "Post feminism and popular culture." *Feminist Media Studies 4(3)* 255-264.

Moya, M., Glick, P., Expósito, F., De Lemus, S., & Hart, J. (2007). It's for your own good: Benevolent sexism and women's reactions to protectively justified restrictions. *Personality and Social Psychology Bulletin, 33,* 1421–1434.

Noll, S. M., & Fredrickson, B. L. (1998). A mediational model linking selfobjectification, body shame, and disordered eating. *Psychology of Women Quarterly, 22(4)*, 623-636.

Nowatzki, J., & Morry, M. M. (2009). Women's intentions regarding, and acceptance of, self-sexualizing behavior. *Psychology of Women Quarterly, 33 (1),* 95-107.

Peat, C. M., & Muehlenkamp, J. J. (2011). Self-objectification, disordered eating, and depression: A test of mediational pathways. *Psychology of Women Quarterly, 35*, 441–450.

Peterson, Z. D. (2010). What is sexual empowerment? Amultidimensional and process-oriented approach to adolescent girls' sexual empowerment. *Sex Roles, 62*, 307–313.

Peterson, R. D., Grippo, K. P., & Tantleff-Dunn, S. (2008). Empowerment and Powerlessness: A closer look at the relationship between feminism, body image and eating disturbance. *Sex Roles, 58*, 639-648.

Quinn, D. M., Chaudoir, S. R., & Kallen, R. W. (2011). Performance and flow: A reviewand integration of self-objectification research. In R. Calogero, S. Tantleff-Dunn & J. K. Thompson (Eds.). *Self-objectification in women: Causes, consequences, and counteractions* (pp. 119– 138). Washington, DC: American Psychological Association.

Russo, N. F. (1995). Women's mental health: Research agenda for the twenty-first century. In B. Brown, B. Kramer, P. Reiker, & C. Willie (Eds.). *Mental health, racism, and sexism* (pp. 373-396). Pittsburgh, PA University of Pittsburgh Press.

Sáez, G., Valor-Segura, I., & Expósito, F. (2012). Is empowerment or women's subjugation? experiences of interpersonal sexual objectification. *Psychosocial Intervention, 21*(1), 41-51.

Saguy, T., Quinn, D. M., Dovidio, J. F., & Pratto, F. (2010). Interacting Like a Body: Objectification can lead women to narrow their presence in social interactions. *Psychological Science, 21,* 178-182.

Shugart, H. A., Waggoner, C. E., & Hallestein, D. L. O. (2001). Mediating third-wave feminism: Appropriation as postmodern media practice. *Critical Studies in Mass Communication 18(2),* 194-210.

Sibley, C.G., & Wilson, M.S. (2004). Men's sexual self-schema and the differentiation of hostile and benevolent sexist attitudes towards positive and negative sexual female subtypes. *Sex Roles, 51,* 687-696.

Smolak, L., & Murnen, S. K. (2011). The sexualization of girls and women as a primary antecedent of self-objectification. In R. M. Calogero, S. Tantleff-Dunn, & J. K. Thompson (Eds.). *Self- objectification in women: Causes, consequences, and counteractions* (pp. 53–75). Washington: American Psychological Association.

Spitzack, C. (1990). *Confessing excess: women and the politics of body reduction.* Albany, NY: State University of New York Press.

Steer, A., & Tiggemann, M. (2008). The role of self-objectification in women's sexual functioning. *Journal of Social & Clinical Psychology, 27(3),* 205-225.

Swim, J. K., Hyers, L. L., Cohen, L. L., & Ferguson, M. J. (2001). Everyday sexism: Evidence for its incidence, nature, and psychological impact from three daily diary studies. *Journal of Social Issues, 57*, 31–53.

Szymanski, D.M. & Henning, S.L. (2007). The role of self-objectification in women's depression: A test of Objectification Theory. *Sex Roles, 56*, 45-53.

Tiggemann, M. & Kuring, J.K. (2004). The role of body objectification in disordered eating and depressed mood. *British Journal of Clinical Psychology, 43*, 299-311.

Tolman, D. L. (2012) Female adolescents, sexual empowerment and desire: A missing discourse of gender inequity. *Sex Roles, 66 (11-12),* 746-757.

Unger, R. K. (1979). *Female and male: Psychological perspectives*. New York: Harper & Row.

Vescio, T. K., Schlenker, K. A., & Lenes, J. G. (2010). *Power and sexism*. In A. Guinote & T. Vescio (Eds.). *The social psychology of power* (pp. 363–382). New York: Guilford Press.

Ward, L. & Friedman, K. (2006) Using TV as a guide: associations between television viewing and adolescents' sexual attitudes and behavior. *Journal of Research on Adolescence, 16.* 133–156.

Ward, L. M. (2002). Does television exposure affect emerging adults' attitudes and assumptions about sexual relationships? Correlational and experimental confirmation. *Journal of Youth and Adolescence, 31*, 1-15.

Wolf, N. (1991). *The beauty myth*. Toronto, ON: Vintage Canada.

Yuval-Davis, Nira (1994) 'Women, Ethnicity and Empowerment', *Feminism and Psychology 4(1)*. 179–97.

In: Empowerment
Editor: Randall Harris
ISBN: 978-1-63484-036-1

Chapter 5

EMPOWERMENT OF WOMEN IN THE TOURISM AND HOSPITALITY INDUSTRY IN ASIA

***Catherine Cheung*[1], *Tom Baum*[2] *and Georgie Passalaris*[3]**
[1]School of Hotel and Tourism Management,
The Hong Kong Polytechnic University,
Hung Hom, Kowloon, Hong Kong, China
[2]Department of Human Resources Management
University of Strathclyde, Glasgow, Scotland
[3]Sustainable Development
Diageo Company, London, United Kingdom

INTRODUCTION

Empowerment is a practical management strategy which has been widely studied and applied by researchers and practitioners in different ways. In the past empowerment concept is related to human resources strategies which include sharing information, rewards, knowledge and power with front line employees or operational staff (Bowen and Lawler, 1992). Operational staff or front line employees can be described as "boundary-spanning workers" (Bateson and Hoffman, 1999). They mediate between the organization and its customers, hence are given the opportunities or empowered to make their own decisions and develop their abilities and job performance skills (Kreitner and Kinicki, 1992). Management researchers seek further to study empowerment concept of unrestricted job decision making power and job autonomy to an individual level. For instance, empowerment has been operationalized as a psychological construct reflecting an individual's feelings of self-control and self-efficacy (Spreitzer, 1995). Hence, the definition of psychological empowerment is found in the literature.

Psychological empowerment captures an individual's orientation towards work role. It is believed to be a motivational construct manifested in namely four types of individual awareness: Meaning, Competence, Self-determination, and Impact (Thomas and Velthouse, 1990). Meaning refers to value of one's work; Competence refers to one's ability; Self-determination refers to one's selection of actions and Impact is one's influences in the workplace (Ashforth, 1989; Deci et al., 1989; Thomas and Velthouse, 1990). These four kinds of awareness or cognitions explain the psychological empowerment of an individual which is directly related to the perception of his or her preferred work role and context. Spreitzer (1995) advocates that psychological empowerment reflects the ongoing changes of employees' perceptions of themselves in connection with their work environment. Nevertheless, empowerment is seen to be influenced by cultural factors (Hui, Au and Fock 2004; Sigler and Pearson 2000). When approved by the management, cultural factor or value of power-distance exerts a strong influence on employees' willingness to accept and exercise discretionary power (Chow, Lo, Sha and Hong 2006). Discretionary empowerment depends more on the individual's preference for control of the power and can be influenced by the individual's cultural background such as power-distance (Hui et al. 2004). Hence, besides psychological empowerment, the definition of psychological empowerment is also found in the literature.

In the hospitality and tourism context, both discretion empowerment and psychological empowerment have been discussed by many researchers. Empowerment issues in hotels such as Ritz Carlton and Scotts' Hotels/Marriott (Carper, 1991; Ghillyer, 1994; Goymour, 1992), restaurants such as Harvester restaurants (Ashness and Lashley, 1995; Pikard, 1993) and airlines such as Scandinavian Airlines and Delta Airlines (Carlzon, 1989; Glover, 1989) are found in the literature.

In the Asian hospitality literature context, relatively little is known about empowerment and related issues, some useful information can be identified in a few researches in China. For instance, Cheung, Baum and Wong (2012) examine the empowerment concepts in the Asian context. Using an open ended questionnaires survey and focus groups, an in-depth examination of the perceptions of hotel managers in China regarding their interpretation and practice of empowerment within their workplace is provided. Their study findings reveal the influences of empowerment practices can be individual-based as well as family based. Individual based influences are employees' virtue, skills and competency. Family or in-group based influence are family relationship between the managers and employees, trusting relationships and commitment from the managers. The significant result is family based empowerment practices are significantly dominant in China hotels. In another hotel study, Humborstad et al. (2008) empirically examines 290 hotel employees in Macau on the impact of empowerment on service willingness. Empowerment is found to have a positive relationship with delivering higher service. In a survey of hotel service employees in Beijing, the successful implementation of empowerment depended on employees' willingness to assume and exercise discretionary power approved by their managers (Hui et, al, 2004). The three studies provide insights on how empowerment works in China hotels which has a predominately high power distance culture. Yet, whether the high power distance culture hinders the empowerment of women is not yet known.

Spreitzer, Kizilos and Nason (1997) test and find a significant relationship between gender and empowerment. Women at the middle and senior managerial positions in the hospitality industry are encountering the most important obstacle of not being thoroughly empowered. The most difficult challenge to struggle in an environment that is male dominated, informal network of "old boy network" (Brownell, 1994). When compare to men, women are more anxious about personal relationships and responsibilities than men (Gilligan, 1982). Stimpson, Neff, Jensen and Newby (1991) compare the rating of adjectives on the social desirability of men and women, women are found to rate adjectives that reflect a concern for relationships, such as likable, friendly, adaptable, etc, as more desirable than men did. Peterson and Hughey (2004) described women felt less empowered than men and proved that gender was a predictor of empowerment.

The impact of empowerment from female managers' perspective are neglected by most literature, most literature seeks insights from the perspective of managers and service employees. To fill this void in the context of a service industry such as hospitality and tourism, the present study focuses on examining the issues of empowering female hospitality and tourism managers in Asia. This study will help to provide useful and practical insights from to the senior management on the implementation of empowerment in the hospitality and tourism industry in Asia. This chapter attempts to examine the empowerment issues of tourism and hospitality women by exploring women's career in the Asia Pacific region. The objectives of this chapter are to review the women's employment situation in the hotel and tourism industry; to discuss the barriers of empowering women in the hospitality and tourism industry and to provide possible practical suggestions.

Literature Review

Women in the Tourism and Hospitality Industry

According to the World Travel and Tourism Council, global tourism will create 70 million new jobs in the next decade, and almost 70% of these will be in Asia. Over the same period, the World Travel and Tourism Council (WTTC) predicts Asia's travel and tourism industry will experience an annual growth of more than 6%, becoming the fastest growth region in the world. In terms of global tourism expenditures, Asian travelers will account for nearly one-half of the total by 2020. Faced with such high growth predictions, especially in Asia, the hospitality industry must adopt a more proactive and strategic approach to talent management.

Taking a global perspective, women in hospitality make up to nearly 70% of the total workforce (Sinclair, 1997); undertake more than 70% of all work in the informal hospitality sector (Sinclair, 1997). Since women already make up a major proportion of the hospitality industry's workforce, it is necessary for any talent management strategy to incorporate a focus on female human capital. It is also vital to pay attention to the barriers to the inclusion of women in the potential supply of talent. Nevertheless, evidence shows that this is not happening.

- Women hold less than 40% of all managerial and supervisory positions in the international hospitality industry (Baum, 2013)
- Women hold less than 20% of general management roles (Sinclair, 1997)
- Women are identified as owners of less than 20% of hospitality businesses and only around 10% of hotels worldwide (Sinclair, 1997)
- Women make up between 5% and 8% of corporate board members of publically-quoted hospitality businesses (Sinclair, 1997)

In 2010, the International Labour Organization (ILO) highlighted the challenges faced by women in the hospitality workplace when it noted that those women who are in a weaker position tended to work in the most vulnerable jobs, where they are more likely to experience poor working conditions, inequality of opportunity and treatment, violence, exploitation, stress and sexual harassment (Baum, 2013). The UNWTO in a 2010 report highlights both the opportunities and challenges of women with respect to employment in tourism. Women workforce dominate the hospitality industry by numbers, however, women remain to be under-represented in senior managerial roles and general management positions. The reality is women in hospitality leadership roles falls below the number of women leaders in other sectors. The issue needs to be addressed and it is necessary to develop strategies that can promote greater gender equality and opportunity in the hospitality industry.

The organizational and structural characteristics of the hospitality industry poses particular challenges for women. These include the shift duties and unsocial working hours on employee; seasonal work during some parts of the year and working in remote regions season. The conditions deprived the time and well-being of women who have family and care responsibilities. These can act as major barriers to women working in the hospitality industry.

Many multinational companies and sectors nowadays have initiatives and objectives which aim to have women in leadership roles. However, the hospitality and tourism industry clearly has not yet succeeded in promoting a significant number of women into leadership positions. What barriers exist in the hospitality industry to prevent women progressing into senior roles and what is being done to break down these barriers?

Barriers Facing Women in Hospitality and Tourism Industry

In the global hospitality industry, the gender challenges highlight a range of barriers that are predominantly socio-cultural but which also impinge on wider economic and political considerations (Baum, 2013, Baum and Cheung, 2015). The opportunities, motivations, and choices of women managers are manipulated by cultural and societal differences in different countries (Izraeli and Adler, 1994). Li and Leung (2001) presents the profile and career challenges of female managers in Asian Hotels. Three major factors, namely work-family conflict, network access and family support were found to be significantly related to the existence of the glass ceiling. In the UK, People 1st identified a number of obstacles to women's advancement to senior positions in the hospitality industry. 1. Difficulty of combining work at senior level with caring responsibilities 2. Dominant masculine organisational culture 3. Preconceptions and gender bias 4. Lack of networking and exclusion from informal networks of communication 5. Lack of visible women in senior positions (cited by Janta, 2011).

Our analysis of the past literature highlights a wider range of barriers to women's participation and opportunity in hospitality:

- Cultural traditions have strong impact in most countries and communities which lay down the traditional care taking gender roles and responsibilities in the home and workplace, thus hinder women to progress to the senior levels in organisations.
- Education systems in many countries that continue to typecast men and women into specific work and domestic roles.

- Ineffective equal opportunities legislation in many countries discriminate against women at all stages of the recruitment and promotion/ opportunity cycle.
- Role stereotyping in specific hotel departments that sees women typecast into operational roles which promotion to senior managerial or leadership roles may be tough.
- Workplace cultures and expectations in hospitality that disadvantage women who aspire to a reasonable balance between work and family (child and elderly) care responsibilities.
- Aspirational and laudable corporate policies in major hospitality companies that support opportunity for women on an equal footing to men and, in some cases, provide additional affirmative action to enable women to progress in organisations.
- Attitude of owners who increasingly influence the employment practices of their management or franchise companies. In a more general comment relating to hotel owners, the 2014 FIU report on talent in China highlights that "Chinese hotel owners have significant influence in the development of properties yet these owners/developers seemingly don't make similar investments on talent acquisition and talent development" (FIU, 2014).
- Undervaluing of women's work is implicit with women often earn less than men for doing equal jobs.

It is vital that all stakeholders move away from the perception that this is a 'women's issue' to which only women have a serious input. It is vital that gender issues in the hospitality workforce are seen as a business matter that demands engagement of key personnel, irrespective of their gender.

Facing up to gender imbalance is an important step for companies to take. In many respects, Google lead the way in this regard. Google recognize that their 30:70 gender imbalance is an issue as are their other diversity demographics relating to ethnicity. However, Google are up-front in addressing the issue when they admit that "We're not where we want to be when it comes to diversity. And it is hard to address these kinds of challenges if you're not prepared to discuss them openly, and with the facts. All of our efforts, including going public with these numbers, are designed to help us recruit and develop the world's most talented and diverse people" (Google Diversity, 2015).

RECOMMENDATION

Baum's (2013) recommendations in his paper for the International Labour Organisation (ILO) were addressed to key stakeholders in Governments, hotel, catering and tourism (hospitality) enterprises, trade unions, educational providers NGOs and international agencies. As recommendations they are, predominantly 'Proposition' in their focus, building a case of equity and equality on moral and entitlement grounds rather than focusing on the business case for women's enhancement in hospitality organisations. The recommendations, nevertheless, are worth reproducing in full here in the following because they highlight the complexity of the challenge that aspiring to gender equality and opportunity in the international hospitality industry poses.

- Hospitality enterprises and trade unions engaging in social dialogue can effect change in terms of equal opportunity by promoting and promulgating talent identification and development on the basis of transparent access for women and men; address practical barriers to international mobility for female executives and senior technical experts, particularly relating to career management, work-life and work-family balance matters; implement and invest in measures to ensure that women on maternity leave can remain in close touch with business developments and wider sector/market trends; design career-entry routes and ladders (similar to graduate entry schemes) for mature entrants, career changers and women returning to work so as to limit opportunities to low skills areas of work; encourage equality of opportunity and treatment and the reduction of wage gaps between men and women for jobs of equal value.
- Hospitality enterprises can engage with their ownership partners in agreeing to the application of gender equality and equal opportunity policies and practices; could promote male careers within areas of work traditionally dominated by women such as housekeeping in order to reduce workplace segregation; address and remove practical obstacles to female participation in the hospitality workplace through the provision of better social and physical security and secure staff accommodation; flexible working conditions and shifts; and access to flexible arrangements for training and development; support suitable childcare provision to enable employees (both male and female) to remain within their workforce.
- Trade unions and employers can agree a joint policy against sexual harassment by customers but also by employees that is visible and applied in hospitality workplaces, recognizing that sexual harassment can have serious implications for the concerned person and represents a major form of discrimination against women; Specific attention should be paid to health and safety. Women are more likely to be in non-standard forms of employment than men in the hospitality sector, they tend not to report illnesses or accidents for fear of losing their jobs. Safe and healthy workplaces are not only important for the workers and their wellbeing but also for the wellbeing of the guests and for the productivity of the enterprise.
- Governments can review employment legislation which may inhibit micro- and small hospitality businesses from employing women of child- bearing/ rearing age and actively promote such workers as a source of skills; governments can support major hotel sector employers in the provision of child-care facilities within the workplace in order to incentivize the employment of women in key roles and positions while offering the same services to male employees;
- Governments, social partners and international development organizations can promote enhanced working conditions and remuneration in hospitality in order to provide sustainable alternatives for women to exploitative options within sex tourism; joint policy to protect women from sexual harassment by customers.
- Well-established social dialogue mechanisms in hospitality enterprises can contribute to improved gender balance across the roles and positions of men and women in the hospitality sector. Increased women's participation in decision-taking could lead to higher female representation in managerial positions.

The challenge with the above recommendations (cited from Baum, 2013) laudable as they might be, is in their implementation. Collectively, they provide an opportunity to drive change in the drive towards greater gender equity and opportunity within the hospitality workplace.

CONCLUSION

The barriers that exist in the hospitality and tourism sectors for women are related to workplace culture and expectations; attitude of owners; discrimination of women at the Human Resources processes; cultural traditions; education system; Role stereotyping and ineffective legislation. The challenge lies with the wide range of stakeholders who play a role in addressing the barriers women are facing and implementing change. Real change will only be possible when collective responsibility for meaningful action and change is taken across the stakeholder community at a local, national and international level.

ACKNOWLEDGMENT

The authors would like to acknowledge an earlier version of this chapter is from the White Paper –Women in Tourism and Hospitality: Unlocking the Potential in the Talent Pool initiated by Diageo Company as part of Plan W, Diageo's Sustainable Development strategy to empower women through learning.

REFERENCES

Ashforth, B. (1989).The experience of powerlessness in organizations. Organizational Behavior and Human Decision Processes. April, 43(2), pp.207-242.

Ashness, D. and Lashley, C. (1995). Empowering service workers at Harvester Restaurants. Personnel Review. 24(8), pp.17-32.

Bateson, J. and Hoffman, D. (1999*). Managing services marketing*. Fort Worth: The Dryden Press.

Baum, T. (2013). International Perspectives on Women and Work in Hotels, Catering and Tourism. International Labour Organization.

Baum, T. and Cheung, C. (2015). Women in Tourism and Hospitality: Unlocking the potential in the talent pool. Retrieved online on 1st November 2015 from http://www.diageoplanw.com/.

Bowen, R. and Lawler, E. (1992). The empowerment of service workers: what, why, how and when. Slogan Management Review, Spring, pp.31-39.

Brownell, J. (1994). Creating strong listening environments: A key hospitality management task, International Journal of Contemporary Hospitality Management, 6(3), pp.3 - 10.

Carlzon, J. (1989). Moments of Truth. Harper and Row: London.

Carper, J. (1991). The ladies and gentlemen of Ritz Carlton. Hotels, 25(5), pp.75-76.

Cheung, C, Baum, T. and Wong, A. (2012). Relocating empowerment as a management concept for Asia. Journal of Business Research, 65(1), pp.36-41.

Chow, I., Lo, T., Sha, Z. and Hong, J. (2006). The impact of developmental experience, empowerment, and organizational support on catering service staff performance. International Journal of Hospitality Management. September, 25(3), pp. 478-495.

Deci, E., Connell, J. and Richard, R. (1989). Self-determination in a work organization. Journal of Applied Psychology, August, 74(4), pp. 580-590.

FIU (2014). Managing growing pains of China's relentless hotel development pipeline. Retrieved online on 1st November 2015 from http://www.macrovisionhospitality.com/uploads/4/3/1/2/43121473/vlef_insight_2014_white_paper_-_english_-_final.pdf.

Ghillyer, A. (1994). An examination of empowerment as the key to service quality in the hospitality industry. MSc dissertation, University of Surrey.

Gilligan C. (1982). In a Different Voice. Harvard University Press, Cambridge.

Glover, W. (1989). The Delta airlines family: a case for supporting service employees. In Shames GW, Glover WG (Eds), World Class Service, International Press: Maine, pp.44-50.

Google Diversity (2015). Foster a fair and inclusive Google. Retrieved online on 1st November 2015 from http://www.google.com/diversity/at-google.html.

Goymour, D (1992). Brand new Marriott. Caterer and Hotelkeeper, 25 June-1 July, pp.42-44.

Hui, M., Au, K. and Fock, H. (2004). Empowerment effects across cultures. Journal of International Business Studies. 35, pp.46-60.

Humborstad, S., Humborstad, B. and Whitfield, R. (2008). Implementation of empowerment in Chinese high power-distance organizations. The International Journal of Human Resource Management, 19(7), pp.1349-1364.

Izraeli, D. and Adler, N. (1994) Competitive frontiers: Women managers in a global economy, in Adler N. and Izreali, D. (eds). Competitive frontiers: Women managers in a global economy, Basil Blackwell, Cambridge, MA, pp. 3-21.

Janta, H. (2011). Polish migrant workers in the UK hospitality industry: Profiles, work experience and methods for accessing employment, International Journal of Contemporary Hospitality Management, 23 (6), pp.803 - 819.

Kreitner, R. and Kinicki, A. (1992). Organizational Behavior (2nd edition). Homewood, IL: Richard D.Irwin Inc.

Li, L. and Leung, R. (2001). Female managers in Asian hotels: profile and career challenges, International Journal of Contemporary Hospitality Management, 13(4). pp.189 - 196.

Peterson, A. and Hughey J. (2004). Social cohesion and intrapersonal empowerment: gender as moderator. Health Education Research. 19(5), pp.533-542.

Pikard, J. (1993). The real meaning of empowerment. Personnel Management. 25(11), pp.28-33.

Sigler, T. and Pearson, C. (2000). Creating an empowering culture: examining the relationship between organizational culture and perceptions of empowerment. Journal of Quality Management, Spring, 5(1), pp.27-52.

Sinclair, T. (1997). Gender, Work and Tourism. London: Routledge.

Spreitzer, G. (1995). Psychological Empowerment in the Workplace: Dimensions, Measurement, and Validation. Academy of Management, 1 October, 38(5), pp.1442-1465.

Spreitzer, G., Kizilos, M. & Nason, S. (1997). A dimensional analysis of the relationship between psychological empowerment and effectiveness satisfaction, and strain. Journal of Management. October 1997, 23(5). pp. 679-704.

Stimpson, D., Neff, W., Jensen, L. and Newby, T. (1991). The caring morality and gender differences. Psychological reports, 69, pp.407-414.

Thomas, K. and Velthouse, B. (1990).Cognitive elements of empowerment: An "Interpretive" model of intrinsic task motivation. Academy of Management. 1 October, 15(4), pp.666-681.

UNWTO (2010). Global report on women in Tourism 2010. Retrieved online on 1st November 2015 from http://www2.unwto.org/sites/all/files/pdf/folleto_globarl_report.pdf.

World Travel and Tourism Council. (2014). Global Talent Trends and Issues for the Travel and Tourism Sector. Retrieved online on 1st November from http://www.wttc.org/-/media/382bb1e90c374262bc951226a6618201.ashx.

In: Empowerment
Editor: Randall Harris

ISBN: 978-1-63484-036-1

Chapter 6

LOVE AND POWER: EMPOWERMENT AND SELF-HELP GROUPS AMONG THE WIVES OF ALCOHOLICS IN BRAZIL

Luciana Araujo Gomes*[1] *and Carla de Meis*[*2]*, MD, PhD
[1]Department of Social Welfare of Angra dos Reis,
Angra dos Reis, Brazil
[2]Department of Psychiatry of the Medical School of
the Federal University of Rio de Janeiro, Rio de Janeiro, Brazil

ABSTRACT

Introduction: In the wake of the feminist movement of the 20th century, women in Western societies have adopted new, more modern values that have brought changes to their lives. However, we observe that traditional values are still important in women's orientations and actions in Brazil, where family values are still uppermost in the female world, territorializing them in a way of life characterized by the maintenance of the bonds of affection and where the role of caregiver, the position of victim, and the idea of suffering as one's destiny and as a feminine virtue is still often present.

Objective: In this study we describe how, through their participation in mutual assistance groups, the wives of alcoholic men are able to re-signify conjugal relationships that are usually deeply marked by physical and psychological violence.

Methods: This is a qualitative research, with open-ended interviews with 12 female partners of male alcoholics who belonged to a support group in the city of Rio de Janeiro, Brazil. The interviews were interpreted based on the gift theory of anthropologist Marcel Mauss.

Discussion: We observed that when the women interviewed begin frequenting the self help group, they fell in with others whose discourse and experiences were similar to their own. Through a mutual self-identification, they began to see themselves in perspective and came to relativize situations that they never dared question before. The figure of "good mother" and "suffering wife" evoked by the majority of the women interviewed when speaking of their arrival at the mutual assistance group tended to disappear from the narratives over time. An aspect of the group's ideology is the rejection of the discourse of victimization. This can be interpreted as being a strategy to move the women towards accountability and away from their passive position as a victim of "someone else" (the partner or the situation), thus promoting a more modern, individualizing type of discourse that helps them to adopt the position of subject, leading to greater autonomy. We observed that as they continue to attend the meetings, the women reflected on their values and started to question their role in the family. It is as if by simultaneously belonging to the family and to the self-help group, the women were able to distance themselves from their environment of origin (the family) and gaze at themselves with a more critical eye in a process of empowerment. We can say that the women developed a relative individualization associated with the process of self-examination that would lead to increased reflection on their part and a broadening of their "inner horizons," which would enable them to re-position themselves in the conjugal relationship in a more satisfactory way.

INTRODUCTION

The social and cultural meaning of marriage in Brazilian society is closely aligned with gender divisions and roles in the dominant culture. Brazil is a huge and complex country. Although a common language is spoken, several cultures coexist within the various white, black, Amerindian and mixed-race populations. Brazilian society is deeply rooted in a traditional patriarchal structure that emphasizes the importance of the family (Freire 1980). It is also a society open to modernization. Consequently, Brazil is a country with a complex juxtaposition of ideas of tradition and modernity, individualism and holism, equality and hierarchy, citizenship and personal relationships, all of which correspond to two different co-inhabiting realms of values (Da Matta 1991).

Gender studies differentiate between sex and gender. While sex is a natural characteristic, gender is a value-laden concept. The traditional view of social roles for women in Brazil, with its mainly Catholic heritage, divides women into two basic opposing categories: one in which they are controlled by men, and the other, in which they are not subordinated by or under the protection of a man, whether husband, father, or brother (Aragão 1983). In the first category, we find the mother, the housewife, reflected in the image of the Virgin Mary, the mother of Christ. She is the saintly woman who has sacrificed the joy of sex to maintain the home, the sacred structure. In the second category, that of the uncontrolled woman, we find the street woman, the whore, the vile woman whose animus is one of malice and destruction (De Meis 2002).

This dichotomy of the housewife versus the prostitute, corresponding to the rationale frequently found in traditional societies where the ideas of 'good' and 'bad,' 'pure' and 'dirty,' and 'high' and 'low' are intrinsic (Dumont 1983), tends to disappear in a more modern culture. Wherever we find a predominance of individualistic values, these dual distinctions tend to become blurred and are replaced by concepts of equality (De Meis 1999). Individualism includes the idea of citizenship in which all human beings - woman or man, married or single, housewife or prostitute - have the same rights and duties (Simmel 1971).

In this chapter, we analyze the narratives of alcoholics' wives who attend mutual help meetings for the families and friends of alcoholics in Rio de Janeiro, Brazil. Although the organization that operates the network of mutual help groups serves both men and women with meaningful ties to alcoholics, for the purposes of our study, we included only the wives of alcoholics. Interviews focussed on these women's often lengthy conjugal relationships with their alcoholic partners in situations that they themselves described as abusive and violent. We explain how, in the self-help groups, by listening to the narratives of other alcoholics' wives and by affirming themselves in their own narratives in a more modern pattern, women are encouraged to question patriarchal values in a process of gaining a more objective awareness of their situations.

METHODOLOGY AND THEORETICAL APPROACH

In this qualitative research study, we conducted open-ended interviews with 12 female partners of male alcoholics. All these women belonged to the same support group in the city of Rio de Janeiro. As visitors are not allowed to attend meetings, the selection of the women was done with the help of the administrative secretary of the mutual assistance group, who received the authorization to help us from headquarters; this woman, who is also a member of the group, acted as a key informant and greatly facilitated our approach to the women interviewed. There was no difficulty in scheduling the interviews, as the research was partly seen as an opportunity to validate the ideas and ideology of the group within the academic world. It is possible that we were encouraged to interview the group's "champions," i.e., women who had integrated well within the group and who may have been chosen by our key informant in the belief that their personal accounts would reflect the discourse the group wishes to propagate when someone "from outside" arrives to observe its activities. However, this apparent bias in the sample selection does not affect our analysis, as our purpose was not to summarize the results of the group's interventions, but to understand how its availability and its ideology, as reflected in the women's narratives, work as factors that bring about change.

The interviews were conducted between November 2008 and February 2009, each one lasting approximately two hours. They were taped and later transcribed. During the process of analysing the transcriptions, the authors met regularly to pinpoint and systematize the common elements in the interview content. When a theme was dealt with repeatedly in the body of interviews, we selected representative quotes for illustrative purposes. The research project was pre-approved by an ethics committee, and the women signed a free-and-informed consent form before being interviewed. The identities of the women interviewed are protected by the use of fictitious names. The first time a woman is quoted in the text, the excerpt is followed by her fictitious name, age, number of years she has been or was married to an alcoholic, and length of time she has been regularly frequenting the self-help group. Expressions and words in quotation marks within the text are those used by the women in the interviews.

The hermeneutical approach used to interpret the narratives of the women interviewed relies on the gift theory as elaborated by Marcel Mauss (1950). Although we did not set out with this theoretical framework in mind, during the analysis process, we saw that Mauss's theory, which holds within it the paradoxical possibility of "winning" while "losing," lends itself well to our analysis, as will be shown below. Love and power form a central duality in our study.

In the gift theory (Mauss 1950), every social relationship is one of exchange. In Mauss's view, the basis of all human social interaction and communication comprises a constant giving-and-receiving in which a person gives something to another person with the aim of creating and maintaining a bond with him or her. The gift is therefore the element that circulates in the service of the social bond and which nourishes it. In this sense, to Mauss, social bonds - or social exchanges - should not be analyzed in terms of the content of the gifts that circulate within them (e.g., goods, affection, words) but rather in terms of the gift-giving itself, that is, the circulation of these goods and symbols between the subjects (Godbout 1992; Lanna 2000). The gift cycle generates the obligation to produce a counter-gift which will eventually be reciprocated in turn, and so forth, setting in motion the endless chain of giving, receiving, and giving back in human relations - in other words, the social bond (Mauss 1950).

To Mauss (1950), nobility and honour are inherent in gift-giving. Therefore, the giver gains prestige by his act, raising his self-esteem and increasing his power in the relationship, power that can only be neutralized by retribution in the form of the counter-gift. To the extent that "one leaves something of one's self" to the other, one is not only giving but also acquiring "something from the other" in the process. Mauss points out that in Germanic languages, *gift* has two meanings: gift and poison. Giving of one's self makes the recipient feel indebted, and even humiliated if he will not or cannot give back the appropriate counter-gift.

For Mauss, even a spontaneous gift is useful and obligatory, as it serves to ensure and perpetuate human relations (1950). The obligation to give something back negates the free nature of the gift, which is only apparent, as the act of giving comes to generate a feeling of inferiority in the recipient, a "quasi-guilt" that can only be eliminated by the act of gifting in return. The debt, when it is deliberately incurred, confirms a hierarchical power relationship between the subjects (Godbout 1992).

In his reading of Mauss's gift theory, Lévi-Strauss (1950) writes that the social bond does not only imply an exchange of gifts, but also a relationship of reciprocity. Reciprocity constitutes the backbone of the bond and is the guarantee of its maintenance, as it generates proportionality, connectivity, and fixity between the subjects. In its more general meaning, reciprocity implies order, equilibrium, and harmony, all elements opposed to chaos, and for this reason, it enables society to function.

Reciprocity is not always a synonym of equality in terms of measurable value. However, in a relationship, a subject can reciprocate even if the counter-gift is not given in the same manner or does not take the same form or currency as the gift. What is important is that both sides of the equation - giver and recipient - feel they are adequately considered in the exchange. As long as this is the case, money can be exchanged for goods, goods for affection, affection for care, and so on, in an endless mutual interplay in which material goods also possess a symbolic and affective character (Lanna 2000). Thus, for Lévi-Strauss, the exchange cannot be understood as a standardized relationship, but a singular, specific one, constructed between two or more subjects over time (Lévi-Strauss 1950).

We referred to above concepts as we questioned the nature of the social bond linking the women and their alcoholic partners during our analysis of the women's narratives.

ALCOHOLISM AND SOCIAL BOND: THE RUPTURE OF RECIPROCITY AND A "CONTAGION"

According to Ramão, Meneghel, and Oliveira (2005), marriage and family occupy an important place in the woman's role in Brazilian society, where women are territorialized within the social functions of nourishing, care-giving, and giving of themselves. The feminine ideal of the 'housewife' thus produced is that of a person who exists for others, the woman having been transformed into a docile and receptive being of whom indulgence, self-restraint, and sacrifice are expected (Rocha-Coutinho 1994).

However, as we have seen in Mauss (1950), sacrifice brings power as much as subordination to the person who makes it. To Mauss, "[...] sacrifice always implies a consecration [...]" (2005, p. 147). This can be illustrated metaphorically by the crucifixion of Christ, a sacrifice that was used as the foundation of the supreme power and authority of the Christian faith. A sense of indebtedness is created in the person for whom the sacrifice is made, much like a debtor who feels he must pay back a loan to restore his dignity. In this manner, the sacrifice constructs a social bond that temporarily places the maker of the sacrifice (or giver) in a "superior" position. Our approach in analyzing our interviews focuses on this dynamic of giving *versus* that of receiving, of prestige *versus* humiliation and violence, of submission *versus* power, in the women´s narratives.

Many of the women members of the mutual help group whom we interviewed in Rio de Janeiro define their lives with their alcoholic partners as unilateral relationships in which they are the only ones who "give" for the sake of maintaining the conjugal bond, reflecting a relationship that has been spoiled by a debt that will not be paid by the partner. The virtual absence of the male figure creates the fantasy of sacrifice, the lack of reciprocity, violence, and illegitimacy. To Mauss (1950), the act of refusing to give or to accept a return gift is equivalent to a declaration of war, as they represent the rejection of the bond and of community.

From the interviews, we observed that the women felt mistreated by having their demands for affection and their offer of love and compromise ignored by their partners. However, from the male perspective, in this same situation, the woman's gift could be interpreted as a form of humiliation, inasmuch as he is unable to reciprocate due to his alcoholism. Thus, we have the paradoxical situation in which the man, upon receiving the gift, feels mistreated and diminished, and responds by acting aggressively towards his partner, as was revealed in the women's narratives.

> "*He told me: 'Who do you think you are, telling me what to do? Have you seen yourself in the mirror lately? Ugly old hag*!'" [Angélica, 51 years old, a widow for one year, married to an alcoholic for 30 years, 8 years in the group]

In this excerpt from a narrative, the man has understood the woman's advice as humiliating to him, placing her above him, and he reacts aggressively with the intention of humiliating her in turn in order to re-establish her lower hierarchical position in the relationship.

What emerged from the women's discourse is a vicious circle of humiliation and mutual destruction: on the woman's part, when she feels that her gift is rejected or diminished, and on the man's part, when, receiving a gift he cannot give back, he loses face in the relationship and feels subjugated by the partner who, paradoxically, in trying to help him and sacrificing herself for him, is locking him into feelings of indebtedness and indignity. The approach promoted in these particular mutual help groups stresses the importance of preventing aggressive behaviour from becoming two-sided. Women are urged not to react to their partners' provocations by entering into what is termed a slanging match (*bate-boca*) and advised to "avoid the first quarrel." This principle was strongly reiterated in the interviews. The women refer to their prior behaviour:

> "*He'd come home and smash up the house, and I'd just stand there. The next day, I'd fix everything up and get things back to normal.*" [Anita, 56 years old, a widow for 7 years, married to an alcoholic for 27 years, 13 years frequenting the group, and separated for 12 years]

> "*He'd leave work, spend the night out, and get home at five or six o'clock in the morning. I'd be furious. But I wouldn't do anything: I just used to cry. He'd wake up the next day feeling depressed and he'd beg my forgiveness. And I'd be capable of forgiving him.*" [Olivia, 62 years old, married for 37 years, living with her partner's alcoholism and frequenting the group for 20 years]

To Mauss (1950), when giving of one's self, there is no guarantee of a return, but the social bond is established nonetheless by the belief that the return exists. However, for the women we interviewed, the knowledge that the debt owed to them by their partners would never be paid has brought them to view the experience of the conjugal relationship with its power games, violence, and humiliation, as a swindle, and the bond that has been constructed as illegitimate. Further humiliation and revolt is felt by being obliged to take part in the swindle.

> *"My life was one big lie! I'd lie to my husband's boss when he didn't show up at work because he'd been drinking; I'd lie to my mother, saying: 'he didn't go to the party because ...' In other words, I was always making up lies."* [Sílvia, 47 years old, married to an alcoholic for 20 years and frequenting the group for 4 years]

In the women's discourse, as revealed in the interviews, there is the belief that alcohol abuse has affected their partner to such an extent that he no longer possesses the "sense of being a husband" or of "living in a conjugal relationship" with his wife.

> "*I saw myself as a woman married to a dead husband. I didn't have a husband! There's no comradeship in a marriage with an alcoholic.*" [Vera, 52 years old, married to an alcoholic for 22 years and frequenting the group for 6 years]

However, in spite of being aware of the failure of the conjugal relationship, many of the women interviewed did not view the marriage contract as revocable. What emerged from their comments was that, although they no longer saw the relationship as a real marriage, they did not decide to end it. Instead, their narratives are ones of falling 'ill,' being abused and humiliated by their partners for the sake of maintaining the relationship. The women consider that they are married but not "really married" as they maintain a situation of relational precariousness.

> "*My self-esteem really took a beating. I became emotionally sick and received psychiatric treatment for a year ... I had to retire at age 44, in the middle of my productive years*." [Selma, 57 years old, married for 27 years and living with her husband's alcoholism for 20 years, frequenting the group for 14 years]

In her study involving mutual-help groups for the families of alcoholics in France, Faizang (1996) affirms that women see their partner's alcoholism as a family illness, in that it affects the people who have an emotional connection with the alcoholic. In this author's view, contagion occurs due to the affective relation, to the social bond. In our interviews as well, the women saw the absence of reciprocity in the conjugal bond as having brought on their illnesses.

> "*When you're involved with an alcoholic ... the whole family gets sick, because alcoholism is contagious; it contaminates the atmosphere*." [Sílvia]

> "*My illness didn't occur on its own ... All the time, I had to go through*: '*When is he coming home from the bar? ...' Dealing with alcoholism makes you sick*!" [Eva, 56 years old, married to an alcoholic for 28 years, frequenting the group for 4 years]

In the women's narratives, the lack of reciprocity in the relationship manifested as a contagious illness that "contaminates the home" with the disillusionment, conflict, and suffering that it causes.

The marriage bond implies reciprocity between husband and wife, an element that was absent in the discourse of our interviewees. These women, in defining their conjugal relationships, made it clear that their pre-nuptial notions of marriage did not correspond to their reality, as their husbands had failed to live up to their commitments in several aspects of family life, thus repeatedly showing their non-respect of the marriage contract.

> "*My children were growing up and he never even bothered to go with them to a (family or community) party*." [Selma]

Thus, the concept of contagion concerns illnesses that affect women through the social bond (Faizang 1996). The women we interviewed came to see themselves as victims of their husband's illness (alcoholism), attributing a collective dimension to the contagion. Among the symptoms and effects caused by living with an alcoholic partner, they cited internal (organ) problems, emotional distress and feelings of revolt, anger, and sadness.

> *"My stomach hurt and my skin broke out. It was because my anger was at the bursting point."* [Luíza, 71 years old, married for 41 years, 15 years of dealing with her husband's alcoholism and frequenting the group]

> *"As he got worse, I got sick. I suffered from depression, I had anorexia nervosa, I lost a lot of weight ..."* [Célia, 55 years old, married to an alcoholic for 35 years, frequenting the group for 4 years]

While her partner becomes ill because of the presence of alcohol in his body, the woman becomes ill because of its presence in the relationship. The partner's alcohol abuse is seen as a sickness that they are suffering from together.

"*... you're getting into the same boat with him. The two of you are going, you're going with him, he's taking you along.*" [Vera]

"*It's all one and the same: they get worse and you get worse too.*" [Olívia]

In the women's accounts, the violence inflicted by their alcoholic partners is not limited to physical, moral, or sexual damage, but is also present in their disillusionment with respect to what they had expected from the marriage.

"*You meet someone, you fall in love, you really admire the person, then you get married and afterwards, all you get are letdowns! That really hurts.*" [Anita]

The women said they do not feel guilty about the lack of conjugal reciprocity in their marriage; rather, they see themselves as victims, the husband being the only one at fault in the relationship. In their discourse, they show a tendency to feel virtuous because, in spite of their bad situation, they are capable of sacrificing themselves for the family.

"*I thought I was the most perfect person in the world: I didn't drink, I didn't smoke, I was a wonderful mother, an excellent homemaker. What faults did I have*?" [Vera]

In our interpretation based on Mauss (1950), by sacrificing themselves, by giving without the prospect of receiving anything in return, these women gain prestige, and by the same token, their male partners are diminished in the relationship. The care, imbued with suffering and sacrifice that the women dedicate to their families brings them prestige within the family group. Their sacrifice brings them power.

"*My father expected me to look after my brothers and sisters. On one hand, it made me a more responsible person. On the other hand, it made me feel all-powerful. So when I married an alcoholic, I thought I could save him from his alcoholism.*" [Selma]

We observed that the main obstacle preventing the women from breaking away from a non-reciprocal relationship, from their partner's lack of commitment, and from mutual abuse, was their adherence to the traditional woman's role in which the wife and mother must do everything possible to hold the family together. As mentioned above, these women belong to a culture in which family values are uppermost in the female world, territorializing them in a way of life characterized by the maintenance of the bonds of affection (Ramão, Meneghel, Oliveira 2005) and leading them to make often counterproductive decisions.

"*I think I spent my whole life ignoring how I felt about the circumstances. Because women are oriented to be wives and mothers, you're oriented towards the external side and not your inner side. So I ended up cancelling myself out to look after the family.*" [Anita]

Despite the adoption of more modern values in the wake of the feminist movement of the last century, which brought changes to many women's lives in Western societies, we observe that in Brazil, traditional values are still important and even predominant in women's attitudes and actions. Breaking with these traditional values is not easy (Biasoli-Alves 2000), as we have seen in these interviews.

> "*I didn't consider separation. Because it's what you've been taught: 'You married him, you've got to stay with him! Things may be bad with him, but they'll be worse without him!*'" [Sueli, 49 old, married to an alcoholic for 26 years, separated for a year and a half, frequenting the group for 10 years].

Dedication to others, selfless care-giving, the feeling that one has to be "perfect," and the sacrifice of one's self for the sake of the family are reflections of values expressed in the discourse of the women we interviewed.

> "*It was my dream to get married and stay married for good. I always thought, if he ever left me, it wouldn't be because of me. But I don't want this; it's not what I'm looking for!*" [Lina, 53 years old, married for 21 years; living with an alcoholic partner and frequenting the group for 20 years].

The "obligation" to give of one's self, to look after one's sick husband, stems from moral values connected to care-giving and to the family that appear to be central in the lives of these women. For Soares (2006):

> [...] *isn't the renunciation of one's own needs and desires for the sake of others, abnegation, and sacrifice considered feminine virtues? If this is what gives a woman value, then wouldn't holding the position of victim in the conjugal relationship also be a virtue*? (p. 86)

Sacrificing one's self for the relationship is the wife's duty, consecrated in the marriage ceremony by the signing of the ethical and religious commitment to fulfill her obligations and responsibilities. (D'Incao 1997; Rocha-Coutinho 1994)

> "*I felt super-responsible for the home, for him, and for the children. I ended up being the only head of the family. So I always saw myself as too protective, but at the same time, I never managed to protect myself.*" [Angélica]

The role of caregiver, the position of victim, and the idea of suffering as one's destiny and as a feminine virtue were continually emphasized in the discourse of the women interviewed in our study.

Empowerment: Rebirth through the Group

It emerged from the women's narratives that, feeling powerless in their struggle to hold the family together, they sought help, including help from the mutual assistance group. The initial motive for this was to obtain guidance and advice on how to help their husbands. However, the women described how, through their participation in the group, they began to develop the reflex of "looking at themselves," and subsequently, looking after themselves, not just the family.

> "*There's something that happens with most of the people who come here: they arrive in the group thinking they'll find a solution for the alcoholics. That's what people want the most, but it's not like that. What we find there is help for ourselves.*" [Célia]

> "*Over time, I understood that whether he drinks or not, the meetings are there for me, so that I can be all right, so that I'll take care of myself.*" [Olívia]

The evocation of the figures of "victim," "good mother" and "suffering wife" by the majority of the women interviewed when speaking of their arrival at the mutual assistance group tended to disappear from the later sections of their narratives. An aspect of the mutual help group's ideology is the rejection of the discourse of victimization. This can be seen as a strategy to move the woman towards responsibilization and away from her passive position as a victim of "someone else" (the partner or the situation), thus promoting a more modern, individualizing type of discourse that helps her adopt the position of subject, leading to greater autonomy.

In joining the group, the women interviewed enter into a new social network composed of people with a common life experience, that of being in a close relationship with an alcoholic. For the women, the group meeting is a space where they are accepted and listened to, where they can tell their stories without fear of being criticized or judged.

> "*You can say what you like in a room where everyone else has the same problem as you do. You say whatever you like, and you hear women saying what all of us think.*" [Olívia]

To Fróis (2007), the mutual help group allows a person to stop seeing him or herself as the only person with a particular problem, thus diminishing feelings of guilt, failure, and shame. In our study, the interviewees became conscious that their problems were shared by others through the narratives of their co-participants. Listening to each other at the meetings and identifying with the other women's stories, they were able to see themselves from new angles and discover possible ways out of situations they previously thought could not be resolved. Identifying with fellow group members made the women feel stronger, improved their self-esteem, and raised their hopes, which resulted in motivating them to continue going to the meetings.

> "*One day, a woman I didn't know was giving testimony and it seemed like she was telling my story. That really affected me! Then and there, I decided to stay, and it's been 21 years now.*" [Olívia]

It is as if the group were a mirror through which the participants see themselves in the others who attend the meeting. By belonging to the group and hearing the stories of their companions, their own experiences take on a new colour.

> "*Here, I can talk, and when I'm talking, I listen to myself. It's when I listen to myself that I realize I can change.*" [Anita]

We observed that as they continue to attend the meetings, the women reflected on their values and started to question their role in the family. Belonging to the family and to the self-help group at the same time, the woman is able to distance herself from her environment of origin (the family) and gaze at herself with a more critical eye in a process of individualization. Based on Duarte & Gomes (2008), we can speak of self-affirmation (or, a relative autonomization) associated with the emergence or ongoing development of domestic nuclei that are distant and independent from the original family situation. However, the rupture with the values of origin varies in consistency and extent according to each case.

> "*When I first came ... I thought I should be pitied, that I'd been abandoned, traded for alcohol ... The group made me change, made me look at things differently.*" [Leonor, 75 years old, married for 22 years, living with an alcoholic partner for 14 years, a widow for 28 years, and frequenting the group for 35 years]

In sharing their experiences, the interviewees glimpse new life possibilities beyond the simple dedication to other people. They transform the capacity to take care of others - with its crucial historical dimension of feminine identity in Brazilian culture - into a capacity that must include taking care of themselves as well. The more a woman had previously seen herself trapped in the "I must look after others" perspective, staking her prestige and her idea of the meaning of her life on it, the more she seems able to open up to the possibility of "I must look after myself." By expressing her feelings, new perspectives arise, widening her range of possibilities (Bourdieu 1979), and by reconstructing the notions of love, marriage, the wife's role, honour, and feminine dignity learned in the past, she is able to re-position herself in the conjugal relationship, in a path to empowerment.

> "*When you start hearing the testimony in the meeting room, you already compare (and you think): 'There are people who are like me!' That comforted me: I arrived in tears and already, I could smile. I started paying attention to my appearance, looking after myself better, feeling happy. I started to realize that there was a way out for me.*" [Sílvia]

Interpreting these narratives through the prism of the gift theory, we can say that for the majority of the women interviewed, the sense of virtuousness in the conjugal relationship functions as an unwanted consolation prize. As the women continue participating in groups meetings, the increase in self-esteem and power gained by occupying the position of martyr within the family loses its attractiveness and tends to be substituted by the increase in self-esteem and prestige that accompanies the demand for greater individuality and self-realization. In other words, the majority of the interviewees preferred to relinquish the traditional kind of power given to the martyr wife in favour of reconstructing narratives for themselves that are more in line with modern values. This attitude, in turn, may culminate in the attempt to take a firm position: to either end a relationship considered violent, illegitimate and unreciprocated, or to transform it by setting limits and arriving at a *modus vivendi* that is more equally-balanced, reciprocated, and satisfactory for the couple, in line with the ideology of the group.

Setting Limits and Seeking Reciprocity

One of the premises of the group is that the partner must avoid entering into a quarrel with the alcoholic from the outset. The mutual-help group's first rule is that limits must be established for the alcoholic to halt the spiral of aggression and mutual humiliation.

> "*Today, when I see that he wants to raise hell, I say: 'I won't enter into your sickness, my husband, oh no!' Today, I set limits for him that I never used to before.*" [Selma]

When they attend the meetings on a regular basis, the women come to achieve self-affirmation, expressing their wishes and their dissatisfactions in the relationship more clearly, and somewhat paradoxically, it is in refusing to rise to quarrels, fights, and provocations that they acquire mediation and negotiating tools which facilitate communication with their partners.

> "*Since I began to attend the group, I learned how to talk without fear, but also without entering into his game ... 'Look, your behaviour is doing this to me. If you get sick, I'm not going to take care of you anymore! I married you to live together, not to take care of you. I don't want that anymore!' It means that by not entering into his game, I was setting limits! With that, I noticed things started going more smoothly.*" [Luíza]

In this sense, the setting of limits contributes to the creation of a new basis for negotiation in the conjugal relationship, centering on the search for a new balance that is more satisfactory for the woman, together with her demand for a reciprocity that she considers minimally fair.

> "*He was already used to a routine: 'I get up, I go to the bar. I come back from the bar. She's at home ... great! In a while, I'll wake up and go out drinking again.' Since I started setting limits, all that is finished: I learned to go out and not feel that I have to come running back home ... So he'd come home and he wouldn't have his maid there, doing everything for him.*" [Vera]

For these women, the setting of limits in the relationship implies taking a firm stand. Their adoption of this attitude contributes to bringing about a change in their alcoholic partners, who begin to take their family responsibilities more seriously, and in consequence, start to feel less like "bad guys:" there is a gain in self-esteem and prestige in the relationship on their part as well. In our perspective based on Mauss (1950), this gain in prestige on the alcoholic partner's part is acquired by becoming less indebted. Consequently, when the man is forced to play the role of the 'good guy' or even of the 'victim' in the relationship, they grow in self-esteem and power. In yet another apparent paradox, it is through the limits set by their partners that the men begin to recover their dignity.

> "*It was as if that was contagious too: when he was drinking, it made me suffer, and when I sought help and started to change, he went for treatment. It shows that, in the same way that bad behaviour is contagious, a [positive] change in behaviour is also contagious.*" [Sílvia]

Thus, through their participation in the mutual assistance groups, the women came to seek a less unilateral, violent relationship and began to set limits. The demand for negotiation emerged - for an agreement that would make the relationship more satisfactory for both partners, establishing the beginning of a search for a new reciprocity. In other words, empowered by the group, taking care of and being responsible for the family ceased to be the women's only ideal as they developed a new, more modern, reading of the way they could cope with the domestic situation.

> "*Since I started the group, I stopped feeling I had to be home by a certain time. The meeting would finish at 5 p. m. If the girls suggested going out to have some ice cream, I would go. But before, I wouldn't do that. It was a prison, you know? I didn't have my own life!*" [Vera]

As mentioned above, the women described how they began to question the role they had previously accepted and started to focus on themselves and their inner world, resolving to take care of themselves and not only of others. Based on Duarte & Gomes (2008), we can say that the women developed a relative autonomization and empowerment associated with the process of self-examination that would lead to increased reflection on their part and a broadening of their inner horizons.

> "*I started to get back to myself: I had a right to live my life! 'Who am I? What am I doing with my life? What am I living for?' I mean, I began asking myself these questions and started trying to make up for lost time, to see what I could do for myself...*" [Vera]

As observed in the narratives, once the women were able to see themselves in perspective, empowerment tended to emerge, enabling them to affirm their desires and decisions.

> "*Since I began attending the group, I started travelling, going to the theatre ... I mean, I was getting back the things I liked, but I'd stopped doing them, because before, I thought if I did them, he'd be upset.*" [Angélica]

According to Da Matta (1991), citizenship is a social condition achieved within the perspective of a public world and implies individuality and equality. Therefore, as long as women remain "imprisoned" in the private world and are prevented from experiencing relationships and achievements in realms beyond the roles of wife and mother, they cannot fully exercise their citizenship. Some of the participants in the group we interviewed were carrying out activities - often for the first time - in the extra-domestic space, which gave a new colour to their identities that was reflected in their changed view of themselves.

> "*Since joining the group, I started working outside, having other occupations besides the ones at home.*" [Vera]

In this way, for several of the women interviewed, the group was the "entrance door" to non-domestic work and the world outside the home.

> "*The group is a way for me to have friends because before, my only relationships were with family members.*" [Leonor]

Beyond **providing the opportunity to transform participants' personal lives, the group acts to widen the field of possibilities (Bourdieu 1979) for these women, who develop new social networks that open new doors for them. Their experience with alcoholism stops being private and becomes collective.**

> "*I started to think that the major gain for me wasn't getting my husband or my marriage back, but that I had turned into a strong, capable woman.*" [Sílvia]

Thus, the narrative of the self-sacrificing, unselfish woman who exists to take care of the family gives way to the woman who is "rewriting the home," carving out a new narrative and a new aesthetic for herself, closer to a more modern and autonomous profile, which is also operating in Brazilian culture.

Conclusion

In this study, we describe the experiences and the evolving perceptions of women in mutual assistance groups regarding their conjugal relationships with their alcoholic partners. We heard accounts of both suffering and inflicting violence, as well as complaints of "loneliness," of "cancelling one's self out," and finally, of "falling ill." Conjugal conflicts are interpreted by the women we interviewed as the consequence of the lack of a minimal degree of reciprocity in the relationship, in which the male partner is seen as absent and as the offending party for his disengagement from the meaning of the marriage contract and from the fulfilment of his "husband's role" due to his alcohol abuse. Despite this view, the women tend to not contemplate separation or breaking up the conjugal bond due to their belief that marriage should be "forever." This position reflects their attachment to traditional values that centre on keeping the marriage and the family together at all costs.

For the women interviewed, before joining the self-help group, their network of social relations was basically limited to their marriage and family connections; they had no significant bonds with anyone other than their husband, their children, or other close relatives. However, the husband's "rupture" of the relationship, i.e., his breaking of the marriage contract due to his alcohol abuse, meant that the women "lost" the figure they had made responsible for the maintenance of their "wife image." Finally, they felt the loss of their life project and saw that they were lacking a new one, which subsequently led to their falling 'ill.'

When they begin frequenting the group, the women interviewed encountered others whose discourse and experiences were similar to their own. Through mutual self-identification, they began to view themselves in perspective and came to relativize situations that they had never questioned before. Paradoxically, it was by seeing the resemblance between themselves and numerous other women that they achieved individualization, experiencing a process of empowerment that brought them greater flexibility and an increased capacity to arrive at a new reading of their roles of wife and mother. Ending the exclusivity of a relationality limited to family members *a priori* and embracing a relationality acquired in the self-help group *a posteriori* helped these wives of alcoholics to see themselves in perspective, and, with this new and greater degree of removal, to reflect on their lives, and hence, to re-signify them.

It was also revealed that by the initial giving of themselves in hopes of "saving" the conjugal relationship, the women had gained in prestige. Paradoxically, the woman's "subordinate" position in the marriage would become a strong reason for feeling "proud" of herself. However, this increase in power came to be seen as undesirable as a new aesthetic and new ways of fitting into the world were discovered. In the narratives, we observed that after participating in the group meetings, the women would eventually arrive at the conclusion that it was better to have a minimum of reciprocity in the marriage than to gain prestige for being virtuous and unhappy, a compensation that came to be seen as "insufficient."

ACKNOWLEDGMENTS

We would like to express our appreciation to the Conselho Nacional de Desenvolvimento Cientifico e Tecnológico (CNPq) and to Darcy Dunton.

REFERENCES

Aragão, L. T. (1983) *Em nome da mãe: Posição estrutural e disposições sociais que envolvem a categoria mãe na civilização mediterrânea e na sociedade brasileira.* In Perspectivas Antropológicas da Mulher 3. (pp. 109-145). Rio de Janeiro: Zahar Editores.

Biasoli-Alves, Z. M. M. (2000) "Continuidades e rupturas no papel da mulher brasileira no século XX." *Psic. Teor. e Pesq.*, Vol. 16, No. 3, pp. 233-9.

Bourdieu, P. (1979) La Distinction: critique social du jugement. Paris: Minuit.

Campos, E. A. (2005) "O alcoolismo é uma doença contagiosa? Representações sobre o contágio e a doença de ex-bebedores." *Ciênc. saúde coletiva*, Vol. 10 (sup), pp. 267-78.

Da Matta, R. (1991) *A casa & a rua*. Rio de Janeiro: Guanabara Koogan.

De Meis, C. (1999) "Subjectivity, Social Suffering, Liminality and Suicide among Prostitutes in Brazil." *Urban Anthropology* Vol. 28 No. 1, pp. 65-101.

De Meis, C. (2002) "House and Street: Narrative of Identity in a Liminal Space among Prostitutes in Brazil." *Ethos* Vol. 30 No. 1/2, pp. 3-24.

Duarte, L. F. D., Gomes, E. C. (2008) Pertencimento familiar, auto-afirmação, individualização. In: Três famílias: Identidades e trajetórias transgeracionais nas classes populares. (pp. 241-73) Rio de Janeiro: FGV.

Dumont, L. (1983) *Essai sur l'individualisme*. Paris: Le Seuil.

Faizang, S. (1996) *Ethnologie des anciens alcooliques: La liberté ou la mort*. Paris: Presses Universitaires de France.

Freire, G. (1980) *Casa-Grande e Senzala*. Rio de Janeiro: Livraria José Olympio Editora.

Fróis, C. O. (2007) "A reinvenção do eu através do discurso: Narrativa, estigma e anonimato nas famílias anônimas." *Mana*, Vol. 13, No. 1, pp. 63-84.

Godbout, J. T. (1992) *L'Esprit du don*. Québec: Boréal.

Lanna, M. (2000) "Notas sobre Marcel Mauss e o Ensaio sobre a Dádiva" *Rev. Sociol. Polit.*, No. 14, pp. 173-94.

Levi-Strauss, C. (1950) *Introduction a l'oeuvre de Marcel Mauss*. In: Mauss, M. Sociologie et Anthropologie. Paris: Presses Universitaires de France.

Mauss, M. (1950) *Sociologie et Anthropologie*. Paris: Presses Universitaires de France.

Hubert, H. & Mauss, M. (2005) *Ensaio sobre a Natureza e a Função do Sacrifício (1899)*. In: (Org.) Guinsburg, J. Marcel Mauss: Ensaios de sociologia. São Paulo: Perspectiva.

Ramão, S. R., Meneghel, S. N., Oliveira, C. (2005) "Nos caminhos de Iansã: Cartografando a subjetividade de mulheres em situação de violência de gênero" *Psicol. Soc.*, Vol. 17, No. 2, pp. 79-7.

Rocha-Coutinho, M. L. (1994) *Tecendo por trás dos panos: a mulher brasileira nas relações familiares*. Rio de Janeiro: Rocco.

Simmel, G. (1971) *On Individuality and Social Forms*. Chicago: University of Chicago Press.

Soares, C. T. (2006) *Ruim com ele, pior sem ele? Limites e possibilidades encontradas por mulheres em processo de ruptura da violência conjugal*. M. A. dissertation in Pschosociology of Comunities and Social Ecology, Universidade Federal do Rio de Janeiro, Rio de Janeiro.

In: Empowerment
Editor: Randall Harris

ISBN: 978-1-63484-036-1

Chapter 7

CHARACTERISTICS OF THE EMPOWERMENT OF JAPANESE FAMILIES REARING CHILDREN

***Rie Wakimizu*[1] *and Hiroshi Fujioka*[2]**

[1]Department of Child Health Care Nursing, Division of Health Innovation and Nursing, Faculty of Medicine, University of Tsukuba, Tsukuba, Japan

[2]Department of Nursing, Tsukuba International University, Tsukuba, Japan

ABSTRACT

We investigated the characteristics of the empowerment of Japanese families rearing children. We conducted multifaceted surveys of the attributes of children from those who are healthy to those who have moderate to serious disabilities. There has been a rapid rise in the falling birth rate and the aging population as well as more nuclear families in Japan during these past few decades, where places and human resources for sharing the struggles and stresses of the child-raising generation are essential, yet the supply or responses have not caught up with these demands, with some mothers having given up on consulting or sharing with others, and others losing confidence in raising their children. The number of incidents of child abuse has continued to escalate since these statistics have been tracked, with prior studies showing a greater sense of failure today by Japanese mothers in raising their children. In addition, Wakimizu et al. developed a Japanese version of the Family Empowerment Scale (FES) in 2010, first developed by Koren of the United States in 1992, and the results of studies on the state of empowerment in Japanese families using the Japanese version of the FES clearly zeroed in on the low values in comparison to families in the United States and Australia. The authors launched an intervention in each region around the university, based on these results, so as to improve family empowerment by combining parent training with providing local resource information. Furthermore, family empowerment in its actuality is not simply tracked cross-sectionally, but temporally and cross-sectionally. We will introduce in the following section 1. The history of Japanese families rearing children, 2. The state of family empowerment and 3. Intervening towards family empowerment and its results.

1. What Is Family Empowerment?

The concept of empowerment can be traced back to the Civil Rights Movement of the 1960s in the United States. The term was originally used in the context of reducing powerlessness arising from the negative treatment due to membership in a socially stigmatized group [1]. Specifically, it referred to the process of awakening the latent power of individuals in negative circumstances imposed by social prejudice, such as the inability to receive a fair wage, appropriate medical treatment, childhood education, or sympathetic legal hearings related to such discrimination. Extended to the field of healthcare, empowerment forms a basis for modern self-help practices [2].

Empowerment is most commonly defined as "an intentional, ongoing process… through which people lacking an equal share of valued resources gain greater access to and control over those resources" [3]. Conversely, unempowerment encompasses stress, frustration, and hopelessness [4].

Empowerment occurs at three main levels: individual, organizational, and community [5]. At the individual level, empowerment incorporates belief in personal competencies such as self-efficacy, locus of control, and self-esteem [6]. Individual empowerment informs an individual's actions and proactive efforts to control their situation [7]. In practical terms, this means devising problem-solving strategies and using them to control the environment [8, 9]. For families (parents) of children with disabilities, Koren et al. revised the three empowerment levels of individual, organizational, and community to family (parents), service system, and community/political empowerment based on their respective scope of activity [10]. The family level reflects the family's (parents') ability to manage daily living; the service system level reflects the degree to which parents are able to work with the service system (professionals); and the community/political level reflects parents' advocacy to politicians and administrative bodies for improved services.

Within these schemas, empowerment appears to comprise two common elements: feeling of control over one's own life and working with outside parties (other family members, organizations, or society) [2]. The present paper defines family empowerment as "families controlling their lives to facilitate caring for a severely disabled child, including being able to work with outside parties."

2. The Actual Situation of Japanese Families Rearing Children

Before we introduce the characteristics of empowerment within Japanese families rearing children, we will first make some cross-cultural comparisons of families raising children in Japan and Western countries, with special focus on the parent-child relationship.

Comparison 1: The relationship between children and parents

There is a difference between Japanese and Western parents' perception of their role as guardians to their children.

In Japan, the belief that the child should be completely protected by the parent from all threats has appeared in daily habits, such as sleep sharing through the night. Parents in Japan generally sleep alongside their children until they are school-aged. It has been reported that

94% of preschool children sleep alongside someone, with 80% sleeping alongside their mother, 30% sleeping between their mother and father, and only 6% sleeping alone [11]. Thus, Japanese families are shown to be more cohesive and protective than Western families, probably due to Confucian values and their sense of seniority, with no particular encouragement of children's autonomy.

On the other hand, in middle-class Western families, children basically sleep alone from birth. Some mothers sleep with their child while breast-feeding, but they do not usually sleep alongside their infants through the night. This custom differs entirely from Japan. Thus, children's autonomy, initiative, and freedom are generally encouraged from early childhood in families in the United States and Europe [12, 13].

Thus, compared with parents in Western countries, Japanese parents generally have a stronger sense of mission to protect their children from all threats and foster stronger ties with their children not only in the hospital environment, but also in daily habits. The discretion of the parents as the preschoolers' proxy has also been more recognized and respected in Japanese society.

Comparison 2: Comparison of the relationships among medical staff, children, and parents

In medical settings involving children in Western countries, nurses generally explain routines, items, procedures, and all events related to any illness, surgery, and hospitalization directly to the child in the presence of his/her parents. Nurses make use of simple language and methods appropriate to the child's developmental level, such as drawing and play, to reduce fear among young patients. In addition, to help absolve the child from any guilt about being hospitalized, nurses also ask the child to explain the reasons for their hospitalization and correct the child if necessary to reassure them that their hospitalization is not their fault [14].

On the other hand, in Japan, nurses generally explain routines, items, procedures, and all other events to the parents, even if the child is old enough to comprehend what is being explained. Then, at home, the parents explain only the contents they believe to be useful to the child. Therefore, in the hospital, children have a narrow window of opportunity for direct contact with medical staff such as doctors and nurses. One recent nationwide study revealed that 66.7% of parents strongly hoped to be an expositor to their child, and that medical staff considered the parents to be the most qualified people for that task [15]. Thus, the medical staff-child-parent relationship in Japan is not necessarily similar to that in Western countries.

3. The Characteristics of Empowerment within Various Families Rearing Children in Japan

To investigate the characteristics of empowerment within Japanese families rearing children, we conducted five multifaceted surveys of the attributes of children with moderate to serious disabilities as well as those of healthy children. Due to the rapid decrease in the birth rate, the aging population, and the increased number of nuclear families in Japan over the past few decades, places and human resources for parents to share the struggles and stresses of child rearing have become essential; however, resources have not caught up with demand, and some mothers have given up on consulting or sharing their experiences with others, while others are losing confidence in their child-raising abilities. The number of child abuse incidents has continued to escalate since such tracking of these statistics began, with some studies showing a greater sense of failure among Japanese mothers today in raising their children [16]. In 2010, we developed a Japanese version of the Family Empowerment Scale (FES) [17], first developed by Koren of the United States in 1992 [10], and the results of studies on the state of empowerment in Japanese families using the Japanese version of the FES clearly zeroed in on the low values of empowerment compared to families in the United States and Australia.

Table 1. Internal consistency and re-test reliability of J-FES score (n = 311)

	Number of items	Mean ± SD	Range	Chronbach's *a*	Intra-class coefficients (n = 244)
FES total (all subscales)	34	92.6 ± 24.1	37–162	0.94	0.91
Family	12	34.5 ± 9.8	15–56	0.89	0.86
Service system	12	34.3 ± 9.2	12–60	0.88	0.81
Community/political	10	20.5 ± 7.8	10–46	0.84	0.82

In our first survey, we showed the FES scores of 311 Japanese mothers raising children in the Greater Tokyo Area (Table 1). The present study revealed lower scores for service system and community/political empowerment among Japanese mothers compared with the previous studies. The mean scores of each subscale in the US were (i) family: 45.8, (ii) service system: 48.6, and (iii) community/political: 31.4. An Australian study also reported a significant difference in the total scores of FES with 119.43 ± 12.53 (mean ± SD) in the US and 108.45 ± 11.96 (mean ± SD) in Australia ($P < 0.001$) [18]. While there is room for improvement with regard to the systems, resources and support base for raising children in the Greater Tokyo Area, the present findings also reflect the attitude within Japan that problems within the family should be resolved at home and the societal character trait of not asserting oneself.

Children with severe disabilities have markedly delayed development and low spare physical capacity, which makes them susceptible to complications when they are ill and leads them to require diverse and highly individualized care. Therefore the stress of families with severely disabled children is very serious [19]. While parents of healthy children are released from the responsibility of care once the children have passed a certain stage of development, parents of children with disabilities must continue to care for them long-term [20, 21]. As the parents themselves age, they worry about the provision of future care. In addition, they feel increasingly isolated and may manifest psychological symptoms. Social and economic problems, such as financial hardship when family members have to quit their jobs in order to care for the child, have also been cited [19]. Families providing home care for children with disabilities in Japan require not only empowerment but also a cooperative structure of family and community support [22]. However, in Japan, difficulty with acceptance and prejudice toward disability from both inside and outside the family, as well as the old-fashioned attitude that problems within the family should be resolved at home, has resulted in insufficient services for families of children with disabilities. Therefore, family members often have decreased emotional capacity and perform care only out of a sense of obligation [23]. Therefore, our second study aimed to evaluate whether there was a difference in the empowerment of family caregivers (mainly mothers) of disabled children between severe physical and mental disabilities and developmental disorders (DDs), which differ in type and required care. Children with severe motor and intellectual disabilities (SMID) are defined in reference to Japan's unique legislation and refer to "children with markedly limited activity due to severe overlapping of physical and intellectual disabilities" [24]. Globally, SMID is synonymous with "children with profound multiple disabilities," i.e., children who cannot use their hands and arms by themselves due to an IQ of less than 20. Starting in the 1960s in Japan, children with SMID were encouraged to enter specialized institutions that provided child rearing and care including whole-body management in order to support these children and their families [25]. However, after the concept of normalization spread following the International Year of Disabled Persons in 1981, the need for support centered on living at home was advocated for those with SMID [26]. Furthermore, in recent years, as a result of changes in medical and welfare policies to shorten hospital stays, there has been a shift toward more of these children being cared for at home from an early age. Of the approximately 40,000 children with SMID in Japan, about 70% live at home [24]. Because of advances in medical care and technology for these children, long-term care and securing of quality of life at home have become possible [27]. On the other hand, Japanese people have long viewed DDs as intrinsic to a child's nature and a result of the parents' methods of child rearing. Although the prevalence rate of DDs in Japan has not been revealed, the incidence of autism in the Tokyo metropolitan area is reported to be 27.2 per 10,000 people [28]. The prevalence rate of autism spectrum disorder varies by region, but the overall rate in Japan is higher than that in North America (odds ratio: 3.60; 95% confidence interval: 1.73–7.46). Furthermore, the prevalence rate of total DDs is said to be triple that of autism [29]. In Japan, the *Act on Support for Persons with Developmental Disorders* took effect in April 2005. This Act defines DDs, such as autism, Asperger's syndrome, pervasive developmental disorder, learning disorder, attention deficit/hyperactivity disorder, and similar cerebral dysfunctions, as having symptoms that usually develop at an early age [30]. The families caring for these children suffer a great deal of distress [31]. The understanding of DDs and the support offered to families rearing a child with DDs have always been limited in Japan.

Table 2. J-FES scores of two different disability groups (N=165)

		Number of Items	*Family Rearing Children With Developmental Disabilities(N=115)* Mean±SD	Range	*Family Rearing Children With Severe Motor and Intellectual Disabilities(N=50)* Mean±SD	Range	p-value
FES total		34	105.7±20.9	65-147	113.0±16.1	75-159	<0.05
	(subscales)						
	Family	12	38.6±8.9	19-56	40.7±6.4	25-56	n.s
	Service system	12	41.3±8.1	25-60	42.3±6.4	27-59	n.s
	Community/ political	10	25.7±6.7	11-43	30.2±6.5	19-47	<0.05

Table 3. Characteristics of subjects (N=225)

			n/mean±SD	%/range
Caregivers				
	Gender	Female	219	97.3%
	Age	20s	10	4.4%
		30s	108	48.0%
		40s	99	44.0%
		50s	8	3.6%
		60s	1	0.4%
	Relationship	Mother	218	96.9%
		Father	6	2.7%
		Grandmother	1	0.4%
	Time spent on the child (weekday)		6.7±3.4	1-19
	Time spent on the child (holiday)		12.6±5.2	1-24
	Employment status	Housewife	86	38.2%
		Part-timer	72	32.0%
		Regular employee	37	16.4%
		Self-employed	14	6.2%
		Temporary employee	7	3.1%
		Government employee	5	2.2%
		Contract employee	3	1.3%
		Domestic worker	2	0.9%
	People who help with child-rearing	Yes	175	77.8%
		No	50	22.2%
	Child-rearing burden scale score		15.0±6.9	1-32
	SS scale score		10.8±4.1	0-15
	Self-efficacy scale score		73.1±13.7	32-113
	Self-esteem scale score		30.6±7.5	12-48
Family				
	Number of family members living with the child		3.4±1.4	1-7
	Number of siblings		1.0±1.2	0-4
	Financial status	Comfortable	9	4.0%
		Moderately comfortable	23	10.2%
		Normal	120	53.3%
		Somewhat hard	46	20.4%
		Hard	27	12.0%
	Use of service	Yes	72	32.0%
		No	153	68.0%
Child				
	Gender	Male	189	84.0%
	Age (years)		9.8±3.6	4-18
	Time after diagnosis (months)		43.5±32.5	8-209
	Diagnosis (multiple answers allowed)	ADHD[1)]	137	60.9%

		n/mean±SD	%/range
	PDD[2]	108	48.0%
	AS[3]	20	8.9%
	Autism	13	5.8%
	LD[4]	13	5.8%
	MR[5](including mild MR)	13	5.8%
	Epilepsy	11	4.9%
	DCD[6]	8	3.6%
	Anxiety disorder	5	2.2%
	Adjustment disorder (truant)	3	1.3%
	Tic disorder	2	0.9%
	Behavior disorder (self-injury)	1	0.4%
	Tourette disorder	1	0.4%
	Situational mutism	1	0.4%
	Nocturnal enuresis	1	0.4%
	Obsessive-compulsive disorder	1	0.4%
	Attachment disorder	1	0.4%
	Dissociative disorder	1	0.4%
	Unknown	15	6.7%
Frequency of hospital visit (time/year)		11.5±9.9	0-65
Medication	Yes	173	76.9%
	No	52	23.1%
Disability certificate	Yes	58	25.8%
	No	167	74.2%
Attendance at (pre)school	Regular class	136	60.4%
	Support class	57	25.3%
	Special-needs class	21	9.3%
	Private nursery	5	2.2%
	None	6	2.7%
Use of Tsukyu	Yes	50	22.2%
	No	175	77.8%

1) ADHD: Attention Deficit / Hyperactivity Disorder.
2) PDD: Pervasive Developmental Disorders.
3) AS: Asperger syndrome.
4) LD: Learning Disorders.
5) MR: Mental Retardation.
6) DCD: Developmental Coordination Disorder.

In 165 parents of children diagnosed by physicians as having severe physical and mental disabilities or DDs, we characterized the empowerment of family caregivers via a questionnaire using the Japanese version of the FES [32]. The FES scores of families of severely physically and mentally disabled children exceeded those of developmentally impaired children, showing that the former families had stronger empowerment than those of the latter (Table 2). The difference in family empowerment between the two groups was possibly caused by several factors including: the differences in the history and social cognition of the disabilities; understanding from surrounding people, which can be affected by whether the disabilities are visible or not; the current availability of well-developed social welfare services; and the psychological burden or a sense of uncertainty felt by the family caregivers. The FES scores of the families caring for children with DDs in the present study were considerably lower than those reported in previous overseas studies. There is an urgent need for further educational activities for the public, an improved treatment and education system, and more extensive social welfare services to assure more comforTable lives for such families and their children.

In our third study, we identified factors associated with the empowerment of Japanese families using the FES with the aim of improving the empowerment of Japanese families raising a child with DDs [33]. The study was conducted with 225 caregivers who raised children with DDs aged 4–18 years in urban and suburban districts in Japan (Table 3).

Multiple regression analysis of data revealed that a decrease in family empowerment level correlated with a higher number of siblings reared together, a shorter period since the diagnosis was made, and lower awareness of social support and self-efficacy in caregivers. Medications, possession of an intellectual disability certificate, infrequent hospital visits of the child, disuse of local services by caregivers, and young caregivers also correlated with a lower level of empowerment (Table 4).

In our fourth and fifth studies, as qualitative research, we examined the empowerment process of families rearing children with DDs and SMID, respectively [34, 35]. First, to clarify the empowerment process for families rearing a child with DDs, we interviewed 20 mothers of children who lived in the Greater Tokyo Area. To analyze the data, we adopted the modified grounded theory approach. The results identified three stages in the empowerment process: confusion over caring for the child, confrontation with the child with the disorder, and expectations of a valuable life for the child (Figure 1). The empowerment process showed the following step-by-step progression: families that were originally ill-equipped to deal with their child's disorders were able to deal with them in collaboration with professionals after approaching the local support services and were able to shift their stance on child-rearing according to their child's growth [34].

As for the empowerment process of families rearing children with SMID, we conducted semi-structured interviews with the main caregivers in 19 families and used the modified grounded theory approach to analyze the data qualitatively. Through the analysis, a process was observed whereby the main caregivers, who had initially felt isolated in child rearing, gained personal inner power through exchanges with others, started approaching others such as service providers and administrative staff, and finally established their own child rearing systems (Figure 2). This process had a feedback effect of replenishing the inner power of individual caregivers and enabling them to continue with appropriate child rearing. This empowerment process of the main caregivers suggested that practical care support can be provided in a specific direction to promote the empowerment of families caring for children with SMID. Examples of this support are encouraging the parents to participate in groups with other parents who are raising children with disabilities, providing advice for daily living, including management of the children's physical conditions, and approaching other family members instead of the main caregiver to coordinate the roles of family members [35].

Table 4. Factors associated with family empowerment1) (N=225)

			sb	*P*-value
Caregivers				
	Gender	F/M#	-	
	Age	1: 20s 2: 30s 3: 40s 4: 50s 5: 60s	0.11	0.10 †
	Relationship	Mother/father/grandmother#	-	
	Time spent on the child (weekday)		0.12	0.21
	Time spent on the child (holiday)		0.14	0.20
	Employment status	1: Housewife/domestic worker 2: Part-timer/temporary employee/contract employee 3: Self-employed 4: Regular employee/government employee	-0.04	0.50
	People who help with help child-rearing	Yes/No#	-0.08	0.21
	Child-rearing burden scale score		<0.01	0.99
	SS2) scale score		0.35	<0.001***
	Self-efficacy scale score		0.28	<0.001***
	Self-esteem scale score		0.06	0.43
Family				
	Number of family members living with the child		0.09	0.33
	Number of siblings		-0.24	0.01 *
	Financial status	1: Hard 2: Somewhat hard 3: Normal 4: Moderately comfortable 5: Comfortable	0.02	0.78
	Use of service	Yes/No#	0.08	0.19 †
Child				
	Gender	M/F#	-0.03	0.64
	Age (years)		-0.54	0.43
	Time after diagnosis		0.28	<0.001***
	Diagnosis		-	
	Frequency of hospital visit		0.10	0.11†
	Medication	Yes/No#	-0.11	0.11†
	Disability certificate	Yes/No#	-0.11	0.10†
	Attendance at (pre)school	1: None 2: Private nursery 3: Special-needs class 4: Support class 5: Regular class	0.01	0.85
	Use of Tsukyu	Yes/No#	0.03	0.59
	R^2		0.44	
	adjusted R^2		0.39	

sb: Values indicate standard partial regression coefficients. †: $P < 0.2$ *:$P < 0.05$ **:$P < 0.01$ ***:$P < 0.001$.
#: reference category.
: Variables not selected for the model as a result of variable selection.
1) Evaluated by the Japanese version of Family Empowerment Scale.
2) Social Support.

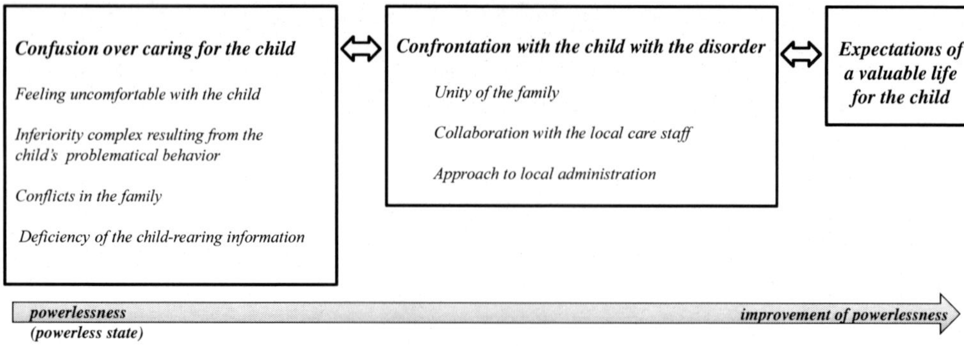

Figure 1. Empowerment process of the family caring for child with developmental disorders. (Wakimizu R, Fujioka H, Yoneyama A. Empowerment process for families rearing children with developmental disorders in Japan. Nurs Health Sci. 2010 Sep 1;12(3): pp. 325).

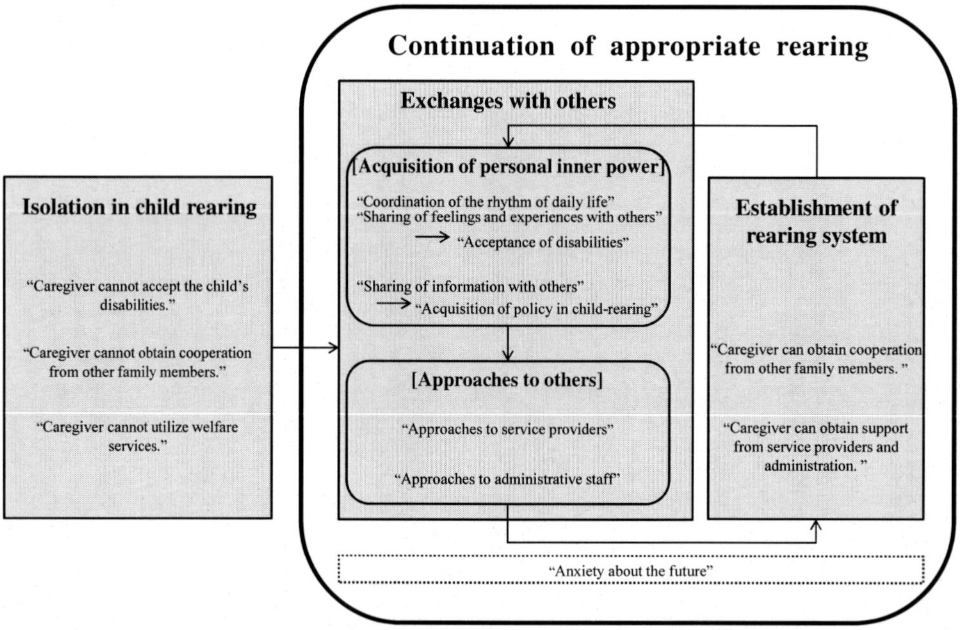

Figure 2. Process of empowerment of families rearing children with severe motor and intellectual disabilities. (Fujioka, H; Wakimizu, R; Okubo, Y; Yoneyama, A. Empowerment of Families Rearing Children with Severe Motor and Intellectual Disabilities at Home. Medical and Health Science Research. 5, pp.45, 2014).

4. Interventions Towards Family Empowerment in Japan

The authors launched an intervention in each region around our university, based on the current situation of empowerment of families raising children in Japan, so as to improve family empowerment by combining parent training with providing local resource information.

Between 2014 and 2015, as the first intervention, we introduced a group-based positive parenting program known as Triple P to mothers raising children aged 1-12 years in Japan and investigated its effectiveness. Participants in both the intervention and control groups were recruited in a local city near Tsukuba and effects of the intervention on parental efficacy and adjustment of the child, parent, and family, as well as family empowerment were examined. We found that child adjustment and parenting adjustment showed a significant intervention effect. In addition, the FES score for the Family subscale and the total score also revealed significant increases only in the intervention group (Table 5).

Table 5. Pre- and post-intervention dependent measures for the intervention and control groups (N=24)

Scale	Score range		Intervention group (N=15)			Control group (N=9)			Group effect	
			Mean	SD	p [a]	Mean	SD	p [a]	F	p
CAPES										
Emotional maladjustment	0-72	Pre	26.80	12.07	0.223	24.22	11.48	0.028	4.154	0.054
		Post	24.73	11.47		27.00	10.84			
Behavioral problems	0-9	Pre	2.20	1.78	0.068	.89	1.05	0.095	2.999	0.098
		Post	1.73	1.33		1.44	1.33			
Total (emotion & behavior)	0-81	Pre	29.00	12.72	0.148	25.11	12.36	0.005	5.814	0.025
		Post	26.47	12.20		28.44	11.61			
Parental self efficacy	19-190	Pre	107.93	50.09	0.063	120.00	38.46	0.476	2.886	0.104
		Post	130.80	43.32		112.67	42.18			
PAFAS										
Parental consistency	0-15	Pre	6.40	1.84	0.003	5.89	1.54	0.466	6.752	0.017
		Post	4.73	2.19		6.33	2.00			
Coercive parenting	0-15	Pre	8.00	3.48	0.001	8.33	3.04	0.206	7.609	0.012
		Post	5.47	1.88		7.33	2.45			
Positive encouragement	0-9	Pre	2.73	2.05	0.250	2.78	1.64	0.147	5.180	0.033
		Post	2.27	1.79		3.78	2.22			
Parent-child relationship	0-15	Pre	4.07	3.61	0.649	3.33	2.92	0.272	.569	0.459
		Post	3.80	3.67		3.78	2.82			
Parenting Total	0-54	Pre	21.20	6.48	0.000	20.33	5.70	0.580	.569	0.459
		Post	16.27	7.13		21.22	7.00			
Parental adjustment	0-15	Pre	7.27	2.66	0.003	7.33	3.67	1.000	4.630	0.043
		Post	5.73	2.09		7.33	2.60			
Family relationships	0-12	Pre	4.07	2.49	0.008	4.89	2.20	0.667	8.339	0.009 [b]
		Post	3.13	2.23		5.22	.97			
Parental teamwork	0-9	Pre	3.60	2.26	0.389	4.22	1.72	0.302	2.669	0.117
		Post	3.33	2.50		4.78	1.56			
Family adjustment Total	0-36	Pre	14.93	6.56	0.002	16.44	7.18	0.674	7.297	0.013
		Post	12.20	6.27		17.33	4.21			
PES										
Parenting is difficult	1-5	Pre	3.46	1.13	0.209	2.57	.98	1.000	.005	0.947 [b]
		Post	3.08	.76		2.57	1.27			
Parenting is rewarding	1-5	Pre	3.13	1.13	0.301	2.67	1.50	0.681	4.596	0.044
		Post	3.40	.99		2.44	.88			

Table 5. (Continued)

			Intervention group (N=15)			Control group (N=9)			Group effect	
PES										
Parenting is demanding	1-5	Pre	3.47	1.36	0.178	3.00	1.41	0.438	.111	0.742
		Post	2.93	1.03		2.67	1.00			
Parenting is stressful	1-5	Pre	3.33	1.18	0.028	2.67	1.32	0.559	.107	0.747
		Post	2.60	.91		2.44	1.24			
Parenting is fulfilling	1-5	Pre	3.20	1.21	0.334	2.11	1.27	0.645	2.229	0.150
		Post	3.47	1.06		2.33	1.12			
Parenting is depressive	1-5	Pre	3.27	1.28	0.045	2.44	1.59	0.447	.157	0.696
		Post	2.60	1.24		2.00	1.50			
Confidence in parenting	1-5	Pre	2.27	1.03	0.013	2.22	1.39	0.225	1.529	0.230
		Post	3.13	.74		2.67	1.22			
Support for parenting	1-5	Pre	2.87	.92	0.055	3.00	1.41	0.782	2.342	0.141
		Post	3.53	.99		2.89	1.54			
Agreement with partner regarding child discipline	1-5	Pre	3.15	.99	0.053	2.88	.99	0.080	16.589	0.001
		Post	3.62	.96		2.13	.64			
Support received from partner	1-5	Pre	3.15	1.41	0.264	3.00	1.31	1.000	1.030	0.324
		Post	3.46	1.13		3.00	1.20			
Happiness with partner	0-6	Pre	3.46	1.61	0.096	3.13	1.36	0.685	.480	0.497
		Post	3.85	1.72		3.25	1.75			
FES										
Family	12-60	Pre	36.13	7.74	0.007	37.67	10.32	0.314	9.295	0.006
		Post	39.40	6.21		36.56	9.02			
Service system	12-60	Pre	34.67	8.33	0.066	37.22	10.73	0.370	3.208	0.088[b)]
		Post	37.47	6.38		35.78	12.36			
Community/political	10-50	Pre	23.80	7.08	0.562	23.89	10.40	0.491	1.824	0.191
		Post	24.33	4.75		22.89	8.33			
Total	34-170	Pre	94.60	21.73	0.037	98.78	29.63	0.323	5.546	0.028
		Post	101.20	14.99		95.22	28.60			

a) paired t test.
b) there was baseline score interaction between intervention group and control group ($p < 0.05$).

In the second intervention, we introduced the group-based Triple P program to Japanese families raising children with DDs in the Greater Tokyo Area and investigated its effectiveness (Table 6). Reductions in children's behavioral problems, changes in dysfunctional parenting practices, and promotion of effects on family empowerment were examined. Fifty-four participants were recruited from two hospitals and two parental groups in the Tokyo metropolitan area. They were assessed in terms of child behavior (Strengths and Difficulties Questionnaire), parenting style (Parenting Scale), parenting adjustment (Depression Anxiety Stress Scale and Parenting Experience Survey), and family empowerment (FES). All outcomes were measured repeatedly from pre-intervention to 6 months after intervention. The Strengths and Difficulties Questionnaire scores for the three subscales of emotional symptoms conduct problems, and difficult behavior indicated a significant intervention effect in the children.

Table 6. Results of repeated measures ANOVA on children, caregivers, and family outcomes (N=54)

Scale		Score range	Time: Pre Mean (SD)	Post Mean (SD)	3 months after Mean (SD)	6 months after Mean (SD)	Effect (time effect): F¶	*p*-value	effect sizes
SDQ									
	Emotional symptoms	0-10	2.98 (2.32)	1.98 (1.65)	1.87 (1.67)*	2.03 (1.97)	4.77	0.003	0.081
	Conduct problems	0-10	3.46 (2.19)	2.89 (1.83)	2.47 (1.87)*	2.79 (2.12)	2.79	0.042	0.049
	Hyperactivity	0-10	6.00 (2.65)	5.11 (2.29)	5.04 (2.33)	5.34 (2.17)	2.05	0.109	0.037
	Peer problems	0-10	4.94 (2.45)	4.19 (2.19)	3.84 (2.38)	4.39 (2.70)	2.26	0.084	0.040
	Difficult behavior	0-40	17.38 (5.89)	14.17 (5.10)**	13.22 (6.00)***	14.55 (5.95)*	6.52	<0.001	0.108
	Prosocial behavior	0-10	4.07 (2.68)	4.50 (2.65)	4.87 (2.63)	4.89 (2.36)	1.31	0.272	0.024
PS									
	Laxness	1-7	2.79 (0.49)	2.29 (0.64)***	2.22 (0.72)***	2.23 (0.64)***	12.16	<0.001	0.184
	Over-reactivity	1-7	3.78 (1.17)	2.75 (1.21)***	2.84 (1.14)***	3.12 (1.19)*	10.39	<0.001	0.161
	Verbosity	1-7	3.65 (0.98)	2.65 (0.84)***	2.81 (1.01)***	2.91 (0.96)***	13.63	<0.001	0.202
	Total	1-7	3.27 (0.62)	2.50 (0.72)***	2.54 (0.78)***	2.63 (0.70)***	17.08	<0.001	0.240
DASS									
	Depression	0-42	8.25 (8.33)	4.72 (5.84)*	4.00 (6.17)**	6.58 (7.32)	4.23	0.007	0.100
	Anxiety	0-42	5.51 (5.00)	3.74 (3.57)	3.29 (5.05)*	5.50 (5.53)	3.61	0.022	0.065
	Stress	0-42	12.45 (7.43)	7.96 (5.95)	7.51 (6.72)	11.39 (8.82)	5.52	0.001	0.127
	Total	0-126	26.22 (18.33)	16.43 (13.72)*	14.80 (16.98)**	22.97 (20.06)	5.21	0.002	0.121
PES									
	Parenting is difficult	1-5	3.38 (0.98)	2.60 (0.90)***	2.51 (0.83)***	3.14 (1.07)	14.69	<0.001	0.217
	Parenting is rewarding	1-5	2.70 (0.97)	3.13 (0.90)*	3.27 (1.10)*	2.81 (1.14)	4.34	0.006	0.076
	Parenting is demanding	1-5	3.43 (1.05)	2.72 (1.10)**	2.93 (1.16)	3.27 (1.11)	5.78	0.001	0.098
	Parenting is stressful	1-5	3.39 (1.01)	2.63 (1.04)***	2.56 (1.01)**	3.16 (1.13)	8.28	<0.001	0.135
	Parenting is fulfilling	1-5	2.87 (1.12)	3.72 (1.04)	2.98 (0.93)	2.66 (0.78)	15.53	<0.001	0.227
	Parenting is depressive	1-5	3.22 (1.21)	2.41 (1.11)***	2.42 (1.02)**	2.76 (1.17)	8.63	<0.001	0.140
	Confidence in parenting	1-5	2.24 (0.90)	2.96 (0.72)***	2.78 (0.84)**	2.74 (0.75)**	9.91	<0.001	0.157

Table 6. (Continued)

Scale		Score range	Pre Mean (SD)	Post Mean (SD)	3 months after Mean (SD)	6 months after Mean (SD)	F¶	*p*-value	effect sizes
PES (Continued)									
	Support for parenting	1-5	2.67 (0.98)	3.39 (1.04)**	3.11 (0.82)*	2.82 (1.07)	6.61	<0.001	0.111
	Support for parenting	1-5	2.67 (0.98)	3.39 (1.04)**	3.11 (0.82)*	2.82 (1.07)	6.61	<0.001	0.111
	Agreement with partner regarding child discipline (n=51)	1-5	2.86 (0.99)	3.08 (1.06)	3.14 (0.89)	3.03 (1.00)	1.07	0.366	0.021
	Support received from partner (n=51)	1-5	2.90 (1.03)	3.18 (1.09)*	3.19 (1.18)	3.05 (1.18)	1.09	0.356	0.021
	Happiness with partner (n=51)	0-6	3.12 (1.25)	3.32 (1.24)	3.62 (1.23)	3.03 (1.13)	3.37	0.020	0.063
FES									
	Family	12-60	37.55 (6.22)	42.07 (7.12)***	41.98 (6.66)**	40.11 (7.09)*	7.65	<0.001	0.126
	Service system	12-60	40.40 (5.29)	43.52 (6.41)***	43.29 (7.49)	43.55 (7.20)	4.10	0.008	0.072
	Community/political	10-50	25.71 (6.57)	27.85 (6.29)**	27.96 (7.08)	28.08 (6.38)	2.09	0.104	0.038
	Total	34-170	103.65 (15.45)	113.44 (17.40)***	112.27 (17.76)*	111.74 (18.50)	5.03	0.002	0.087

ANOVA adjusted for the baseline score at each measurement time.
$^{*}p < 0.05$, $^{**}p < 0.01$, $^{***}p < 0.001$,
F statistic in repeated measures ANOVA adjusted for each baseline score.
ANOVA, analysis of variance; SD, standard deviation.

Moreover, the Parenting Scale scores for all subscales, the Depression Anxiety Stress Scale scores for all subscales, and the Parenting Experience Survey scores for all but three subscales (the fulfilling subscale, the perception of agreement with the partner regarding child discipline subscale, and the perception of support received from partner subscale) indicated a significant intervention effect in the caregivers. In addition, the FES scores for all subscales indicated a significant intervention effect in the family as a whole. These results provided promising evidence for the group intervention-based Triple P program as an effective intervention for Japanese families raising preschool and school-aged children with DDs.

Other interventions focusing on family empowerment in Japan include those targeting adult patients with cancer [36], children with disabilities [37], and leukemia [38], and patients with schizophrenia [39]. While there are many methods of family-centered intervention, the ultimate goals are the same: to enable families to utilize the various problem-solving and decision-making capabilities acquired during family life to date or to acquire such skills [40]. However, the efficacy of these interventions has yet to be assessed with pre- and post-intervention measurements using a standardized scale.

The present findings regarding empowering families raising children in Japan are summarized below. These points represent important factors for family empowerment both in Japan and other countries.

Table 7. Results of the client satisfaction for participating the parenting program (N=78)

	mean	SD
1. How would you rate the quality of help you and your child received? (7 = Excellent, 1 = poor)	5.84	1.18
2. Did you receive the type of help you wanted from the programme? (7 = Yes definitely, 1 = No, definitely not)	5.81	0.92
3. To what extent has the programme met your child's needs? (7 = Almost all have been met, 1 = No needs have been met)	4.99	1.26
4. To what extent has the programme met your needs? (7 = Almost all have been met, 1 = No needs have been met)	5.18	1.24
5. How satisfied were you with the amount of help you and your child received? (7 = Very satisfied, 1 = Quite dissatisfied)	5.98	0.98
6. Has the programme helped you to deal more effectively with your child's behaviour? (7 = Yes it has helped a great deal, 1 = No it has made things worse)	5.29	1.32
7. Has the programme helped you to deal more effectively with problems that arise in your family? (7 = Yes it has helped a great deal, 1 = No it has made things worse)	4.90	1.44
8. Do you think your relationship with your partner has been improved by the programme? (7 = Yes definitely, 1 = No, definitely not)	4.14	1.55
9. In an overall sense, how satisfied are you with the programme you and your child received? (7 = Very satisfied, 1 = Quite dissatisfied)	5.86	1.25
10. If you were to seek help again, would you come back to Triple P? (7 = Yes definitely, 1 = No, definitely not)	4.93	1.39
11. Has the programme helped you to develop skills that can be applied to other family members? (7 = Yes definitely, 1 = No, definitely not)	4.92	1.40
12. In your opinion, how is your child's behaviour at this point? (7 = Greatly improved, 1 = Considerably worse)	5.51	0.84
13. How would you describe your feelings at this point about your child's progress? (7 = Very satisfied, 1 = Very dissatisfied)	5.44	1.08

1) Regional Differences in Service Systems

Based on the *Child Welfare* and *Services and Supports for Persons with Disabilities Acts*, service systems for children and their families are developed on a regional (city, ward, town and village) basis, leading to potential differences in availability depending on location. The number of facilities providing the advanced specialist care required by severely disabled children is limited and access to such services is particularly problematic in areas outside large municipalities. Available social resources in non-central areas are also scarce. Differences in services impact the amount and quality of social support received from outside the family [41]. Thus, regional differences affect family empowerment through social support.

2) Life Events

Life events occurring within the family, particularly to the primary caregiver, may affect care for the child. The effects may be positive or negative depending on the type of life event. Life events that positively affect home care include changes to the living environment such as moving or building/renovating a house, making friends, and living with parents [42]. Conversely, events such as another family member requiring care due to serious illness in addition to caring for the child increase feelings of care difficulty and burden.

The "feeling of control over one's own life" element of empowerment is strengthened by experience with successfully controlling one's life or handling difficult situations [43]. For primary caregivers of severely disabled children, the experience of overcoming a difficult situation is linked to increased self-confidence [44]. Therefore, life events that are undesirable for the family do not have to be damaging for empowerment.

3) Social Support

No common definition for social support has been reached; however, it can be described as various types of physical and psychological support received from important people in an individual's life. Such support includes diverse elements, which can be broadly categorized as emotional support (empathy and encouragement) and instrumental support (advice and practical assistance). Social support can also be classified based on its source (family and friends, or professionals).

Support from people surrounding an individual, i.e., social support, is also essential to the other element of family empowerment, "working with outside parties." For families of children with disabilities, social support is directly linked to increased empowerment [45, 46].

4) Evaluation of Caregiving (Feelings of Burden, Positivity toward Care)

The positive aspects of caregiving, such as satisfaction, fulfillment, and self-growth, have attracted recent attention in the field of elderly care. Similarly, it is important to consider both positive and negative aspects when evaluating caregiving in families of severely disabled children who require considerable medical treatment. Studies have reported that families caring for severely disabled children experience parental satisfaction [47] and maternal self-growth [48] in addition to feelings of burden [41, 49].

Parental feelings of burden in caregiving increase with the severity of the child's disability and the need for medical treatment; however, this can be mitigated by social support [41]. Positive and negative evaluations of caregiving appear to be, respectively, positively and negatively correlated with family empowerment [45].

REFERENCES

[1] Solomon, B. (1976). *Black empowerment: Social work in oppressed communities.* New York: Columbia University Press.

[2] Gibson, C.H. (1991). A concept analysis of empowerment. *J. Adv. Nurs. 16(3)*, 354-361.

[3] Cornell Empowerment Group. (1989). Empowerment and family support. *Networking Bulletin, 1,* 1-23.

[4] Koegel, R.L., Brookman, L., Koegel, L.K. (2003). Autism: Pivotal response intervention and parental empowerment. *Trends in Evidence-Based Neuropsychiatry, 5,* 61-69.

[5] Shulz, A.J., Israel, B.A., Zimmerman, M.A., Checkoway, B.N. (1995). Empowerment as a multi-level construct: Perceived control at the individual, organizational, and community levels. *Health Education Research, 10,* 309-327.

[6] McCammon, S.L., Spencer, S.A., Friesen, B.J. (2001). Promoting family empowerment through multiple roles. *J. Fam. Soc. Work, 5,* 1-24.

[7] Mitchell, W., Sloper, P. (2002). Information that informs rather than alienates families with disabled children: developing a model of good practice. *Health Soc. Care Community, 10,* 74-81.

[8] Schuler, M.E., Nair, P., Black, M.M. (2002). Ongoing maternal drug use, parenting attitudes, and a home intervention: effects on mother-child interaction at 18 months. *J. Dev. Behav. Pediatr, 23,* 87-94.

[9] Harrigan, R.C., Ratliffe, C., Patrinos, M.E., Tse, A. (2002). Medically fragile children: an integrative review of the literature and recommendations for future research. *Issues Compr. Pediatr Nurs, 25,* 1-20.

[10] Koren, P.E., DeChillo, N., Friesen, B.J. (1992). Measuring empowerment in families whose children have emotional disabilities: A brief questionnaire. *Rehabil. Psychol. 37(4),* 305-321.

[11] Sankei Living Shimbun Inc. (2006). *Enfant: enji to mama no deta* [data of kids and mother in Japan] (vol.3). [Brochure]. Tokyo.

[12] Azuma, H. (1994). *Nihon-jin no sitsuke to kyouiku hattatsu no nitibeihikaku ni motoduite* [Japanese parenting and education: based on cultural comparison between America and Japanese notions of development]. Tokyo: University of Tokyo Press.

[13] Tamura, T. (1997). Seijuku-suru to iukoto ha douiukotoka — kosei to mikata no bunkahikaku [What is to be mature? Comparison of cultures about the perspective of personality]. *Child Study, 674,* 42-47.

[14] Hockenberry, M.J., Wilson, D., Winkelstein, M.L., Kline, N.E. (Eds.) (2003). *Wong's Nursing Care of Infants and Children* (7th ed.). St. Louis: Mosby.

[15] Ebina, M. (2004). *Kodomo to oya heno purepareishon no jissen-hukyu—iryou-koui wo okonau sai no kodomo heno kakawari ni tsuite—* [Practice and diffusion of psychological preparation for pediatric patients and their parents undergoing medical practice]. pp. 85-126, In: Kamoshita, S. (head honcho), *Shounika-sanka wakate ishi no kakuho ikusei ni kansuru kenkyu* [A study of fostering and securing of younger obstetrician and pediatrician]. Report to the Ministry of Health, Labour and Welfare Grant-in-Aid for Scientific Research in Japan.

[16] Children's Rainbow Center. Child abuse in Japan today. http://www.crc-japan.net/contents/situation/. Accessed: 29 July 2015.

[17] Wakimizu, R., Fujioka, H., Furuya, K., Miyamato, S., Iejima, A., Yoneyama, A. (2010). Development of the Japanese version of Family Empowerment Scale (J-FES). *Journal of Health and Welfare Statistics, 11,* 33–41.

[18] Dempsey, I., Dunst, C. (2004). Help giving styles and parent empowerment in families with a young child with a disability. *Journal of Intellectual and Developmental Disability, 29,* 40–51.

[19] Sloper, P., Turner, S. (1993). Risk and resistance factors in the adaptation of parents of children with severe physical disability. *J. Child Psychol. Psychiatry. 34,* 167-188.

[20] Raina, P., O'Donnell, M., Schwellnus, H., Rosenbaum, P., King, G., Brehaut, J., Russell, D., Swinton, M., King, S., Wong, M., Walter, S.D., Wood, E. (2004). Caregiving process and caregiver burden: conceptual models to guide research and practice. *BMC Pediatr. 4,* 1.

[21] Hallum, A., Krumboltz, J.D. (1993). Parents caring for young adults with severe physical disabilities: psychological issues. *Dev. Med. Child Neurol. 35,* 24-32.

[22] Tanaka, C., Hamabe, F., Tawaratumita, Y., Sugawara, S., Miyake, S. (2011). Actual conditions and issues regarding in-home support for children with severe motor and intellectual disabilities requiring medical care and their family (part2). *Journal of severe motor and intellectual disabilities. 36,* 141-146.

[23] Monma, T., Maeda, K. (2011). Longitudinal changes of attitude and thinking toward social supports in families rearing children with severe motor and intellectual disabilities. *Journal of severe motor and intellectual disabilities. 31,* 289-295.

[24] Okada, K. (2006). *Juushoushinshinshougaiji no rekishi* [The history of children with severe motor and intellectual disabilities], pp15-20, In: Asakura, T. (Eds), *Juushoushinshinshougaiji no total-care* [The total care of children with severe motor and intellectual disabilities], 1st edn, Herusu Shuppan, Tokyo.

[25] Ezoe, T. (2006). *Juushoushinshinshougaiji no gainen to teigi* [The definition of children with severe motor and intellectual disabilities], pp4-6, In: Asakura T (Ed), *Juushoushinshinshougaiji no total-car*e [The total care of children with severe motor and intellectual disabilities], 1st edn, Herusu Shuppan, Tokyo.

[26] Hori, T. (2006). Lobbying movements by parents of children with severe motor and intellectual disabilities during high economic growth and their background. *Japanese Journal of Social Welfare. 47,* 31-44.

[27] Origuchi, Y., Miyanomae, T., Imai, M., Nishima, S. (2008). Annual changes in the death rate among patients with severe motor and intellectual disabilities (SMID) show a downward trend. *Journal of Severe Motor and Intellectual Disabilities 33,* 83-86.

[28] Honda, H., Shimizu, Y., Imai, M., Nitto, Y. (2005). Cumulative incidence of childhood autism: a total population study of better accuracy and precision. *Dev. Med. Child Neurol. 47,* 10-18.

[29] Williams, J.G., Higgins, J.P., Brayne, C.E. (2006). Systematic review of prevalence studies of autism spectrum disorders. *Arch. Dis. Child. 91,* 8-15.

[30] Ministry of Health, Labour and Welfare. (2005). *Establishment of the Support Law for People with Developmental Disorders*. [Cited 2 Mar 2010.] Available from URL: http://www.mhlw.go.jp/english/wp/wp-hw2/part2/p2c8s2.pdf.

[31] Yamada, A., Suzuki, M., Kato, M., Suzuki, M., Tanaka, S., Shindo, T., Taketani, K., Akechi, T., Furukawa, T.A. (2007). Emotional distress and its correlates among parents of children with pervasive developmental disorders. *Psychiatry Clin. Neurosci. 61,* 651-657.

[32] Wakimizu, R. (2012). Survey on the empowerment of the family rearing children with special needs－Comparison of two different kinds of disabilities of severe motor and intellectual disabilities and developmental disabilities. *The Journal of Ambulatory and General Pediatrics, 15(1),* 25-30.

[33] Wakimizu, R., Fujioka, H., Yoneyama, A., Iejima, A., Miyamoto, S. (2011). Factors associated with the empowerment of Japanese families raising a child with developmental disorders. *Res. Dev. Disabil. 32(3),* 1030-1037. doi: 10.1016/j.ridd.2011.01.037.

[34] Wakimizu, R., Fujioka, H., Yoneyama, A. (2010). Empowerment process for families rearing children with developmental disorders in Japan. *Nurs. Health Sci. 12(3),* 322-8. doi: 10.1111/j.1442-2018.2010.00533.x.

[35] Fujioka, H., Wakimizu, R., Okubo, Y., Yoneyama, A. (2014). Empowerment of Families Rearing Children with Severe Motor and Intellectual Disabilities at Home. *Medical and Health Science Research. 5,* 41-53.

[36] Fujita, S., Shoji, M. (2015). Care for families whose functions are fragile. *Japanese Journal of Cancer Care. 20(2),* 277-284.

[37] Sakai, M., Ishii, K. (2012). Support toward home care for a family that mother and a child have disabilities. *Family Nursing. 10(1),* 140-147.

[38] Koyama, K. (2010). Nursing that respect the will of children with leukemia and their families at the time of chemotherapy introduction. *The Japanese Journal of Child Nursing. 33(1),* 88-94.

[39] Usuda, N., Uehira, E. (2007). Nursing intervention for decreasing anxieties of families of persons with schizophrenia. *Journal of the Japanese Psychiatric Nursing Association. 50(2),* 260-264.

[40] Nojima, S. (2005). Family Empowerment Nursing Model. pp.8-14, In: Nojima, S., Nakano, A. (Eds) Nursing practice for family empowerment. Herusu Shuppan: Tokyo.

[41] Kuno, N., Yamaguchi, K., Morita, C. (2006). The sense of burden of mothers with severely disabled children at home and the related factors. *Journal of Japanese Society of Nursing Research. 29,* 59-69. (In Japanese).

[42] Zensho, M. (2006). A study of children with severe motor and intellectual disabilities and their family's home care needs and social supports. *The Bulletin of Saitama Prefectural University. 7,* 51-58. (In Japanese).

[43] McCammon, S.L., Spencer, S.A., Friesen, B.J. (2001). Promoting family empowerment through multiple roles. *J. Fam. Soc. Work. 5,* 1-24.

[44] Morita, K. (2009). Factors in the management of home care for patients with severe motor and intellectual disabilities: interviews with principal caregivers. *Journal of Severe Motor and Intellectual Disabilities. 34,* 375-381.

[45] Nachshen, J.S., Minnes, P. (2005). Empowerment in parents of school-aged children with and without developmental disabilities. *J. Intellect Disabil. Res. 49,* 889-904.

[46] Orr, R.R., Cameron, S.J., Day, D.M. (1991). Coping with stress in families with children who have mental retardation: an evaluation of the double ABCX model. *Am. J. Ment. Retard. 95,* 444-450.

[47] Toki, M., Washio, M., Furukawa, A., Narita, H., Yokogushi, K., Ishiai, S. (2010). Investigating Parental Caregiver Burden for Children with Disabilities using a Japanese version of the Zarit Caregiver Burden Interview (J-ZBI). *Jpn J. Rehabil. Med. 47,* 396-404.

[48] Itzhaky, H., Schwartz, C. (2000). Empowerment of parents of children with disabilities: The effect of community and personal variables. *J. Fam. Soc. Work. 5,* 21-36.

[49] Gibson, C.H. (1999). Facilitating critical reflection in mothers of chronically ill children. *J. Clin. Nurs. 8,* 305-312.

In: Empowerment
Editor: Randall Harris
ISBN: 978-1-63484-036-1

Chapter 8

ASSESSING HOPE IN HIV-POSITIVE WOMEN LIVING IN RURAL WEST NILE UGANDA: THE DEVELOPMENT AND PILOT IMPLEMENTATION OF A FIELD TOOL

Brenna Lynn McGuire[1], Katherine Gnauck[1], Lynne Fullerton[1], Teresa Leslie[1], Moses Anguzu[2] and Lucy Adiru[2]
[1]University of New Mexico Health Science Center, Albuquerque, New Mexico, US
[2]Arua Regional Referral Hospital, Arua, Uganda

ABSTRACT

Depression and a sense of hopelessness have been shown to impact HIV testing, treatment adherence and health outcomes for HIV-positive women in sub-Saharan Africa. However, little has been reported on the impact of participation in Economic Empowerment (EE) programs and a sense of hope for HIV-positive individuals. We report the development and pilot implementation of a Hope Questionnaire with HIV-positive women living in West Nile Uganda. Focus groups with HIV-positive women in Uganda provided domains of mental health attributes which were reworded into positive affirmation statements of hope. yielding the Hope Questionnaire. This tool was piloted with HIV-positive women with 18 months of participation and women completely new to an EE sewing initiative. Each hope question score was compared to the sum of these scores using ANOVA. Results show that hope scores did not differ between women with continued participation and those new to the program. Hope may be an important by product of EE initiatives and appears to be an individually subjective outcome difficult to compare between groups.

Keywords: economic empowerment, HIV + women, hope, depression, PMTCT

INTRODUCTION

In sub-Saharan Africa there are currently 25 million people living with HIV/AIDS and 71% are women (WHO 2015). The incidence of maternal to child transmission (MTCT) is roughly 33% (WHO/PMNCH 2006) in mothers not receiving antiretroviral (ARV) medications with 90% of all childhood HIV infections acquired through vertical transmission during pregnancy, labor/delivery, or breastfeeding (AIDSinfo 2014). Since 2000, Uganda has made efforts to reduce the HIV/AIDS epidemic and prevent MTCT through increased access to ARV's and Prevention of Maternal to Child Transmission (PMTCT) programs (Larsson 2015). There are many factors that contribute to high HIV prevalence including the social factors that influence PMTCT uptake: AIDS-related stigma, low self-efficacy, hopelessness and depression (Belenky, 2014).

AIDS-related stigma, hopelessness and depression are especially challenging for HIV-positive women in resource poor settings of sub-Saharan Africa. Upon disclosure of their HIV-positive status, women face social stigma from their community and blame, separation and domestic violence from their partners (De Paoli 2004; Eide M. 2006). Complicating these challenges are gender inequality, poverty, and low-self efficacy which contribute to decreased clinical compliance and lost to follow up (LFU) in PMTCT programs (Vaz 2012; Moges Z. 2011).

Hope and Depression in HIV/AIDS

Recent work by Jen Cheavens, describes depression as the loss of hope. Hope has been extensively studied in psychology amongst US populations and its definition subsequently broadened. For example, the perception of hope includes the idea that "something desired might happen" (Hansen 2015); and hope is a positive motivational state based on goal-directed energy (planning to meet set goals) which incorporates aspects of self-efficacy (Snyder 1991). Studies have shown these hope attributes improve patient compliance and clinical outcomes in times of medical illness. (Moon 2000). Furthermore, research examining psychological aspects of HIV/AIDS show that "high-hope" HIV-positive individuals generate new goals, remain flexible in approaches to achieving those goals and are more resourceful when faced with extreme challenges (Romero 2006).

On the other hand, a distinct relationship between depression and HIV non-adherence amongst HIV positive individuals living in Sub-Saharan Africa has been shown. In a systematic review and meta- analysis, poor medication compliance was not limited only to HIV-positive individuals with overt clinical depression but also occurred in individuals with mild symptoms of clinical depression (Gonzales 2011). Therefore, Gonzales 2011 argues that interventions aimed at reducing depressive symptoms should be a goal of behavioral interventions for HIV-positive individuals. While previous research with PLWH has attempted to quantify depression, little has been done on the quantification of a "sense of hope" and the impact of economic empowerment initiatives on mental health attributes such as hope.

Hope and Economic Empowerment in HIV/AIDS

Recently, microenterprise and economic empowerment (EE) programs have been identified as successful strategies to alleviate gender related poverty, social exclusion and health disparities (Organization for Economic Co-operation and Development 2012). EE initiatives have shown promise in increasing women's economic independence, decreasing their HIV risk and enabling women to have more control over their healthcare choices (UNAIDS 2012; Romero 2006; Wallerstein 2006).

Similarly, our previous qualitative research with HIV-positive women participating in an EE program in Uganda suggested that an overlooked benefit of economic empowerment programs may be their ability to redirect participant's attention towards productive and positive thoughts of hope (Kellett 2015). Themes emerged unexpectedly in this work which spoke to benefits impacting psychological well being and imbuing hope in the individual. These included: sense of happiness, turning uselessness to usefulness, planning for the future, better peace of mind and ability to concentrate for example:

Sense of happiness

> If you come in the group, you come relax, you'll start rejoicing those burdens which you are having at home, that psychologists call torture, you'll no longer have it.

Future expectations –

> We are right now, the HIV people are more useful than the negative people because what we are doing is more useful than the negative people because we are planning for our future. But people who are negative, they don't plan for their future.

banishing idleness, positive focus, ability to concentrate-

> If you learn that skill, you'll not mind or think, thoughts of evil things. Your mind will always be busy on what you want to do. Because if you'll be dormant, you don't do something, you'll be thinking of evil things. But, if you'll be working, you'll be doing your own things. You'll not be thinking of any bad things because you'll be concentrating strictly on what you are doing ...

Thus the literature and our previous research with HIV-positive women in Uganda, suggested that participants in our EE initiative would benefit from gaining feelings of, happiness, having a future and having concentration and positive focus. We felt this would be an optimal opportunity to study the impact of an EE initiative on the level of hope amongst the initiative participants and hypothesized that hope scores would be higher amongst participants with continued participation in the initiative as compared to participants just starting the initiative.

METHODS

Development of the Hope Questionnaire

Many hope tools have been developed for use in psychological studies (Hansen 2015; Lopez 2003; Snyder 1991; Snyder 1996). However, these tools have not been translated, tested or validated in developing country setting with HIV-positive individuals. Using the previously describe relationship between hope and depression we turned first to a diagnostic tool for depression, the PHQ-9 depression scale, which has been validated in sub- Saharan Africa with HIV-positive individuals (Adewuya 2006).

Table 1. Adapted PHQ-9 with Item 1, 2,6,7 used for basis of Hope Questionnaire

PATIENT HEALTH QUESTIONNAIRE-9 (PHQ-9)

Over the last 2 weeks, how often have you been bothered by any of the following problems? *(Use "✔" to indicate your answer)*	Not at all	Several days	More than half the days	Nearly every day
1. Little interest or pleasure in doing things	0	1	2	3
2. Feeling down, depressed, or hopeless	0	1	2	3
3. Trouble falling or staying asleep, or sleeping too much	0	1	2	3
4. Feeling tired or having little energy	0	1	2	3
5. Poor appetite or overeating	0	1	2	3
6. Feeling bad about yourself — or that you are a failure or have let yourself or your family down	0	1	2	3
7. Trouble concentrating on things, such as reading the newspaper or watching television	0	1	2	3
8. Moving or speaking so slowly that other people could have noticed? Or the opposite — being so fidgety or restless that you have been moving around a lot more than usual	0	1	2	3
9. Thoughts that you would be better off dead or of hurting yourself in some way	0	1	2	3

FOR OFFICE CODING 0 + ______ + ______ + ______

=Total Score: ______

If you checked off any problems, how difficult have these problems made it for you to do your work, take care of things at home, or get along with other people?

Not difficult at all	Somewhat difficult	Very difficult	Extremely difficult
☐	☐	☐	☐

Developed by Drs. Robert L. Spitzer, Janet B.W. Williams, Kurt Kroenke and colleagues, with an educational grant from Pfizer Inc. No permission required to reproduce, translate, display or distribute.

We found four questions from the PHQ-9 depression scale (Table 1) which expressed opposite concepts to our hope attributes: sense of happiness, future expectations, positive focus and ability to concentrate. We then reworded these PHQ-9 questions into a positive affirmation statements which became the four questions on our Hope Questionnaire.

Table 2. Steps in Development of the Hope Questionnaire

Step I	**Step III**	**Step IV**	**Step V**	
Patient Health Questionnaire-9 (PHQ-9) question	**Hope Questionnaire positive affirmation statement**	**Field confirmation/cultural appropriateness**	**Final Hope Questionnaire**	**Corresponding Hope Domains**
Little interest or pleasure in doing things	*I find pleasure in the things that I do*	"pleasure" was not a culturally recognized concept, changed to "happy"	*Q1 I am happy in the things that I do.*	Sense of Happiness
Feeling down, depressed, or hopeless	*I am hopeful and happy about my life*	"planning" substituted because it suggests anticipation due to hope	*Q2 I am hopeful and planning for my life.*	Future Expectations
Trouble concentrating on things, such as reading the newspaper or watching television	*I am able to forget about my troubles and problems and I can concentrate on things such as making and preparing a meal*	split into two statements for clarity	*Q3 I am able to forget about my troubles and problems.*	Positive focus and ability to concentrate
			Q4 I can concentrate on things such as making and preparing a meal.	
Feeling bad about yourself - or that you are a failure or have let yourself down	*I feel good about myself*	"feeling good" was not easily understood or translated in this culture. The question was omitted.	–	–

We returned to West Nile Uganda to vet the Hope questions with HIV-positive women to assure cultural appropriateness. The final Hope Questionnaire contained four questions/ statements (Table 2). Study participants were asked to report on a Likert scale how often the positive Hope statement described how they had been feeling in the past two weeks. We recoded the ordinal responses as numeric scores, i.e., Not at all = 1; Some days = 2; More than half of the time = 3; Every day = 4. Hope scores were coded such that increasing scores were associated with increasing agreement with each statement.

Study Design

Study location. Our study took place in 2014 in the West Nile region of Uganda which has a population of approximately 2 million people. The prevalence of HIV in Uganda was 7.2% (8.3% among women and 6.1% among men) (Uganda, Ministry of Health 2011).

Maracha, our study community is situated 40 km from a main trade center for the West Nile region and has proximity to South Sudan (60 km North) and the Democratic Republic of the Congo (10 km West). Maracha is composed of subsistence farmers in a newly formed district with limited electricity and water resources. There are cell towers with variable cell phone service and no stable internet. There are no banks or ATM's in the town. St Joseph's Hospital community (bed #) has obstetric and surgical services and the only HIV/PMTCT clinic. The PMTCT program began operation in 2005.

Study intervention. In November 2012, a grassroots EE initiative (sewing workshop) was linked to a hospitals HIV/ PMTCT clinic program and open to HIV-positive mothers enrolled in the clinic on a first come, first served basis. Interested women who exceed workshop capacity were 'wait listed' and incorporated into the initiative as capacity permitted. The workshop was accessible five days per week and provided equipment, sewing instructors, sewing materials and paid the mothers for good quality finished products.

Study Sample

A convenience sample of the HIV-positive women participating in the EE initiative were enrolled in the study when the initiative was opened, November 2012. Participation in EE initiative was not contingent on participation in any aspect of the study. The women did not risk forfeiture of access to the HIV/PMTCT clinic for themselves or their infants for refusal to participate or early withdrawal from the study.

Measurement

The Hope Questionnaire was administered by trained local national staff. All questions were translated into the local language, Lugbara or Kiswahili in real time by the national staff. A total of thirty-nine HIV-positive women enrolled in the EE initiative participated in our study. Twenty-six of these women had continued participation for eighteen months since start- up of the EE initiative in 2012, (Group I). Thirteen women were newly enrolled in the EE initiative in 2014, (Group II). One woman in Group II was excluded from the analysis because of incomplete demographic data. A demographic survey was administered to all participants at (time = 0) which asked: participants' age, number of children, distance living from workshop, education level, civil status, time since HIV diagnosis.

Statistics

Groups I and II were compared using chi squared analysis for all categorical variables (e.g., education) and the Wilcoxon rank sum test for ordinal and ratio scale data (e.g., Hope Scores).

The study was reviewed and approved by Institutional Review Boards at the University of New Mexico and the Makerere University in Kampala, Uganda.

RESULTS

There were no significant differences between Groups I and II in participant age, education, marital status, number of children, or year of HIV-positive diagnosis. Median values, stratified by group, are presented in (Table 3).

Table 3. Participant Demographic Data

	18 mo Participants (n = 26)	New Participants (n = 12)
Age (median)	34 years	33.5 years
Education		
None	11.5%	8.3%
Primary	73.1%	66.7%
Secondary	15.4%	25.0%
Marital status		
Married/living with	53.8%	66.7%
Divorced	23.1%	16.7%
Widowed	23.1%	16.7%
Number children (median)	3.0	4.0
Distance to workshop (median)	3.3	2.3
Year to diagnosis (median)	2007.5	2003.5

Hope scores did not differ between groups of women with continued participation in the EE initiative for 18 months (Group I) and those new to the program (Group II). Median Hope scores were generally high among both groups, with most women indicating that they were hopeful more than half of the time. Group I and Group II Hope scores are presented in Table 4.

Table 4. Median Hope Scores* (IQR'S) compared between 18 mo Participants (Group I) and New Participants (Group II)

Positive Statements	18mo Participants (n = 26) (IQR)	New Participants (n = 12) (IQR)	p-value**
I am happy in the things that I do	2.0 (2.0, 3.0)	3.0 (2.5, 3.0)	0.89
I am hopeful and planning for my life	3.0 (2.0, 3.0)	2.5 (2.0, 3.0)	0.17
I am able to forget about my troubles and problems	3.0 (2.0, 3.0)	3.0 (2.0, 3.0)	0.42
I can focus on things in my life such as making and preparing meals	3.0 (2.0, 3.0)	3.0 (2.5, 3.0)	0.73

*Hope scores were coded such that increasing scores associated with increasing agreement with each statement.

** One-sided test of median hope score among 18 mo Participants > median Hope score for New Participants.

The overall Hope Score, calculated as the sum of scores for each of 4 questions, was examined to determine if it varied with demographic factors among the total sample (n = 38). The overall score was significantly associated with only one of the demographic variables: Women who were widowed had lower Hope scores than divorced women or women who were married/living with a partner (p = 0.038).

The overall Hope Score, calculated as the sum of scores for each of 4 questions, was examined to determine if it varied with demographic factors among the total sample (n = 38). The overall score was significantly associated with only one of the demographic variables: Women who were widowed had lower Hope scores than divorced women or women who were married/living with a partner (p = 0.038).

CONCLUSION

Economic empowerment programs have been shown to improve PMTCT uptake and decrease transmission of HIV/AIDS (Kennedy 2014). Recent studies looking at the impact of EE programs have shown the complex relationship between poverty and the HIV epidemic with increased attention being paid to the importance of increasing women's social capital (Kim JC 2008). Part of this social capital is improving the mental and psychological state of mind of the individual which helps to overcome psychological barriers that exist in accessing HIV/AIDS care (hIarlaithe 2014). There is currently a need to assess the psychological impact of EE programs as this aspect of participation has yet to be fully understood as a potential benefit to expanding these types of initiatives.

Results from this initial pilot study using the Hope Questionnaire showed high levels of hope amongst all participants regardless of the time spent in the EE initiative. Similarly, the wide variability in score for each Hope question within groups would suggest that assessing levels of hope between participant groups in relation to time spent involved in an EE program may not show the change in hope experienced by each individual participant when compared to herself. Research looking at the effects of self-efficacy with participation in EE programs showed significant results when participants were compared to themselves at pre and post time points in the intervention (Gnauck 2015). Hope may be similar in that it is a personalized and individualized measure with each woman having different levels of baseline hope.

Anticipation of participation in an EE program may have had the effect of increasing positive feelings of hope amongst our new participants. To date two experimental fMRI studies have demonstrated dopamine activation of brain reward centers during anticipation of monetary rewards (Knutson, 2001. Breiter 2001). This research suggests that there may be a phenomenon in which individuals experience psychological feelings of reward or benefit prior to actually experiencing the intended outcome. This may be present in our population as feelings of hope were high among all participants regardless of time spent involved in the EE initiative.

The creation of a "hope tool" provides a measure to assess the protective mechanism that hope may have against AIDS related stigma and its associated depression leading to improved health uptake behaviors and outcomes. Future work measuring hope amongst women in the sewing workshop compared to demographically similar women not participating in our intervention might demonstrate the psychological effect that EE programs have on participants.

REFERENCES

Adewuya, A.O., Ola, B.A., & Afolabi, O.O. (2006). Validity of the patient health questionnaire (PHQ-9) as a screening tool for depression amongst Nigerian university students. *J Affect Disord,* 96(1-2), 89-93. Retrieved from: http://dx.doi.org/10.1016/j.jad.2006.05.021.

AVERT- Averting HIV and Aids (2014). 'HIV Prevention: Preventing Mother-to-Child Transmission of HIV.' Retrieved from: http://www. avert.org/prevention-mother-child-transmission-pmtct-hiv.htm#footnote1_cw0c4oy.

Belenky N.M., Cole S.R., Pence B.W., Itemba D., Maro V., & Whetten K. (2014). Depressive symptoms, HIV medication adherence, and HIV clinical outcomes in Tanzania: a prospective, observational study. *Plos One,* 9(5):e95469. doi:10.1371/journal.pone.0095469.

Breiter H.C, Aharon I., Kahneman D., Dale A., & Shizgal P. (2001). Functional Imaging of Neural Responses to Expectancy and Experience of Monetary Gain and Losses. *Neuron* 30, 619 – 639. Retrieved from http://www-psych.standford.edu/~knutson/rab/breiter01.pdf.

De Paoli M.M., Manongi R., & Klepp K.I., (2004). Factors influencing acceptability of voluntary counseling and HIV testing among pregnant women in northern Tanzania. *AIDS Care.* 16(4): 411-425. doi: 10.1080/09540120410001683358.

Eide M., Myhre M., Lindbaek M., Sundby J., Arimi P., & Thior I. (2006). Social consequences of HIV-positive women's' participation in prevention of mother-to-child transmission programmes. *J Patient Education and Counseling.* 60: 146-151. doi:10.1016/j.pec.2004.11.014.

Gnauck, K., Leslie T., Fullerton L., McGuire B., Adiru L., Seevers B., & Anguzu M. (2015). An Economic Empowerment Initiative Partnered with Prevention Mother to Child Transmission (PMTCT) Programs for HIV-positive Women in West Nile Uganda: Does Participation Increase Self-Efficacy Related to HIV-Aids Stigma?. Manuscript submitted for publication.

Gonzalez J.S., Batchelder A.W., Psaros C., & Safren SA. (2011). Depression and HIV/AIDS treatment nonadherence: a review and meta-analysis. *J Acquir Immune Defic Syndr* 58(2), 181-187. doi: 10.1097/ QAI. 0b013e 31822d490a.

Hansen, K. (2015). What is hope and how can we measure it? Positive Psychology UK. Retrieved from: http://positivepsychology.org.uk/pp-theory/hope/100-what-is-hope-and-how-can-we-measure-it.html.

hIarlaithe, M.O., Grede, N., De Pee, S., & Bloem, M. (2014). Economic and social factors are some of the most common barriers preventing women from accessing maternal and newborn child health (MNCH) and prevention of mother-to-child transmission (PMTCT) services: a literature review. *AIDS Behav* 18(5), 516-530. doi: 10.1007/s10461-014-0756.

Kennedy, C.E., Fonner, V.A., O'Reilly, K.R., & Sweat, M.D. (2014). A systematic review of income generation interventions, including microfinance and vocational skills training, for HIV prevention. *AIDS Care,* 26(6), 659-73. doi: 10.1080/09540121.2013.845287.

Kellett, N.C., Gnauck, K., Sussman, A., Levin, N., Seevers, B., Hanselman, J., & Adaku, A. (2015). AIDS, stigma and economic empowerment: Exploring notions of belonging and masculinity in West Nile Uganda. Manuscript submitted for publication.

Kim, J.C., Pronyk, P., Barnett, T., & Watts, C. (2008). Exploring the role of economic empowerment in HIV prevention. *AIDS,* 22(4), S57-71. doi: 10.1097/01.aids.0000 341777.78876.40.

Knutson B., Adams C.M, Fong G.W,, & Hommer, D. (2001). Anticipation of Increasing Monetary Reward Selectively Recruits Nucleus Accumbens. *Journal of Neuroscience,* 21, 1-5. Retrieved from http://www-psych.edu/~span/Publications/bk01jn.pdf.

Larsson, E., Ekström, A., Pariyo, G., Tomson, G., Sarowar, M., Baluka, R., Galiwango, E., & Ekéus Thorson, A. (2015). Prevention of mother-to-child transmission of HIV in rural Uganda: Modelling effectiveness and impact of scaling-up PMTCT services. *Global Health Action,* 8. doi:http://dx.doi.org/10.3402/gha.v8.26308.

Lopez S.J., Snyder C.R., & Pedrotti J.T. Hope: Many definitions, many measures. Lopez SJ., Snyder CR. Positive psychological assessment: A handbook of models and measures. Washington, DC: American Psychological Association; 2003; 91-106.

McIntyre, J. (2006). Strategies to prevent mother-to-child transmission HIV. Current Opinion in Infectious Diseases, 19 (1),33-8. Retrieved from http://www.ncbi.nlm.nih.gov/ pubmed/16374215.

Moges, Z., & Amberbir, A. (2011). Factors Associated with Readiness to VCT Service Utilization among Pregnant Women Attending Antenatal Clinics in Northwestern Ethiopia: A Health Belief Model Approach. *Ethiopian Journal of Health Sciences*, 21(1), 107–115. Retrieved From: http:// www.ncbi.nlm.nih.gov/pmc/articles/PMC3275874/.

Moon C. Chapter 18 - Hope and the Journey with AIDS. Snyder, CR. Handbook of Hope Theory, Measures, & Applications. San Diego, CA: Academic Press; 2000; 341-351.

Organization for Economic Co-operation and Development (OECD). (2013). Poverty Reduction and Pro-Poor Growth. The Role of Empowerment. Retrieved from OECD website: http://www.oecd.org/dac/poverty reduction/50157953.pdf.

Romero l., Wallerstein N, Lucerr J., Fredine H.G., Keefe J.,& O'Connell J. (2006). Woman to Woman: Coming together for positive change - Using empowerment to prevent HIV in women. *AIDS Education and Prevention,* 18(5), 390-405. doi: 10.1521/aeap. 2006.18.5.390.

Snyder, C.R., Harris, C., Anderson, J.R., Holleran, S.A., Irving, L.M., Sigmon, S.T., Yoshinobu, L., Gibb, J., Langelle, C., & Harney, P. (1991). The will and the ways: Development and validation of an individual-differences measure of hope. *Journal of Personality and Social Psychology*, 60(4), 570-585. Retrieved from: http://dx.doi.org/ 10.1037/0022-3514.60.4.570.

Snyder, C.R., Sympson S.C., Ybasco F.C., Borders T.F., Babyak M.A., & Higgins, R.L. (1996). Development and validation of the State Hope Scale. *Journal of Personality and Social Psychology,* Vol 70(2), 321-335. Retrieved from: http://dx.doi.org/10.1037/0022-3514.70.2.321.

Uganda Ministry of Health. (2011). Uganda AIDS Indicator Survey. Retrieved from: https://www.usaid.gov/sites/default/files/documents/1860/Uganda_AIDS_Indicator_ Survey_2011.pdf.

UNAIDS. (2012). Global Report: UNAIDS Report on the Global AIDS Epidemic. Retrieved from UNAIDS website: http://www.unaids.org/en/media/unaids/contentassets/ documents/epidemiology/2012/gr2012/JC2434_WorldAIDSday_results_en.pdf.

Vaz L.M., Maman S., Eng E., & Barbarin O.A. (2012). Patterns of Disclosure of HIV-status to Infected Children in a Sub-Saharan African Setting. *J Dev Behav Pediatr,* August 2012:1. Retrieved from http://www. ncbi.nlm.nih.gov/pmc/articles/PMC3128187/.

Wallerstein N. (2006). What is the evidence on effectiveness of empowerment to improve health? WHO Regional Office for Europe Health Evidence Network Report. Retrieved from: http://www.euro.who.int/Document/ E88086.pdf.

World Health Organization (WHO). (2015). Global Health Observatory Data: HIV/AIDS. Retrieved from WHO website: http://www.who.int/gho/ hiv/en/.

In: Empowerment
Editor: Randall Harris
ISBN: 978-1-63484-036-1

Chapter 9

FOSTERING INDEPENDENCE AND EQUALITY: LESSONS LEARNED FROM AN ECONOMIC EMPOWERMENT MODEL IN WEST NILE UGANDA

***Brenda Seevers*[1] *and Katherine Gnauck*[2]**
[1]New Mexico State University, Las Cruces, New Mexico, US
[2]University of New Mexico Health Sciences Center, Albuquerque, New Mexico, US

ABSTRACT

Economic empowerment is recognized as a crucial component for alleviating poverty, social exclusion and reducing health disparities. It is necessary to build the capacity of women with technical and entrepreneurial skills in order to broaden their range of choices and give them a voice in their households and communities. In the last decade, rural non-farm (RNF) initiatives have been recognized as major actors of women's economic empowerment in developing countries. We report, a low-budget grassroots RNF economic empowerment model started in 2008, for HIV-positive women in West Nile Uganda. The goal of the LifeStitches model is to empower women with income-generating skills to improve their quality of life and to decrease the burdens of AIDS-related stigma. In 2012, replication in a nearby community demonstrated the model's viability. The structural aspects of this model include empowerment, sustainability and participatory evaluation and are discussed in the context of an established paradigm. The outcomes assessed by a demographic/socioeconomic outcome tool; DataThreads, supported the effectiveness of this model to address poverty and highlighted barriers to participation. Lessons learned are discussed. In conclusion, the incremental building of technical and entrepreneurial skills constitutes essential elements of empowerment.

Keywords: rural non-farming, economic empowerment, model, gender inequity, HIV/AIDS

INTRODUCATION AND THEORETICAL FRAMEWORK

Importance of RNF Approach

Rural non-farm (RNF) initiatives in developing countries have been increasingly recognized in importance for economic development. This trend has continued even as agriculture becomes a greater part of global markets and as rural areas develop stronger links to urban centers (Nagler, P, & Naude, 2014; Zezza, Carletto, Davis, Stamoulis, & Winters, 2009).

Women's contributions to RNF initiatives have also been confirmed in global reports (FAO, 2011). RNF activities include a spectrum of livelihood strategies taken on by rural communities (Dary, S.K, & Kuunibe, N. (2012; Cliché, G. (2011; Davis et al., 2010). In developing countries, most rural households still maintain agricultural production, but the larger share of income in rural households is non-agricultural. However, Africa may currently lag in this trend. For example, agriculture for African countries remains the more important income resource ranging from 59% to 78% of overall income (Davis et al., 2010). Building the capacity of women with technical and entrepreneurial skills in both agricultural and non-agricultural areas broadens the range of choices women can make and give them a voice in their own households and communities (FOA, 2011; Zezza et al., 2009).

Poverty, Vulnerability, Gender and Health Disparities

The benefits in women's healthcare and empowerment have been inferior to those accomplished by men despite many decades of international development programs which have had a clear emphasis on women (Banerjee & Duflo, 2011; Collins, Morduch, Rutherford, & Ruthven, 2009; Jacob et al., 2006).

Nearly half (47.5%) of the world's population in sub-Saharan Africa lives on the equivalent of $1.25 US Dollars per day (World Bank, 2015). Women shoulder a disproportionate share of the poverty burden which increases their vulnerability to marginal employment, and insufficient health care (UNAIDS, 2008; UNAIDS, 2010, UNIFEM, 2008/2009). Women also lack control over key decisions in their lives such as: personal health care; daily purchases; family visits and diet.

Approaches that link women's healthcare to economic development are growing in recognition and support as developing countries and international NGO's struggle to achieve the Millennium Development Goals (UNDP 2012). In sub-Saharan Africa where over sixty-one per cent of the people living with HIV/AIDS are women (UNAIDS, 2010), RNF initiatives in Kenya, Ethiopia, and South Africa show promise in addressing economic and health disparities (Odek, Busza, Morris, Cleland, Ngugi, & Ferguson, 2009; Pronyk et al., 2008; Mohammad, 2007).

Sustainability, Empowerment and Outcome Evaluation

Historically the strategy of initiating a development intervention without providing for sustainability has not provided long-term benefits (Voth, 2004; Islam, Gray, Feid, Kelly, & Kemp, 2011). Despite many development interventions, sub-Saharan Africa continues to be one of the most aid-dependent regions of the world (Moss, 2005). A list of countries receiving foreign aid (based on official development assistance) shows Africa received more than double the amount of aid in 2013 than Asia, its' next counterpart (Wikepedia, 2015). In an economic context, development enterprises have been defined as sustainable when they can survive stresses and maintain or enhance a region's capabilities and assets, while not undermining the natural resource base (Chambers & Conway, 1992). Successful interventions that empower their participants have repeatedly demonstrated sustainability (UNAIDS, 2010; Beckley, Martz, Nadeau, Wall, & Reimer, 2008; Kim, Pronyk, Barnett, & Watts, 2008; Emery & Flora, 2006; Malhotra, Schuler, & Boender, 2002). Cooperation in development evidenced by increasing community involvement in project design and project management has shown to be key to sustainability (Janssens, 2010).

Economic empowerment project frameworks must use participatory approaches in determining needs and priorities, and also promote the continued involvement of participants in implementation, monitoring, and outcome evaluation (Manderson & Mark, 1997; Mahmud & Shah, 2012). The identification and tracking of sustainability indicators provides valuable guidance feedback for decisions. It also provides for community empowerment, an entity which has thus far eluded conventional development approaches (Fraser, Dougill, Mabee, Reed, & McAlpine, 2006).

The literature provides several models for economic empowerment. For example, a framework based on microfinance suggests that its impact occurs on four levels:

individual, *household*, *enterprise*, and *community*. *Individual* level pathways include: *material*, *cognitive*, *perceptual* and *relational.* Table 1 shows individual levels of impact of this economic empowerment model.

Table 1. Individual Level Impacts

Material	Cognitive	Perceptual	Relational
Income	Knowledge	Self-confidence	Intra house-hold
Resources	Skills	Self-esteem	Extra house-hold
Basic needs	Awareness	Visibility	
Earning			

Adapted from Chen 1997.

A second example would be the Livelihoods Approach. A theoretical framework for viewing the complex issues and resources that can impact RNF initiatives (Duncombe, 2006). In the framework, assessing the six capital assets available in a community: human, financial, cultural, political, physical and natural, are imperative to bringing about change.

The LifeStitches Model

The LifeStitches model has several components which are similar to the Livelihoods Approach. For example, the Livelihoods Approach encompasses both empowerment and sustainability and views the poor as operating in a context of vulnerability. Additionally, the approach proposes participatory methods for data collection and analysis that fully involve the participants (Zezza et al., 2009; Duncombe, 2006).

Applying the Livelihoods Approach to the LifeStitches (LS) Model

Human capital. Many local indigenous human capitals such as: information, networks, and contacts are utilized. For example, a partnership was developed with local tailors who became sewing instructors and valuable resources for sewing machine repair, pricing and markets for materials, and referral resources in the community.

Financial capital. No initial capital was available at the start of the program. The supporting NGO provided 'start up' funds and assisted in marketing ventures with a high profit margin. Profits subsequently went back to the project start-up, development and diversification.

Social capital. LS participants already had significant social capital within their medical community operating on the hospital grounds. They also networked with other established HIV/AIDS peer support groups in the community. Each of the women had religious affiliations in the community and several had small business associations in the community.

Physical capital. For the first three years, the workshop was run out of space in the hospital laundry loaned by the hospital. Two sewing machines were acquired in the initial period with nine acquired over time by various means such as by donation and also eventual purchase using the workshop profits.

Natural capital. The hospital contributed municipal water and electricity costs for the workshop and hospital land where a new small workshop space was constructed using workshop profits.

LifeStitches Model Setting

Uganda has a population of approximately 39 million people with approximately 1.4 million people infected with HIV/AIDS. Thirty-eight percent of Ugandans live below the national poverty line (UNGASS, 2010; World Bank, 2015). Arua, the first project model site, is located in a district of 200,000 people in West Nile Uganda and is the main trade center for the region. The economy of this region is mixed agriculture and commerce based. West Nile, is located in northern Uganda bordered by Sudan and the Democratic Republic of Congo (See Figure 1).

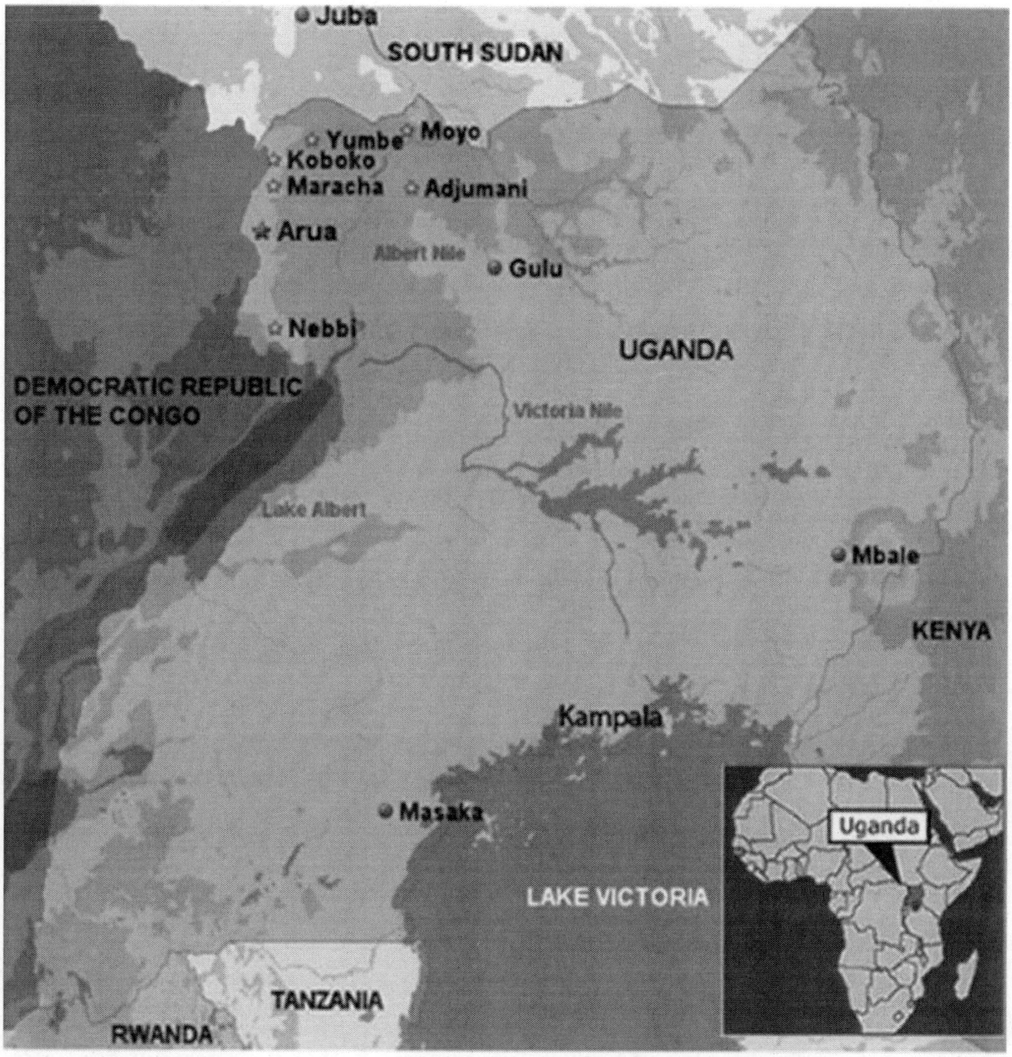

Figure 1. Map of Uganda.

In 2008, a grassroots, RNF economic empowerment initiative—the LifeStitches Project sewing workshop—was linked to the Prevention of Mother To Child Transmission (PMTCT) HIV/AIDS medical clinic at the Arua Regional Referral Hospital. The project is sponsored by a US not-for-profit NGO based in Albuquerque, New Mexico. The LifeStitches Project was initially funded by private donor funds but soon became supported by the sewing workshop's sales profits. The model initially depended on export of products to be sold in the US but is currently transitioning to local market based production.

Building Strategies for Empowerment

The LifeStitches model shown in Figure 2 describes the workshop structure and the incremental process of building empowerment through the acquisition of sewing skills.

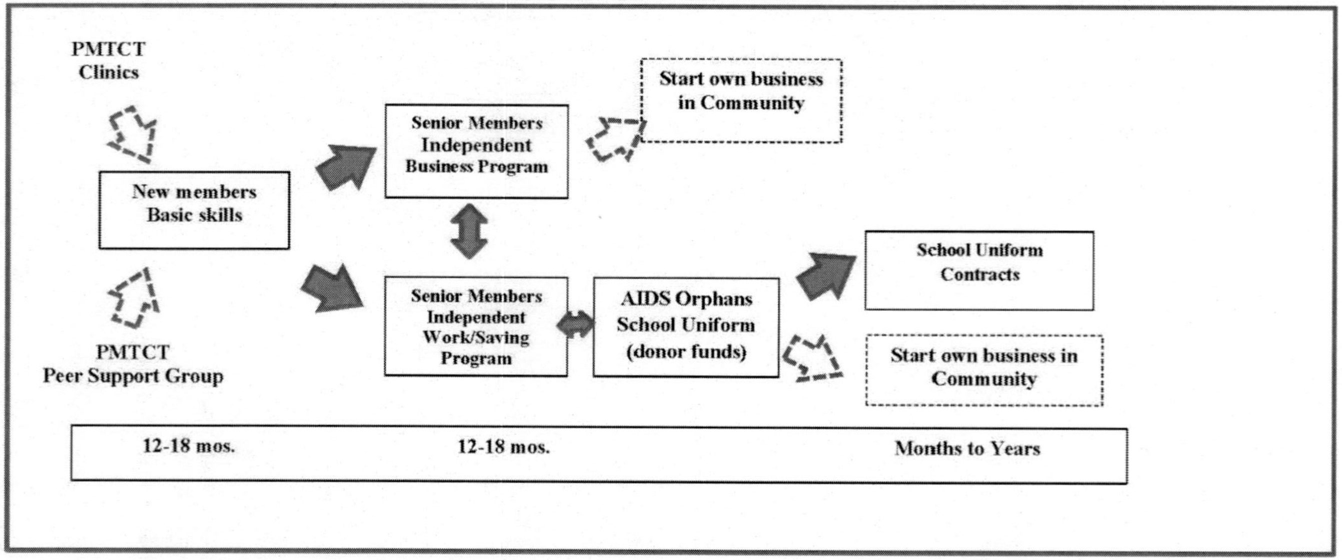

Figure 2. LifeStitches Workshop Empowerment Model.

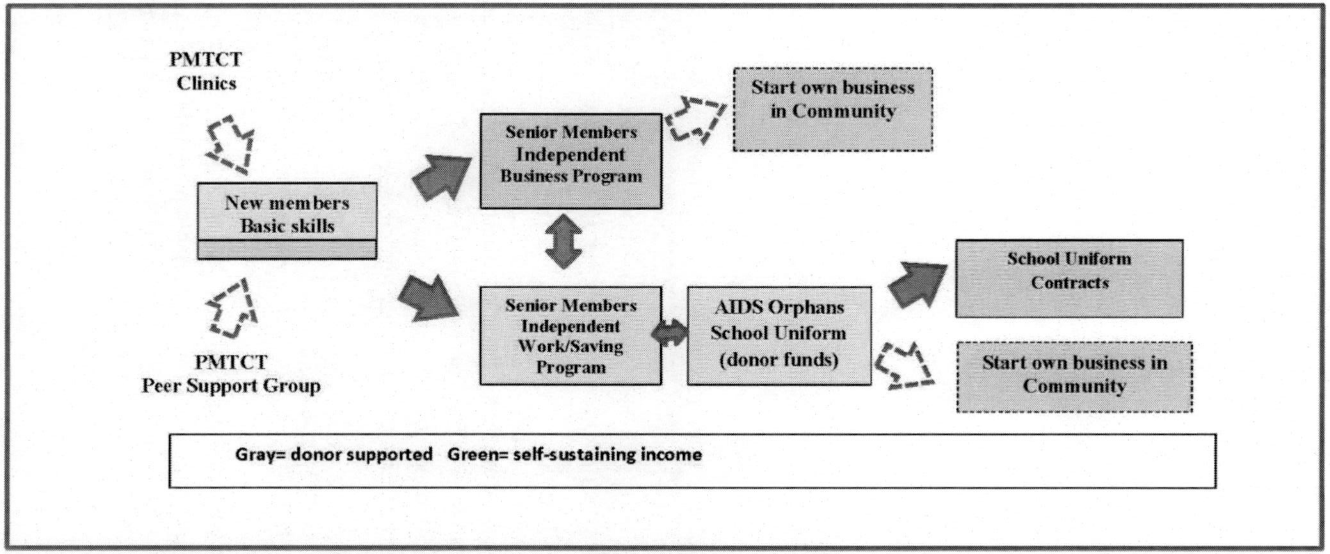

Figure 3. The LifeStitches Model – Movement to Self-Sustaining Income and Economic Empowerment.

In the New Members Basic workshop, women begin with an income generating task that is fabric related but requires no sewing skills. They advance over the next six to twelve months to acquire basic sewing skills sufficient to produce finished high quality cotton table products, such as napkins and placemats. Women spend up to 18 months in the Basic workshop where they are mentored by senior participants and professional teacher tailors hired from the community.

After mastering basic skills, women can progress to the Senior workshop. In the Senior Independent Business Program, there is much autonomy and a market business program prevails. Women purchase all their own fabric, needles, threads, and pay rent for equipment and workshop space. Senior women can also participate in the Work/Savings program to learn advanced tailor skills from a community tailor, and can exit this program with tailor skills and enough money saved to purchase her own pedal sewing machine and start-up capital to begin her own business.

Building Sustainable Outcomes

Four elements were incorporated into the LifeStitches workshop model to help insure sustainability: Capacity building; Self-governance; Focused feedback; and Ongoing redesign.

Capacity Building

Figure 3 shows the evolving steps toward economic autonomy in the workshop model which is completely market based. Women are paid monthly for completed high quality products. As women gain more skill and economic independence, they move toward the option of leaving the workshop structure and starting out in a tailoring business.

Self-Governance

The workshop participants group has an elected Chairperson, treasurer and secretary and also a liaison from the hospital PMTCT peer support group. Meetings are held monthly. Ideas, policy changes, and management changes are vetted by the participants with ample opportunity for discussion. Most final decisions are made based on majority vote.

Focused Feedback

Key participant interviews with the hospital community and the community at large (including other HIV/AIDS peer support groups) occur on a regular basis as issues and thresholds in the model develop. The governance board for the US based NGO receives quarterly reports on the project and also provides valuable market feedback on the workshop quality, production and sales. Ideas and recommendations travel both ways between Uganda and United States.

Ongoing Re-Design

A strength of being small and operating with a low budget means more flexibility and inevitable obstacles are not catastrophic and can be usually overcome. For example, when cotton prices surged, workshop staff went out to negotiate for 'price adjustment' in the cost of fabric.

Growth of Model Program

Since the program began in 2008, more than 80 mothers have participated in the Arua Life Stitches Basic workshop. Through referrals from the PMTCT clinic, new participants are continually contacted and recruited to participate in the workshop. Growth of the program resulted in finding additional space for senior mothers. The Mvarra Workshop was opened in 2012. Located approximately one half miles from the Hospital workshop, Mvarra houses the Senior Mothers Independent Business and Work/Savings Programs.

To address the barriers to participation, two new programs were also introduced in 2015. The Ride to Own Bike Purchase, allows mothers to use salaries to purchase bicycle transportation to and from the workshop. The Bike Repair Shop Program is an alternative income generating employment program to those women who do not want to learn to sew or whose sewing skills are not strong enough to support sustainable employment.

Measurement of Outcomes

Indicators of success involved the use of a demographics/socioeconomic tool, DataThreads, developed in 2011. The DataThreads tool was validated in Arua. Two indicators were included in this tool: demographic and economic ("proxies for wealth"). Demographic descriptions included: age, education, marital status, number of children less than five years old living at home, length of time HIV-positive, distance traveled to the workshop from home, means of transportation to the workshop, and numbers of days per week involved in the workshop. Through semi structure interviews, economic information that was context specific to the women and their lives in the community was gathered and guided the development of the economic indictors, both short-term (e.g., income, food purchased at the market) and long-term (e.g., bicycle purchases, improvements to home roofs) (Table 2).

Table 2. Socioeconomic Indicators

Cash	Household Items	Real Estate	Education/Healthcare Access
Lending or borrowing Savings Project earnings	Wheeled transportation Livestock Food security	Type of dwelling Dwelling owned Dwelling land owned	Private school Member medication bought other than ARVs

The tool was administered Fall 2011, to workshop members (59 of 60) by trained national project staff. Workshop participation levels Low= 0-2 day/week; High= 3 or more days/week and personal demographics were queried.

Demographics as Predictor of Participation

There were 30 High and 29 Low participators. Grouping all members, the median age was 36 years, median number of years since HIV/AIDS was diagnosed, 7.5 and median number of years enrolled in the workshop was three.

We found that high participation in this economic empowerment initiative predicted a higher median income and may reflect higher skill and proficiency development. The amount of earnings achieved was correlated to the level of participation. Participation was associated with two major factors, the ability to get to the workshop and once there the ability to complete high quality products. At the time of the analysis, two thousand Ugandan Shillings were roughly the equivalent of one US dollar. The median six month income for High participators (33,900 Ugandan Shillings) was significantly greater than Low participators (15,000 Ugandan Shillings) ($p=0.003$).

Distance living from the workshop was a significant predictor of participation. Two-thirds (65%) of women who lived ≤ 3 miles from the workshop were High participators, in contrast with 39% of women who lived farther away ($p=0.047$). In addition, 71% of High participators had access to owned or hired wheels v 43% of high participation among women who always walked ($p=0.054$).

The number of small children in the home was also a predictor of participation, with the likelihood of being in the High participation group decreasing nearly 52% with each additional child. We found the number of small children may limit participation and cause distractions affecting the ability to learn and complete high quality products.

Strategies to increase access to the model program include decentralized workshops, including home-based work; workshop sponsored child care and bike-loan programs,

MODEL REPLICATION

Does the model work? Can it be replicated in another community? Each community is unique and it is unrealistic to assume that what works in one place can automatically be transferred to another location. In 2011, visits were made to two rural communities in the West Nile area (Maracha and Koboko). The Participatory Rural Appraisal (PRA) approach to assessing community situations, was utilized to gain a sense of each community. In focus groups, we learned that women diagnosed with HIV/AIDS believe they have little hope for a successful future for themselves or their children in poor rural communities. The stigma of living with HIV/AIDS means risking family and community support. Low education levels and lack of employment skills leave them unable to support themselves and their children. These HIV-positive women saw a future with little hope and much despair. The community of Maracha was used to replicate the LifeStitches model.

Maracha is an extremely rural and poverty stricken community. There is limited infrastructure with no banks or state run electricity and only limited internet service. The primary economic base for the community is agriculture with subsistent crops (beans, cassava, maize) being the major source of income.

The Maracha workshop opened in Fall 2012 at St Joseph's Regional Hospital. Within weeks of the workshop opening, the number of participants outgrew the available space.

Recognizing the positive impact the LifeStitches program had on the local community, the hospital generously donated additional workshop spaces. This space houses the level two – advanced skills workshop. The Maracha workshop has outreached growth capacity and has shown to provide support and income to the target population.

LESSONS LEARNED

The preliminary outcome results support the effectiveness of this low budget grassroots RNF model and its ability to address poverty among HIV-positive women in developing countries. Lessons learned include:

Economic empowerment can become a reality. The LifeStitches model demonstrates that a RNF initiative can be both empowering and sustainable. An argument can be made for a distinction between simple income generating initiatives and economic empowerment initiatives. The former, often driven by outside donor funds and a top-down management approach, provide income for participants but do not necessarily empower participants to survive autonomously as entrepreneurs. Economic empowerment implies the development of skills, business training and community networking along with a stable economic base operating over time. This allows participants to acquire the necessary technical skills and equipment, along with business practices that work in the community, while maintaining a financial base to support a few years of trial and error growth. The outside supporting agency provides the initial training and start up technology, and the stable economic base to cushion the enterprise during the startup period. However, it is the participant who, through trial and error, develops the ultimate entrepreneur skills and community networking that will insure sustainability over time.

Empowerment means giving up power. Successful development projects are those that come from the people and are maintained by the people. Self-governance and autonomy are essential for sustainability. Over the past four years, Life Stitches has moved from extensive NGO involvement to minimal support. Each year, more and more of the operation is assumed by the women in the project. Local leadership is essential for sustainability. Identifying women in the project with leadership and management potential and giving them the opportunity to demonstrate it gives ownership and control to the participants. A true sustainability model provides the mechanisms for the NGO to provide guidance and support but to eventually step away.

Success does not happen overnight. A gradual step by step approach allowed women the opportunity to develop trust, self-confidence and the skills necessary to conduct a business. In many developing countries the ability to learn may be very high but education and literacy levels are often very low. Basic skills that others take for granted such as using a pair of scissors or a simple ledger may take weeks or months to master. Patience, practice and the opportunity to learn through trial and error in a non-threatening environment are essential characteristics.

You do not need a lot of money. A small amount of start-up funds can be turned into a sustainable successful venture. Starting small allows opportunities for small successes and minimizes losses in the trial and error period. Achieving and documenting success on a small scale permits potential donors to make a better assessment about a future investment.

Quality v Quantity. An important business lesson was the emphasis on quality versus quantity. Participants are paid based on the number of completed products, therefore some challenges existed in ensuring that all products must achieve a standard level of quality. Each product produced is evaluated to ensure a quality standard. Mothers are not paid until the product meets minimum standards. This initially created stress and tension since work produced was not quality and mothers had to "redo" products.

Using local management. Finding a local workshop manager with the necessary educational skills and potential leadership abilities also proved difficult. As is true in many rural areas, the pool of available applicants was small as it was easier to make more money in Arua or Koboko. It took hiring and firing two managers before achieving success. In all three situations, the manager hired was male. This is relevant because 1) there were no qualified female applicants and 2) culturally (especially in rural areas) women have primarily seen or experienced only men in leadership positions. Despite limited formal education, the women participating in the workshop have proven themselves to be capable. A future goal of the project is to develop leadership and managerial skills among the participants and promote from within.

Indirect benefits can have powerful impacts. Often in the attempt to address one problem, other opportunities will arise. The decision to initiate an own to ride bicycle program was targeted at addressing long travel distances. Facilitating accessibility to the workshop increased attendance, decreased learning time and ultimately increased earning capacity. Bicycle attainment also facilitated pride in ownership, an increased sense of independence and an understanding of the responsibilities of upkeep and maintenance. It also created an awareness that repair facilities were minimal. This created the opportunity to participants to diversify the economic empowerment model by teaching bicycle repair.

Listen, learn, change, grow. The positive aspects of growth are also tempered with new issues. Evaluation and assessment must be on-going and options must remain flexible so that once barriers/needs are identified, program redesign can occur. Both formal and informal assessment strategies are critical. Appropriate community assessment strategies such as the Participatory Rural Appraisal (PRA) model ensure community involvement and support.

Outcome evaluation using tools such as DataThreads identify predictors of as well as barriers to success. Using the data produced allows structured program design including the bike ownership program to address the distance barrier, organized day care to increase participation and alternative income generation operations such as the bike-repair program for those who cannot or do not want to sew. At the same time, participatory or experiential evaluation is also relevant.

Unlike the model workshop in Arua, finding a suitable workshop manager in Maracha proved to be difficult. The lack of experienced and qualified applicants led to short time hires, program fluctuation and inconsistency at a crucial time to start-up. This established the need for creativity and flexibility by using Arua staff to ensure that the new and fledgling program in Maracha succeeded. Perhaps this is the greatest lesson of all – *have a plan, be prepared, be flexible, adapt!*

CONCLUSION

Future directions for this project should include: continued monitoring for sustainability and economic empowerment; and continued evaluation of long term outcomes, such as increased self-esteem, reduction of AIDS-related stigma, and improved health care access. The gradual evolution of technical and entrepreneurial skills as well as networking with the community constitute the essential elements of empowerment and sustainability of this model. Preliminary results support its effectiveness to address poverty among vulnerable women in developing countries. The replication and diversification of the model has shown it can be successful.

REFERENCES

Awojobi, O. (2014). Empowering women through micro-finance: Evidence from Nigeria. *Australian Journal of Business and Management Resources. 4* (1) 17-26.

Banerjee, A. V., & Duflo, E. (2011). *Poor economics: A radical rethinking of the way to fight global poverty*. New York: Public Affairs.

Beckley, T.M. Martz. D., Nadeau, S., Wall, E., Reimer, B. (2008). Multiple capacities, multiple outcomes: Delving Deeper into meaning of community capacity. *Journal of Rural and Community Development, 3*(3), 56-75.

Centers for Disease Control. (2011). Epi Info™ for Windows, version 7.0. Retrieved from http://wwwn.cdc.gov/epiinfo/html/downloads.htm.

Cheston, S. & Kuhn, L. (2002). Empowering women through micro-finance. New York: UN Development Fund for Women.

Chambers, R., & Conway, G. (1992). *Sustainable rural livelihoods: Practical concepts for the 21st century*. Brighton, England: Institute of Development Studies.

Chen, M.A. (1997). A Guide for Assessing the Impact of Miroenterprise Services at the Individual Level. Aims Project Report. USAID/G?EG?MD. Washgington D.C.:Systems International.

Chen, M.A. & Snoddgrass, D. (2001). Managing Resources, Activities and Risk in Urban India. The Impact of the Sewar Bank. Aims Project Report. USAID/G?EG?MD. Washgington D.C.: Systems International.

Cliché, Gilles, (2011). Rural Womens' Empowerment in Nonfarm Employment: Issues for ICT Initiatives and Territorial Policies for Latin America. Retrieved from http://www.un.org/womenwatch/daw/csw/ csw56/egm/Cliche-EP-7-EGM.

Collins, D., Morduch, J., Rutherford, S., and Ruthven, O. (2009). *Portfolios of the Poor: How the World's Poor Live on $2 a Day.* Princeton, NJ: Princeton University Press.

Daniels, L. (1999). The role of small enterprises in the household and national economy in Kenya: A significant contribution or a last resort? *World Development*, *27*(1), 55-65.

Dary, S. & Kuunibe, N. (2012). Participation in Rural Non-Farm Economic Activities in Ghana. *American International Journal of Contemporary Research. 2* (8) 154-161.

Davis, B., Benjamin, D., Winters, P., Carletto, G., Covarrubias, K., Esteban, Q., Zezza, A., Stamoulis, K., Azzarri, C., Digiuseppe, S. (2010). A Cross-Country Comparison of Rural Income Generating Activities. *World Development,* 38(1), 48–63.

Duncombe, R. (2006). Using the Livelihoods Framework to Analyze ICT Applications for Poverty Reduction through Microenterprise. *Information Technologies and International Development*, *3*(3), 81-100.

Emery, M. & Flora, C. (2006). Spiraling-Up: Mapping community transformation with community capitals framework. *Journal of Community Development Society, 37*(1), 19-35.

Food and Agriculture Organization of the United Nation (FAO). (2011). *Women in Agriculture: Closing the Gender Gap for Development.* Retrieved from http://www.fao.org/docrep/013/i2050e/i2050e.pdf.

Fraser, E., Dougill, A., Mabee, W., Reed, M., McAlpinec, P. (2006). Bottom up and top down: Analysis of participatory processes for sustainability indicator identification as a pathway to community empowerment and sustainable environmental management. *Journal of Environmental Management, 78*, 114–127.

Islam, M., Gray, D., Reid, J., Kelly, T., Kemp, P. (2011). Beyond Recurrent Costs: An Institutional Analysis of the Unsustainability of Donor-Supported Reforms in Agricultural Extension. *Journal of International Agricultural and Extension Education, 18*(1),5-18.

Jacob, M., Abraham, S., Surya, S., Minz, S., Singh, D., Abraham, V.,…Jacob, K. (2006) A community health programme in rural Tamil Nadu, India: the need for gender justice for women. *Reproductive Health Matters,* 14,101-108.

Janssens, W. (2010). Women's Empowerment and the Creation of Social Capital in Indian Villages. *World Development, 38*(7), 974–988.

Kato, M. & Kratzer, J. (2013). Empowering Women through micro-finance: Evidence from Tanzania. *ACRN Journal of Entrepreneurship Perspectives. 2* (1) 31-59.

Kim, J., Pronyk, P., Barnett, T., Watts, C. (2008). Exploring the role of economic empowerment in HIV Prevention. *AIDS, 22*, S57-S71.

List of countries by foreign aid received. (2015) Wikipedia. Retrieved from: http://wikipedia.org/skik/list.

Mahmud, S., Shah, N. M., & Becker, S. (2012). Measurement of Women's Empowerment in Rural Bangladesh. *World Development, 40*(3), 610-619.

Malhotra, A. Schuler, S.R., Boender, C. (2002) *Measuring women's empowerment as a variable in international development*. Gender and Development Group, World Bank, Washington. Retrieved from www.siteresources.WorldBank.org.

Manderson, L. & Mark, T. (1997). Empowering women: participatory approaches in women's health and development projects. *Health Care for Women International, 18*(1), 17-30.

Mohammad, R. (2007). A community program for women's health and development: Implications for the long-term care of women with fistulas. *International Journal of Gynecology and Obstetrics, 99*, S137–S142.

Moss, T. (2005). Current issues in development assistance to sub-Saharan Africa. Retrieved from http://www.cgdev.org/doc/expert%20pages/ moss/ToddEIU.pdf.

Nagler, P. & Naude, W. (2014). Non-Farm Enterprises in Rural Africa: New Empirical Evidence. Policy Research Working Paper, World Bank Group.

Odek WO, Busza J, Morris CN, Cleland J, Ngugi EN, Ferguson, AG. (2009). Effects of micro-enterprise services on HIV risk behaviour among female sex workers in Kenya's urban slums. *AIDS and Behavior*, *13*(3), 449-461.

Odell, K. (2010). *Measuring the Impact of Microfiance.* Washington DC: Grameen Foundation. Retrieved from: www.grameenfoundation.org.

Pronyk P., Kim J., Abramsky T., Phetla G., Hargreaves J., Morison L,... Porter, J. (2008). A combined microfinance and training intervention can reduce HIV risk behavior in young female participants. *AIDS, 22*, 1659-1665.

UNAIDS. (2008). *Joint United Nations Programme on HIV/AIDS. Report on the global AIDS epidemic.* Geneva. Retrieved from http://data.unaids.org/ pub/GlobalReport/ 2008/ jc1510_2008_global_report_pp1_10_en.pdf.

UNAIDS. (2010). *Joint United Nations Programme on HIV/AIDS. Report on the global AIDS epidemic.* Geneva. Retrieved from http://www. unaids.org/ documents/ 20101123_Global Report_em.pdf.

United National Development Programme (UNDP). (2011).The Millennium Development Goals: Eight Goals for 2015. Retrieved from http://www. undp.org/content/undp/en/ home/mdgoverview.html.

UNGASS Country Progress Report Uganda. (2010). *UN Special Session on HIV/AIDS.* Retrieved from http://data.unaids.org/ pub/Report/ 2010/ uganda_2010_country_ progress_report_en.pdf.

UN Development Fund for Women (UNIFEM). (2008). *Progress of the World's Women 2008/2009: Who Answers to Women? Gender & Accountability*, retrieved from http://www. unhcr.org/refworld/ docid/ 4a09773a2.html.

Voth, D. (2004). *An Overview of international development perspectives in history: Focus on agricultural and rural development.* Retrieved from University of Arkansas, Department of Agricultural Economics and Agribusiness. http://ageconsearch. umn.edu/bitstream/ 15776/1/sp040005. pdf.

World Bank. (2012). *World Development Indicators (Edition: 2012)* World Bank Publications, Washington DC. Retrieved from http://data. worldbank.org/topic/poverty.

World Bank. (2015). *World Development Indicators (Edition: 2012)* World Bank Publications, Washington DC. Retrieved from http:// data.worldbank.org/topic/poverty.

Zezza, A., Carletto, G., Davis, B., Stamoulis, K., Winters, P. (2009). Rural Income generating Activities: Whatever Happened to the Institutional Vacuum? Evidence from Ghana, Guatemala, Nicaragua and Vietnam. *World Development, 37*(7), 1297–1306.

In: Empowerment
Editor: Randall Harris
ISBN: 978-1-63484-036-1

Chapter 10

AN ECONOMIC EMPOWERMENT INITIATIVE PARTNERED WITH PREVENTION MOTHER TO CHILD TRANSMISSION (PMTCT) PROGRAMS FOR HIV-POSITIVE WOMEN IN WEST NILE UGANDA: DOES PARTICIPATION INCREASE SELF-EFFICACY RELATED TO HIV-AIDS STIGMA?

Katherine Gnauck[1], Teresa Kate Leslie[1], Lynne Fullerton[1], Brenna Lynn McGuire[1], Lucy Adiru[2], Brenda Seevers[3] and Moses Anguzu[2]

[1]University of New Mexico Health Sciences Center, Albuquerque, NM, US
[2]Arua Regional Referral Hospital, Arua, Uganda
[3]New Mexico State University, Las Cruces, NM, US

ABSTRACT

AIDS-related stigma is a formidable barrier to uptake in Prevention Mother To Child Transmission (PMTCT) programs in sub-Saharan Africa. Poverty, lack of education, low self-efficacy, and living in rural communities also contribute. We report an economic empowerment initiative for HIV-positive women linked to PMTCT programs in West Nile Uganda. The classic self-efficacy model was used to develop an AIDS-related Stigma Self-Efficacy Questionnaire. Results show self-efficacy increased with participation and generalized across empowerment and stigma domains. Self-efficacy may be an effective way to measure the impact of economic empowerment initiatives on reducing AIDS-related stigma for HIV-positive women in sub-Saharan Africa.

Keywords: AIDS-related stigma, HIV-positive women, PMTCT, self-efficacy, economic empowerment

INTRODUCTION

Twenty-five million people with HIV/AIDS live in sub-Saharan Africa. Sixty percent of these are women and 2.3 million are children (WHO 2015, UNAIDS 2012). Despite dramatic steps towards prevention and treatment the epidemic continues. Lack of infrastructure and access to antiretroviral (ARV) treatment contributes, but the larger issue especially for women are AIDS-related stigma, gender inequality and poverty (Adetokunboh and Oluwasanu 2015, Brusamento, Ghanotakis, Car, L., Majeed and Car, J. 2012, Gourlay, Birdthistle, Mburu, Iorpenda and Wringe 2013, Duff, Kipp, Wild, Rubaale and Okech-Ojony 2010, Watts, Zimmerman, Nyblade and Eckhaus 2010). Women fear social stigma, blame, and separation or even domestic violence from partners if they disclose their HIV status (Colombini et al. 2014, De Paoli, Manongi and Klepp 2004, Eide et al. 2006, Varga et al. 2006). These factors lead to women's decreased uptake into PMTCT programs, poor compliance, and eventually loss to follow-up (LFU) (Gourlay et al. 2013). For example, in 2010, more than half (54%) of HIV-positive individuals in sub-Saharan Africa took ARV's, while only 30% of HIV-positive pregnant women got involved in PMTCT programs to receive antiretroviral medications to prevent transmission of HIV to their infants (UNAIDS 2012). The most common socioeconomic reasons women are unable to participate in PMTCT programs are the high transportation cost and long travel distances required to get to the clinics (Escamilla et al. 2015, Hlarlaithe, Grede, de Pee and Bloem 2014, Lubega et al. 2013). While antiretroviral drugs (ARVs) are available free of charge in Uganda (Gusdal et al. 2009), physically accessing health care facilities can be difficult for HIV mothers and exposed infants (Adetokunboh and Oluwasanu 2015).

The principle strategies for addressing AIDS-related stigma since the 1990's have been education, counseling and sensitization but these have been inadequate to reduce stigma despite sufficient funding and platforms (Ayiga, Nambooze, Nalugo, Kaye and Katamba 2013, Jurgensen, Sandoy, Michelo and Fylkesnes 2013). Economic empowerment (EE) has been recognized as being a vital component in the developing world for alleviating poverty and health disparities in women. EE while increasing women's self-efficacy (Kim, Pronyk, Barnett and Watts 2008, Wallerstein 2006) and also reduces HIV risk by decreasing gender inequality and income generating options (Odek et al. 2009, Pronyk et al. 2008). A recent model employed to encourage women to join PMTCT clinics also involves them in economic empowerment programs and are aimed at enabling women to take control of their lives and health care through economic opportunities (OECD 2013).

Since 2007, we have worked in West Nile Uganda with grass roots EE initiatives (sewing workshops) for skills training and income generation for HIV-positive women of child bearing age. The goal was to use economic empowerment to help pregnant women and mothers to overcome the burden of poverty and AIDS-related stigma that stood between them and effective PMTCT programs. In cooperation with the Uganda Ministry of Health (MOH) in the West Nile region, we linked our EE initiative to the MOH AIDS/PMTCT clinics with the expectation of addressing AIDS-related stigma and subsequently improving PMTCT uptake and compliance. We anticipated that as women acquired skills resulting in income generation in a supportive workshop environment, we would likely see an improved socioeconomic status tracked through income and proxies for wealth (Levin et al. 2012). A more difficult task was demonstrating that the economic empowerment generalized to an empowerment for these women to deal with the daily AIDS-related stigma. To accomplish this we sought a measure of self-efficacy which is a construct from social cognitive theory strongly anchored in skill attainment and capable of generalization that would help evaluate the impact of our EE initiatives on AIDS-related stigma.

Self-Efficacy (SE) Definitions and Theoretical Dimensions

Self-efficacy theory was introduced by Bandura (1977) as a cognitive mechanism underlying behavior change. It is defined as an individual's belief in their perceived capability to execute a necessary behavior to accomplish a task (Bandura 1977, 1982, 1994, 2006).

Self-efficacy is very domain specific and is manifested by differences in magnitude, strength and generalization.

Therefore, self-efficacy measurement should include: gradations in challenge, i.e., increasingly difficult levels of task demands; and response scales that reflect the strength of belief in one's capability, i.e., 'cannot do,' 'moderately certain can do,' 'highly certain can do' to 'completely certain can do' (Bandura 2006). Self-efficacy measurement should always be linked to behaviors over which people can exercise control (Bandura 2006).

Building Self-Efficacy

Self-efficacy builds on input from performance attainment, verbal persuasion/feedback, and vicarious experiences, i.e., observing role models. It is key to measure self-efficacy at more than one point in time, generally before an intervention then afterward (Bandura 1977, 1982). Gist and Mitchell (1992) argued that self-efficacy is also influenced by external factor, e.g., task complexity as well as internal factors, e.g., knowledge/skills, general health, personality and self- esteem.

There has been a long history of investigation and discussion in the psychosocial literature which supports self-efficacy as a common mechanism for explaining the impact of interventions on changing behaviors (Cervone 2000, Chen, Gully and Eden 2001, Gist and Mitchell 1992). Self-efficacy has frequently been reported for interventions around HIV-positive women in sub-Saharan Africa and specifically interventions which involved economic empowerment (Kim et al. 2007, Kim et al. 2008, Pronyk et al. 2008).

To our knowledge there are no reports in HIV-positive women in sub Saharan Africa linking economic empowerment generalizing to self-efficacy in reducing AIDS-related stigma.

EE Initiative

Parallels to the Building Blocks of Self-Efficacy

In reviewing Bandura's theory of self-efficacy and the classic factors which contribute to building self-efficacy we found many parallels of components within our EE initiative. *Performance accomplishment* - Our EE initiative allowed mothers to acquire basic sewing skills, which represented large increments of knowledge and skills above their baseline.

Verbal persuasion and Vicarious experience - Our EE initiative provided peer contact with other HIV-positive participants and live modeling with teachers and peers via the acquisition of sewing skills and the observation of others living with HIV.

Parallels to Economic Empowerment and Self-Efficacy

The second motivation factor for this study was based on qualitative focus group work with HIV-positive women demographically similar to our study participants who were participating in a the same EE initiative in a nearby community (Kellett 2015).

The results strongly suggested that self-efficacy and empowerment around poverty and AIDS-related stigma may be indirect byproducts of participation in the EE initiative. Additionally the responses easily fit into the structure of the classic building blocks of self-efficacy as follows:

Performance attainment - As women learned income generating sewing skills, they had the following comments which reflected an increased sense of economic empowerment and personal worth:

> You'll make your own things, then you'll get your own money out of what you have made. Out of the skills you have learned. You'll not always be asking for things from people. You'll not ask for, you'll not go and borrow it from somebody.

Verbal persuasion and vicarious experiences - Being a part of the social interaction in the EE initiative helped break down stigma associated with being HIV-positive and provided valued role model support as women stated:

> You'll be free, you'll say that there are very many, you'll not fear that you're alone having the virus.

General physical health, personality and self-esteem - Women claimed that being involved in the workshop and staying busy helped them take their mind off their worries and feel better about themselves (psychologically):

> If you'll have, if you learn that skill, you'll not mind or think, thought of evil things. Your mind will always be busy on what you want to do.

Additionally, having income generating ability allowed these HIV-positive women to purchase food to better maintain health:

> If you're now getting, if you learn the skill, you'll be doing your work, you'll get your own money, you can buy all things which you own to eat. You'll get the money, you'll maintain yourself even no one will know that you're HIV positive.

Hypothesis

Because of the strong suggestion that empowerment and self-efficacy would result from participation in our EE initiative, we proposed the following study hypothesis. Our primary study question examined changes in SE over time with continued participation in the program as women were compared to themselves. Specifically, we hypothesized that among program participants, SE scores at 18 months would be higher than scores for the same individuals at the beginning of the study. We further hypothesized that changes in SE related to skill attainment and economic empowerment would correlate with changes in AIDS-related stigma SE scores.

Methods

AIDS-Related Stigma Self-Efficacy Questionnaire

Stigma Domains

Three AIDS-related stigma domains were identified from the preliminary qualitative focus group analysis: Disclosure of HIV status, Advocacy in the community, and Advocacy in the home. Five self-efficacy questions within these domains were then developed based on tasks and challenges dealing with stigma identified in the focus group responses. Sub questions of 2 to 3 levels of task difficulty were added. For example, question 1 concerned disclosure of HIV status. The question had three levels measuring self-efficacy relating to disclosure *to* different people, i.e., a woman's best friend, husband, and mother-in-law. Sub questions were ordered such that task difficulty increased sequentially within each overall question (Table 1).

Skills Attainment and Economic Empowerment Domains

One question pertaining to sewing skills and one question pertaining to income generating ability were developed to measure self-efficacy related to skills attainment and economic empowerment.

Table 1. AIDS-related stigma domains used to develop self-efficacy questions and sub-questions

Domain	Main Question	Sub-questions
Disclosure of HIV status	The antenatal nurse enrolls you in PMTCT. How sure are you that you can go home and tell people you are going to PMTCT clinic,	Best friend?
		Husband?
		Mother in law?
	How sure are you that you can wear a t-shirt (with PMTCT logo) like this,	At home?
		To visit family?
		At the market?
Advocacy in the community	Your HIV-positive child tells you that the children at school chase him away, how sure are you that you can,	Go to the teacher?
		Ask for help to stop discrimination?
	People do not let you get water from the bore hole. How sure are you that you can,	Ignore them?
		Still get your water?
Advocacy in the home	If your husband is not tested yet, how sure are you that you can,	Ask your husband to get tested?
		Insist if he says no initially?

Table 2. Skills Attainment and Economic Empowerment domains used to develop self-efficacy questions and sub questions

Domain	Main Question	Sub-question
Skills Attainment	You need some money to purchase items at the market, how sure are you that,	You can learn sewing skills through the workshop?
		You can earn money using these skills?
		Women at the market treat you with respect because you have earned money?
Economic Empowerment	How sure are you that you can do the following very well in the sewing workshop,	Cut fabric?
		Iron fabric?
		Sew straight line?

Figure 1. Domain – Disclosure of HIV status. *Question - The antenatal nurse enrolls you in PMTCT. How sure are you that you can go home and tell people you are going to PMTCT clinic. Sub Questions - Your best friend? Your Husband? Your Mother-law?*

Here again, sub questions of 2 to 3 levels of task difficulty were included and ordered such that task difficulty increased sequentially within each overall question. The final version of the AIDS-related Stigma Self-Efficacy Questionnaire included 7 questions, each of which had 2-3 levels within the question (Table 2).

Cultural Adaptation

The researchers worked with key community members in our study setting to ensure the questions adapted culturally to the Uganda setting. All questions were translated into the local language, Lugbara or Kiswahili as needed by the trained national staff study assistant. Culturally appropriate colored illustrations were developed as a talking adjunct for each question (Figure 1).

Study Design

Study Location

Our study took place from 2012 to 2014 in the West Nile region of Uganda which has a population of approximately 2 million people. The prevalence of HIV in Uganda was 7.3% (8.3% among women and 6.1% among men).

Access to antiretroviral (ARV) treatment and PMTCT programs from the Ugandan Ministry of Health began in 2000 (UNAIDS 2013). Maracha, our study community is situated 40 km from a main trade center (Arua) for the West Nile region and has proximity to South Sudan (60 km North) and the Democratic Republic of the Congo (10 km West). The PMTCT program in Maracha was opened in 2012. Maracha is in a newly formed district with limited electricity and water resources.

The main source of livelihood is subsistence farming. There are jobs in the district government offices and with St Joseph community hospital. Some individuals travel to Arua for employment. Cell towers provide variable cell phone service but no stable internet.

There are no banks or ATM's in the town. St Joseph's Community Hospital has two hundred beds with obstetric and surgical services and the only HIV/PMTCT clinic in the district. The HIV/AIDS program began operation in 2005.

Economic Empowerment (EE) Initiative

In November 2012, a grassroots EE initiative (sewing workshop) was linked to St Joseph's Hospital HIV/PMTCT clinic program and was open to HIV-positive mothers enrolled in the PMTCT clinic on a first come, first served basis.

Subsequent to the initial enrollment, interested women who exceeded workshop capacity were 'wait listed' and incorporated into the initiative as capacity permitted. The workshop was accessible five days per week and provided equipment, sewing instructors, and sewing materials. Mothers were paid for good quality finished products which were sold in the country capital or in the West, such as the United States, Ireland, and Germany.

Study Sample

A convenience sample of the HIV-positive women participating in the EE initiative were enrolled in the study when the initiative was opened, November 2012. Access to the EE initiative was not contingent on participation in any aspect of our study.

The women did not risk forfeiture of access to the HIV/PMTCT clinic for themselves or their infants for refusal to participate or early withdrawal from the study. All our participants were enrolled in the PMTCT/HIV/AIDS clinic and were receiving ARV's per World Health Organization (WHO) guidelines. All were in basic good health.

Measurement

The questionnaire was administered to participants in November 2012 (time = 0) and again after eighteen months of participation (t = 18 months). A demographic survey was administered at (time = 0) which included questions regarding: participants' age, number of children (biological or that they have assumed responsibility for, i.e., AIDS orphans), distance living from workshop, education level, civil status, and time since HIV diagnosis.

To examine the hypothesis that women's self-efficacy scores would increase over time, self-efficacy responses were coded using a Likert scale with five values relating to how sure women were that they could accomplish the tasks identified in the stigma and economic empowerment domains. Responses were recoded ordinally as follows: not sure (assigned a value of 1); maybe (2); moderately sure (3); pretty sure (4); totally sure (5).

This study was reviewed and approved by Institutional Review Boards at the University of New Mexico and the Makerere University in Kampala, Uganda.

Analysis

Frequency distributions and measures of central tendency were used to describe demographic variables. Nonparametric tests were used to evaluate hypotheses with an alpha error of 0.05 as the threshold of significance. All data were uploaded to Microsoft Access™ and analyzed in Stata™ v13.

Individual participants' self-efficacy scores in 2012 were compared to their scores in 2014 (t = 18 months) using a one sided nonparametric matched pairs sign test (StataCorp. 2013. Stata 13 Base Reference Manual. College Station, TX: Stata Press). nonparametric matched pairs signtest (insert reference: StataCorp. 2013. Stata 13 Base Reference Manual. College Station, TX: Stata Press).

The hypothesis that changes in the Skill Attainment and Economic Empowerment domains (questions 6 and 7) were associated with changes in the three AIDS-related stigma domains (questions 1-5), composite variables were generated. The AIDS-related self-efficacy composite variable was created by summing the changes in scores for all parts of questions 1-5. Similarly, composite variables were prepared for the Economic Empowerment domain by summing the scores of the three parts of question 6, and for the Skills Empowerment domain by summing the scores of the three parts of question 7.

For all three variables, positive numbers indicate that scores improved from 2012 to 2014. A composite Economic/Skills Empowerment domain score was generated by summing the scores from the composite Economic Domain and Skills Empowerment Domain. Regression analysis was used to quantify these relationships.

Results

Demographic Data

There were 40 participants enrolled in the study (time = 0). Twenty-six women (65%) continued participation and were reevaluated (t = 18 months), and fourteen women (35%) were lost to follow up (LFU).

Results report 24 participants (92.6%) who completed all of the self-efficacy questions. There were no differences between participants and LFUs in age, education, year of diagnosis, number of children, or distance to workshop (Table 3). However, participants were less likely to be married (53.8%) than LFUs (85.7%) (chi square, df = 1, $p = 0.044$).

Table 3. Demographic characteristics of women enrolled in the Economic Empowerment initiative (sewing workshop)

	Participants (n = 26)	LFU (n = 14)
Age (median)	34 years	33 years
Education		
none	11.5%	14.3%
primary	73.1%	78.6%
secondary	15.4%	7.1%
Marital status		
Married	53.8%	85.7%
Divorced	23.1%	0.0%
Widowed	23.1%	14.3%
Number children (median)	3.0	3.5
Distance to workshop (med)	3.3	3.5
Year of diagnosis (median)	2007.5	2005

Outcome Variables

Self-efficacy scores were higher after 18 months than they were at study onset (Table 4).

For most (10 of 12) questions in the first three domains: Disclosure of HIV Status; and Advocacy in the Community; Advocacy at Home, median self-efficacy values were 4 and 5 at (t = 0) and (t = 18mo). In these domains, self-efficacy increased significantly for all questions except two, both of which concerned women talking with their spouses.

Self-efficacy scores varied more in the Skills Attainment and Economic Empowerment domains, but all scores were significantly higher at (t = 18mo) than at the beginning of the intervention (t = 0).

Predictive Variables

The prediction that increase in task difficulty would be associated with decreasing self-efficacy was not upheld. Median self-efficacy scores for sub questions were not different for any questions except question 7, and those differences were not in the expected direction.

Table 5. shows that the combined changes in self-efficacy scores from questions in the three AIDS-related stigma domains (Disclosure of HIV Status domain, Advocacy in the Community domain, and Advocacy at Home domain) were significantly correlated with changes in self-efficacy for both the Skills Attainment and Economic Empowerment domains. Self-efficacy changes in the Economic Empowerment domain predicted nearly 20% of the variability in changes in the composite AIDS-related Self-Efficacy score ($\beta = 0.19$; $p = 0.018$).

In the Skills Attainment domain, self-efficacy changes were also associated with changes in AIDS-related Stigma self-efficacy ($\beta = 0.26$; $p = 0.019$), and changes in the combined Skills Attainment/Economic Empowerment domain score predicted over one-third of the variability in AIDS-related Stigma self-efficacy changes.

Table 4. Median self-efficacy scores with (IQR) at the start of the EE initiative (t = 0) and after 18 months of participation (t = 18 months)

	t = 0	t = 18 months	p-value*
Disclosure of HIV status domain			
1. The antenatal nurse enrolls you in PMTCT. How sure are you that you can go home and tell [people] you are going to PMTCT clinic?			
best friend	4 (3.5,5)	5 (4,5)	0.048
husband	4 (4,5)	5 (4,5)	0.13
mother-in-law	4 (4,5)	5 (4,5)	0.048
2. How sure are you that you can wear a t-shirt (with PMTCT logo) like this			
at home	4 (4,5)	5 (5,5)	0.0065
to visit family	4 (4,5)	5 (5,5)	0.0017
at the market	4.5(4,5)	5 (5,5)	0.011
Advocacy in the community domain			
3. Your HIV-positive child tells you that the children at school chase him away, how sure are you that you can ...			
go to the teacher	4 (4,5)	5 (4,5)	0.0059
ask for help to stop discrimination	4 (3,4)	5 (4,5)	0.0001
4. People do not let you get water from the bore hole. How sure are you that you can ...			
ignore them	4 (4,5)	5 (4,5)	0.0012
still get your water	4 (4,5)	5 (5,5)	0.0065
Advocacy in the home domain			
5. If your husband is not tested yet, how sure are you that you can			
Ask your husband to get tested	5 (4,5)	5 (4,5)	0.29
Insist if he says "no" initially	4 (3,5)	5 (4,5)	0.029
Economic/skills empowerment domain			
6. You need some money to purchase items at the market, how sure are you that ...			
You can learn sewing skills through the workshop	4 (3,4.5)	5 (4,5)	0.0096
You can earn money using these skills	4 (3,5)	5 (4,5)	0.0064
Women at the market treat you with respect because you have earned money	4 (3,4)	5 (4,5)	0.0009
7. How sure are you that you can do [the following] very well in the sewing workshop?			
cut fabric	2 (2,2)	3 (2,4)	0.0096
iron fabric	3 (2.5,4)	4 (4,5)	0.021
sew straight line	2 ((1,2)	3 (2,5)	0.0001

*One-sided test of SE score at t = 18 months >SE score at t = 0.

CONCLUSION

LFU and Role of Demographics

Our study participants had similar age/education profiles as HIV-positive women in stigma, disclosure studies from Uganda (Karamaji, Tumwine, Tylleskar and Heggenhougen 2006, King et al. 2008, Ssali et al. 2012) and South Africa (Simbayi et al. 2007, Varga et al. 2006). Thirty-five percent of our participants were LFU and several factors may have contributed.

Table 5. Associations between changes in the Skills Attainment and Economic Empowerment domains with changes in AIDS-related stigma self-efficacy

Domains	Correlation with AIDS-related stigma self-efficacy change composite score	r-squared	coef	p-value
Skills Attainment	0.474	18.90%	0.26	0.019
Economic Empowerment	0.479	19.40%	0.19	0.018
Combined Skills Attainment/Economic Empowerment	0.62	35.50%	0.45	0.001

The AIDS- related stigma self-efficacy change composite score for each participant was calculated by summing the changes in questions 1-5 from t = 0 to t = 18 months.

The Skills Attainment domain score was calculated by summing the changes in scores for the two parts of question 7 from t = 0 to t = 18 months.

The Economic Empowerment domain score was calculated by summing the changes in scores for the three parts of question 6 from t = 0 to t =1 8 months.

Although we found no significant difference in level of education between participants and the LFU group, the women with continued participation tended to have some secondary education and may have more readily recognized the opportunity inherent in the EE initiative.

Distance living from the initiative and number of children were not contributing factors in this study even though we found these factors contributed in a nearby community to decreased participation in an EE initiative (Gnauck et al. 2012) and LFU at the PMTCT clinic (Ahoua et al. 2010).

Relocation to follow a partner in search of work may have played a large role in LFU. Varga et al., in South Africa (2006) found just over half of participants had moved in the previous three years to follow a partner in search of work. Ahoua et al. in Uganda (2010) found 12% PMTCT LFU due to relocation for economic reasons.

In our study, at least half of LFU (7/14) moved away. Marital status may have indirectly selected out these women as the majority (85.7%) of our LFU women were married, contrasted with (53.8%) of those who continued participation.

Generalization of Self-Efficacy

Our hypothesis that SE scores would improve with participation in the EE initiative was supported and included both the AIDS-related stigma and the Skills Attainment/EE domains. These findings were consistent with expectations based on Bandura's SE theory.

The correlation of improved SE across domains, i.e., from the Skills Attainment/ Economic Empowerment to AIDS-related stigma domains supports our secondary hypothesis that SE can generalize and reinforce participant's perceived capability across a variety of domains.

While support of our second hypothesis would be predicted by Bandura's theory, it is perhaps better explained by the Generalized Self-efficacy (GSE) theory which encompasses the broad range of human behaviors needed in coping with AIDS stigma.

GSE is characterized as operating across varied domains and helps to effectively navigate across a variety of challenging situations (Cervone 2000, Chen, Gully and Eden 2001, Luszczynska, Scholz and Schwarzer 2005). GSE is a dynamic entity, appears to buffer the negative influence of low education (Zahodne et al. 2015), and is operative across cultures (Luszczynska et al. 2005). In GSE, individuals think about multiple components of a task in a number of different ways that are interrelated (Cervone 2000). The broadness of GSE may also explain why we found no differences in task difficulty levels as predicted by the classic Bandura model.

Many other factors of participation in the EE initiative probably influenced the increase we observed in self-efficacy. Certainly the improved health of the individual participants contributed. Improved health has been shown to improve SE in HIV-positive individuals at clinic settings in Uganda (Wagner et al. 2011). Our participants were taking ARV's which kept their HIV infection in check and during the 18 month period of the study as earnings increased, participants were noted to upgrade their clothing, bring healthy food to prepare at lunch and gain weight. Another positive factor could have been the influence of the almost daily peer support interaction in the EE initiative.

The verbal persuasion/feedback, and vicarious experiences of Bandura's model cannot be underestimated and has been reported as a result of program exposure in Malawi (Berendes and Rimal 2011). Lastly the role of income generating ability, which our study participants enjoyed, overlaps all of the above factors. Economic empowerment has been found in to have a multitude of positive benefits for overcoming AIDS-related stigma for HIV-positive women living in sub-Saharan Africa (Kim et al. 2008, Odek et al. 2009, Pronyk et al. 2008).

SE and Spousal/Community Interactions

Women in our study expressed high confidence at the start of the study in their ability around spousal issues of HIV disclosure and advocating HIV testing. We therefore did not see an increase in SE scores resulting from participation in the EE initiative.

It is unclear why disclosure to spouses was not the problem that others have reported in the literature. For example, Ssali et al. (2012) in urban Uganda found only half of the women who had spouses disclosed to the spouse and those disclosing tended to be younger and King et al. (2008) in Uganda found the ability of women to disclose to partners was related to being married. Looking at the subset of the fourteen married women in our study, their responses to questions concerning spouses were statistically similar to the overall participant sample, so marital status appeared not to play a role in our study. It is possible with greater numbers of participants the role of self-efficacy, EE initiatives, spousal issues and marital status could be better understood.

Our participants reported living in extended family households and had long standing ties to their community - all disincentives for disclosure (Varga et al. 2006).

However, our participants showed increased SE for disclosure to friends and mother in laws with participation in the EE initiative and increased SE to be associated with PMTCT clinic by wearing the project t-shirts in public.

Limitations

Stigma with its fear of desertion and intimate partner violence has long been key in motivation for women to not disclose their positive HIV status to partners and the community. Dependency on the partner for food/rent/school fees, also lowers the motivation for disclosure (Gnauck et al. 2013, Karamaji et al. 2006, Kiula, Damian, J., Damian, D. J. and Msuya 2013, Simbayi et al. 2007).

We did not explore the issue of EE initiatives, self- efficacy and intimate partner violence (IPV) in this study and it was a missed opportunity. Karamaji et al. (2006) found it common in eastern Uganda with a prevalence for lifetime IPV, 54% and for physical violence occurring within the past year, 14%. Living in rural communities and husbands having another partner increased this risk. We learned over the course of the study that our participants did have issues of IPV especially around situations with co-wives.

This would have been an opportunity to examine more fully the role of EE initiatives, IVP and spousal interactions in general. Certainly, interventions which embraced EE initiatives in South Africa showed decreased IPV particularly when associated with partner involved education/counseling (Kim et al. 2008, Pronyk et al. 2008).

For the HIV-positive women living in West Nile Uganda, we found participation in an EE initiative increased self-efficacy in AIDS-related stigma. This effect was evidenced in specific tasks and generalized across tasks for AIDS-related stigma. The AIDS-related Stigma Self-Efficacy Questionnaire piloted in this study may be a useful tool to measure the impact of EE initiatives in decreasing AIDS-related stigma. Understanding of the role of EE initiatives and self-efficacy around spousal relationships and intimate partner violence warrants further investigation.

References

Adetokunboh, O. and Oluwasanu, M. (2015). Eliminating mother-to-child transmission of the human immunodeficiency virus in sub-Saharan Africa: The journey so far and what remains to be done. *J. Infect. Public Health. Advance online publication.* doi: 10.1016/j.jiph.2015.06.010.

Ahoua, T., Ayikoru, H., Gnauck, K., Odaru, G., Odar, E., Ondoa-Onama, C., Pinoges, L., Balkan, S., Olson, D. and Pujades-Rodriguez, M. (2010). Evaluation of a 5-year programme to prevent mother-to-child transmission of HIV Infection in Northern Uganda. *J. Trop. Pediatr.*, 56(1), 43-52. doi: 10.1093/tropej/fmp054.

Ayiga, N., Nambooze, H., Nalugo, S., Kaye, D. and Katamba, A. (2013). The impact of HIV/AIDS stigma on HIV counseling and testing in a high HIV prevalence population in Uganda. *Afr. Health Sci.*, 13, 278–286. doi: 10.4314/ahs.v13i2.12.

Bandura, A. (1977). Self-efficacy: Toward a unifying theory of behavioral change. *Psychological Review*, 84(2), 191-215. Retrieved from http://dx.doi.org/10.1037/0033-295X.84.2.191.

Bandura, A. (1982). Self-efficacy mechanism in human agency. *American Psychologist*, 37 (2), 122-147. Retrieved from: http://dx.doi.org/10.1037/0003-066X.37.2.122.

Bandura, A. (1994). Self-efficacy. In: V. S. Ramachaudran (Ed.), *Encyclopedia of human behavior* (Vol. 4), pp. 71-81. New York: Academic Press. (Reprinted in H. Friedman [ED.], Encyclopedia of mental health. San Diego: Academic Press, 1998).

Bandura, A. (2006). Guide for constructing self-efficacy scales. In: F. Pajares and T. Urdan (Eds.), *Self-efficacy beliefs of adolescents* (pp. 307-337). United States: Information Age Publishing.

Berendes, S. and Rimal, R. N. (2011). Addressing the slow uptake of HIV testing in Malawi: The role of stigma, self-efficacy, and knowledge in the Malawi BRIDGE Project. *J. Assoc. Nurses in AIDS*, 22(3), 215–228. doi: 10.10/16/j.jana.2010.08.005.

Brusamento, S., Ghanotakis, E., Car, L., Majeed, A. and Car, J. (2012). Male involvement for increasing the effectiveness of prevention of mother-to-child HIV transmission (PMTCT) programmes. *Protocols Cochrane Database of Systematic Reviews*, 2012, 10, 1-22. doi: 10.1002/14651858.CD009468.pub2.

Cervone, D. (2000). Thinking about self-efficacy. *Behav. Modif.*, 24(30), 30-56. doi: 10.1177/ 0145445500241002.

Chen, G., Gully, S. M. and Eden, D. (2001). Validation of a new general self-efficacy scale. *Organizational Research Methods*, 4, 62-83. doi: 10.1177/109442810141004.

Colombini, M., Stöckl, H., Watts, C., Zimmerman, C., Agamasu, E. and Mayhew, S. H. (2014). Factors affecting adherence to short-course ARV prophylaxis for preventing mother-to-child transmission of HIV in sub-Saharan Africa: a review and lessons for future elimination. *AIDS Care*, 26, 914-26. doi: 10.1080/09540121.2013.869539.

De Paoli, M. M., Manongi, R. and Klepp, K. I. (2004). Factors influencing acceptability of voluntary counseling and HIV testing among pregnant women in northern Tanzania. *AIDS Care*, 16, 411-425. doi: 10.1080/09540120410001683358.

Duff, P., Kipp, W., Wild, T., Rubaale, T. and Okech-Ojony, J. (2010). Barriers to accessing highly active antiretroviral therapy by HIV-positive women attending an antenatal clinic in a regional hospitall in western Uganda. *Journal of the International AIDS Society J. Int. AIDS Soc.*, 13, 37. doi: 10.1186/1758-2652-13-37.

Eide, M., Myhre, M., Lindbaek, M., Sundby, J., Arimi, P. and Thior, I. (2006). Social consequences of HIV-positive women's participation in prevention of mother-to-child transmission programmes. *J. Patient Education and Counseling*, 60, 146-151. doi: http:// dx.doi.org/10.1016/j.pec.2004.11.014.

Escamilla, V., Chibwesha, C., Gartland, M., Chintu, N., Mubiana-Mbewe, M., Musokotwane, K., … Chi, B. H. (2015). Distance from household to clinic and its association with the uptake of prevention of mother-to-child HIV transmission regimens in rural Zambia. *JAIDS Journal of Acquired Immune Deficiency Syndromes. Advance online publication.* Retrieved from http://www.ncbi.nlm.nih.gov/pubmed/26135197.

Gist, M. E. and Mitchell, T. R. (1992). Self-efficacy: A theoretical analysis of its determinants and malleability. *The Academy of Management Review*, 17(2), 183-211. Retrieved from http://www.jstor.org/stable/258770.

Gnauck, K., Levin, N., Fullerton, L., Jackson, A., Anguzu, M., Seevers, B. and Adaku, A. (2012). An economic empowerment initiative linked to Prevention Mother-to-Child Transmission (PMTCT) peer support groups in West Nile Uganda: Part II, barriers to participation [Abstract]. *AIDS 2012*, Washington DC.

Gnauck, K., Ruiz, J., Kellett, N., Sussman, A., Sullivan, M. A., Montoya, M., Levin, N., Tomedi, A. and Mwanthi, M. A. (2013). Economic empowerment and AIDS-related stigma in rural Kenya: A double edged sword? *J. Culture, Health and Sexuality*, 15(7), 851-865. DOI: 10.1080/13691058.2013.789127.

Gourlay, A., Birdthistle, I., Mburu, G., Iorpenda, K. and Wringe, A. (2013). Barriers and facilitating factors to the uptake of antiretroviral drugs for prevention of mother-to-child transmission of HIV in sub-Saharan Africa: A systematic review. *Journal of the International AIDS Society*, 16(1), 185-88. doi: 10.7448/IAS.16.1.18588.

Gusdal, A. K., Obua, C., Andualem, T., Wahlstrom, R., Tomson, G., Peterson, S., … INRUD-IAA project. (2009). Voices on adherence to ART in Ethiopia and Uganda: a matter of choice or simply not an option? *AIDS Care*, 21, 1381-7. doi: 10.1080/09540120902883119.

HIarlaithe, M. O., Grede, N., de Pee, S. and Bloem, M. (2014). Economic and social factors are some of the most common barriers preventing women from accessing maternal and newborn child health (MNCH) and prevention of mother-to-child transmission (PMTCT) services: a literature review. *AIDS* 18, 516-30. doi: 10.1007/s10461-014-0756-5.

Jürgensen, M., Sandøy, I., Michelo, C. and Fylkesnes, K. (2013). Effects of home-based Voluntary Counselling and Testing on HIV-related stigma: Findings from a cluster-randomized trial in Zambia. *Social Science and Medicine*, 81, 18-25. doi: 10.1016/j.socscimed.2013.01.011.

Karamagi, C. A. S., Tumwine, J. K., Tylleskar, T. and Heggenhougen, K. (2006). Intimate partner violence against women in eastern Uganda: implications for HIV prevention. *BMC Public Health*, 6, 284-296. doi: 10.1186/1471-2458-6-284.

Kellett, N. C., Gnauck, K., Sussman, A., Levin, N., Seevers, B., Hanselman, J. and Adaku, A. (2015). AIDS, stigma and economic empowerment: Exploring notions of belonging and masculinity in West Nile Uganda. *Manuscript submitted for publication.*

Kim, J. C., Pronyk, P., Barnett, T. and Watts, C. (2008). Exploring the role of economic empowerment in HIV prevention. *AIDS*, 22(4), S57-71. doi: 10.1097/01.aids.0000341777.78876.40.

Kim, J. C., Watts, C. H., Hargreaves, J. R., Ndhlovu, L. X., Phetla, G., Morison, L. A. et al. (2007). Understanding the impact of a microfinance-based intervention on women's empowerment and the reduction of intimate partner violence in South Africa. *Am. J. Public Health*. 97(10), 1794-1802. doi: 10.2105/AJPH.2006.095521.

King, R., Katuntu, D., Lifshay, J., Packel, L., Batamwita, R., Nakayiwa, S., Abang, B., Babirye, F., Lindkvist, P., Johansson, E., Mermin, J. and Bunnell, R. (2008). Processes and outcomes of HIV serostatus disclosure to sexual partners among people living with HIV in Uganda. *AIDS Behav*. 12, 232–243. doi: 10.1007/s10461-007-9307-7.

Kiula, E. S., Damian, J., Damian, D. J. and Msuya, S. E. (2013). Predictors of HIV serostatus disclosure to partners among HIV-positive pregnant women in Morogoro, Tanzania. *BMC Public Health*, 13, 433-442. Retreived from http://www.biomedcentral.com/1471-2458/13/433.

Levin, N., Gnauck, K., Fullerton, L., Jackson, A., Anguzu, M. and Adaku, A. (2012). An economic empowerment (EE) initiative linked to Prevention Mother-to-Child Transmission (PMTCT) peer support groups in West Nile Uganda: Participation as a predictor of socioeconomic changes [Abstract]. *American Academy Pediatrics*, New Orleans.

Lubega, M., Musenze, I., Joshua, G., Dhafa, G., Badaza, R., Bakwesegha, C., Reynolds, S. (2013). Sex inequality, high transport costs, and exposed clinic location: reasons for loss to follow-up of clients under prevention of mother-to-child HIV transmission in eastern Uganda - a qualitative study. *Patient Prefer Adherence*, 22, 447-54. doi: 10.2147/PPA.S 19327.

Luszczynska, A., Scholz, U. and Schwarzer, R. (2005). The general self-efficacy scale: Multicultural validation studies. *J. of Psychology*, 139(5), 439-457. doi: 10.3200/JRLP. 139.5.439-457.

Odek, W. O., Busza, J., Morris, C. N., Cleland, J., Ngugi, E. N. and Ferguson, A. G. (2009). Effects of micro-enterprise services on HIV risk behavior among female sex workers in Kenya's urban slums. *AIDS Behav.*, 13, 449-461. doi: 10.1007/s10461-008-9485-y.

Organization for Economic Co-operation and Development (OECD). (2013). Poverty Reduction and Pro-Poor Growth. The Role of Empowerment. Retrieved from OED website: http://www.oecd.org/dac/povertyreduction/50157953.pdf.

Pronyk, P. M., Kim, J. C., Abramsky, T., Phetla, G., Hargreaves, J. R., Morison, L. A. et al. (2008). A combined microfinance and training intervention can reduce HIV risk behavior in young female participants. *AIDS*, 22, 1659-1665. doi: 10.1097/QAD.0b013e328307a 040.

Simbayi, L. C., Kalichman, S. C., Strebel, A., Cloete, A., Henda, N. and Mqeketo, A. (2007). Disclosure of HIV status to sex partners and sexual risk behaviours among HIV-positive men and women, Cape Town, South Africa. *Sex. Transm. Infect.*, 83, 29–34. doi: 10. 1136/sti.2006.019893.

Ssali, S. N., Atuyambe, L., Tumwine, C., Ssegujja, E., Nekesa, N., Nannungi, A., Ryan, G. and Wagner, G. (2010). Reasons for disclosure of HIV status by people living with HIV/AIDS and in HIV care in Uganda: An exploratory study. *AIDS Patient Care and STD*, 24(10), 1-7. doi: 10.1089/apc.2010.0062.

UNAIDS. (2012). *Global Report: UNAIDS Report on the Global AIDS Epidemic*. Retrieved from UNAIDS website:http://www.unaids.org/en/media/unaids/contentassets/documents/ epidemiology/2012/gr2012/JC2434_WorldAIDSday_results_en.pdf.

UNAIDS Uganda Country Report. (2013). Retrieved from http://www.unaids.org/sites/ default/files/country/documents/UGA_narrative_report_2014.pdf.

Varga, C. A., Sherman, G. G. and Jones, S. A. (2006). HIV-disclosure in the context of vertical transmission: HIV-positive mothers in Johannesburg, South Africa. *AIDS Care*, 18(8), 952-960. doi: 10.1080/09540120500356906.

Wagner, G. J., Holloway, I., Ghosh-Dastidar, B., Kityo, C. and Mugyenyi, P. (2011). Understanding the influence of depression on self-efficacy, work status and condom use among HIV clients in Uganda. *J. Psychosom. Res.*, 70(5), 440–448. doi: 10.1016/j. jpsychores.2010.10.003.

Wallerstein, N. (2006). *What is the evidence on effectiveness of empowerment to improve health?* (Europe Health Evidence Network Report). Retrieved from WHO website: http:// www.euro.who.int/Document/E88086.pdf.

Watts, C., Zimmerman, C., Nyblade, L. and Eckhaus, T. (2010, July). Stigma as an important barrier to universal access to PMTCT: Model projections. *Paper presented at the XVIII International AIDS Conference*, Vienna, Austria. Abstract retrieved from http://pag.aids 2010.org/Abstracts.aspx?AID=14274.

World Health Organization (WHO). (2015). *Global Health Observatory data: HIV/AIDS.* Retrieved from WHO website: http://www.who.int/gho/hiv/en/.

Zahodne, L. B., Nowinski, C. J., Gershon, R. C. and Manly, J. J. (2015). Self-efficacy buffers the relationship between educational disadvantage and executive functioning. *J. Int. Neuropsychol. Soc.*, 4, 297-304. doi: 10.1017/S1355617715000193.

INDEX

C

D

E

I

J

K

L

M

N

Y